Story Celebrations

Story Celebrations

A Program Guide for Schools and Libraries

Jan Irving

with illustrations by Joni Giarratano

LIBRARIES

UNLIMITED

A Member of the Greenwood Publishing Group

Westport, Connecticut • London

Library of Congress Cataloging-in-Publication Data

Irving, Jan, 1942-
  Story celebrations : a program guide for schools and libraries / Jan Irving.
      p. cm.
  Includes bibliographical references and indexes.
  ISBN 978-159158-432-2 (alk. paper)
    1. Children's libraries—Activity programs—United States. 2. Elementary school libraries—
Activity programs—United States. 3. Children's literature—Study and teaching (Elementary)—
Activity programs. 4. Children—Books and reading—United States. I. Title.
  Z718.3.I786   2008
  027.62'51—dc22   2007037072

British Library Cataloguing in Publication Data is available.

Library of Congress Catalog Card Number: 2007037072
ISBN: 978-1-59158-432-2

First published in 2008

Libraries Unlimited, 88 Post Road West, Westport, CT 06881
A Member of the Greenwood Publishing Group, Inc.
www.lu.com

Printed in the United States of America

∞™

The paper used in this book complies with the
Permanent Paper Standard issued by the National
Information Standards Organization (Z39.48–1984).

10   9   8   7   6   5   4   3   2   1

The publisher has done its best to make sure the instructions and/or recipes in this book are correct. However, users should apply judgment and experience when preparing recipes, especially parents and teachers working with young people. The publisher accepts no responsibility for the outcome of any recipe
included in this volume.

Contents

v

Introduction

This is a book for the curious librarian, the adventurous educator who is looking for a new twist on an old theme, a creative spark to engage students, an opportunity to venture beyond humdrum, well-trodden paths. *Story Celebrations* does not follow a rote set of standards or rules. It is not prescriptive. It does not promise quantitative results. Rather, it is meant to inspire the reader—teacher or librarian or caregiver—to become engaged in learning, in explorations, right along with students.

Why the title *Story Celebrations*? My grown son questioned my use of the word "celebrations," as I was covering topics like plagues and gross science. To him, the word automatically suggested "participating in a party, having a good time."

Did he think I would be treating serious topics irreverently? Will teachers and librarians think they need to avoid tough issues and choose only programs that appeal to the mass-market, superstore culture of our day? Is there room left in schools for exploring ideas beyond the standards-driven curriculum? Will public libraries shy away from planning programs on endangered animals or on cooking healthy food?

To quell my uncertainty, I checked several dictionaries, only to discover the preferred meanings of "celebration" use these phrases: "to observe," "to extol," and, significantly "to praise." So "Story Celebrations" asks us to praise and even revere the story—the story of disease, the story of history, the story of human accomplishment. Despite the demands on schools to adhere to standards and for public libraries to appeal to media-obsessed kids, we can celebrate stories in schools and find room for them in our public library programs.

Although this book does not directly follow core content standards as proscribed by the No Child Left Behind Act, educators will find numerous benchmarks are addressed. Reading skills and understandings are taught through the writing, speaking, and thinking activities in all chapters. Writing springboards, worksheets for planning speeches and understanding puns, and models for interpreting stories behind paintings are typical of the handouts in this book. Sample science projects and learning centers are given in chapter 7, "Gross Science," and research topics suggested in the chapter on plagues will challenge young scientists to use scientific methods of testing assumptions and making predictions based on information.

This volume, along with its predecessors (*Stories NeverEnding* [2004] and *Stories, Time and Again* [2006]), combines books and research materials for you to plan programs and activities on a wide range of topics. Each chapter has a bibliography as well as a list of selected Web sites. The ten subjects covered in this book are interrelated, and they also relate to the twenty subjects developed in the other two books in this series. For example, Chapter 8 teaches public speaking skills. It can be combined with chapter 10, on endangered animals, as students prepare informational speeches on ways in which zoos are helping nearly extinct animals to survive. Use the chapter "Barrel of Fun," in *Stories NeverEnding* along with the chapter 2, "Puns of Fun: Word Play for Kids," in this book to explore similar themes. Language and literature weave together all areas of the curriculum and the world of information from science to math, from art to history. This book series helps you make the connections.

One of the new features in this volume is the list of Web sites. Students use the Internet for much of their research today, and on some subjects, when currency is very important, the electronic sources can be invaluable. For example, up-to-date books may not be readily available in such areas as endangered animals. The Web sites of major wildlife organizations can be a helpful extension of a student's learning. Careful researchers, however, need to examine sites for authenticity by checking more than one electronic source. Teachers and librarians must be active researchers themselves as they guide kids through the morass of information available. Slavish adherence to any source without interpretation of data and sound reasoning never results in quality work.

In addition, notations of reading levels of books are now included in the chapter bibliographies. Different reading indexes have been employed to determine reading levels, as it is impossible to find one uniform scale to evaluate all books listed. I have attempted to provide a guide for teachers and made a good faith effort to document the various formulas.

Story Celebrations has been written for adults working with kids in grades 4 through 8, or ages 10–14. Since this is a fairly wide range, some topics lend themselves to the elementary level while others work better with middle school kids. There is something for everyone and, as always, savvy teachers can scale a project to a more simple or more advanced level as they wish.

For each chapter, two complete programs are described in a step-by-step approach—one for a school setting and one for a public library. In many cases the activities will work in either setting. Generally, school programs involve more research and activities that can be evaluated. The public library programs use games, food fairs, crafts, and lighthearted fun. This doesn't mean a school librarian can't use the program ideas offered for public libraries, or vice versa. After all, in each setting the purpose is to stimulate reading, learning, and the love of reading.

Because upper elementary and middle school students tend to focus their interests in specific areas, a "club" approach can be appealing with this age group. Organizing a speaker's club and a special interest wildlife group may work better than planning a general program for a large, diverse audience.

The common thread in this book and the entire series is the importance of story in our lives, past, present, and future. Stories from our own family roots or stories of pandemics from ancient times to our own day will continue to be told and retold. Understanding the enormous changes that defined the Victorian age gives us a prism to explore the rapid acceleration of ideas in our own complex times. Learning about healthy diets and approaching science in new ways keeps young people attuned to expanding horizons, to new worlds of information. May those who delight in the heart of story and the joy of exploration find much to discover in these pages!

1

Paintings That Tell Stories

Despite a recent news story about a capuchin monkey who paints pictures, most of us agree that creating art is a human activity. It is one of the oldest accomplishments of humans, and it dates as far back as the cave paintings created sometime between 13,000 and 8000 B.C. found in Lascaux, France. The details of these paintings are sketchy, but the simple animal shapes and stick figures from Lascaux seem to tell a story about early man hunting for food.

Some 5,000 years later the ancient Egyptians painted murals on the walls of pyramids that provide far more elaborate accounts of people hunting, fishing, dancing, enjoying feasts, waging war, and burying their dead. Art from early times chronicled human activity, and through visual art, stories have been told. The noted art historian H. W. Janson tells us that art is a "visual dialogue," but for there to be a dialogue the viewer needs to become involved with the piece of art.

This chapter about paintings that tell stories centers on the interaction between art and viewer. Since this is but one chapter in a book of many topics, the scope has been narrowed to paintings with a narrative quality, works of art that tell a particular story as well as pictures that suggest stories for the viewer to tell. In addition, the focus is on select paintings from Western art from the late Middle Ages and early Renaissance to the present day. Although religious art is often narrative, it has been excluded because these programs are intended for public schools and libraries. Furthermore, to explain stories from the Bible and Christian symbolism takes more time than allotted for these programs. Portraits, landscapes, and most abstract art have been excluded, since telling stories is not central to the importance of these genres.

As an alternative, homeschooling teachers and religious educators may adapt the ideas in this chapter using examples from Christian art. For example, students could compare Giotto's scenes from the life of Christ with Michelangelo's many religious paintings. Rembrandt and Pieter Brueghel were prolific artists of religious works that make interesting comparisons.

Some periods of art lend themselves especially well for our purposes. Sixteenth- and seventeenth-century Dutch and Flemish paintings by master artists-storytellers such as Pieter Brueghel and Jan Steen are filled with rich narrative details. American historical paintings offer exciting records of our past and present-day struggles. *Washington Crossing the Delaware,* by Emanuel Leutze, the Harriet Tubman series of paintings by Jacob Lawrence, and Thomas Hart Benton's murals in the Missouri Capitol serve as good examples.

Because today's youth live in a visual world, they readily respond to art and art projects. Even after a long school day, restless children will settle down to drawing and pouring over books of paintings of exciting subjects. They will tell you frankly what they like and what they don't like. They talk about things in pictures and ask all kinds of questions. Art is not a hard sell in or out of school. And what kid doesn't respond to a good story? Combining art and story becomes a natural topic loaded with appeal for this age group that looks for new ways to communicate and question.

Public schools and libraries are natural venues for these kinds of programs. Yes, museums and art galleries constantly plan art programs for kids fortunate enough to take advantage of the opportunities. However, not all children live in large communities with art museums or galleries. Many families cannot afford art classes and trips. Not all parents take their children to museums, nor do they go on their own. Many schools either can't afford class trips or may find it difficult to take time away from a rigid curriculum focused on basic classes. This is not to suggest that those who go to museums would find a library art program superfluous. Children who love art often welcome any new opportunity to explore something they like.

Including paintings and stories in the classroom or library curriculum gives students interesting new ways to study history, geography, sociology, and language arts. The student who becomes caught up in the story of the Spanish Civil War will likely linger over Picasso's *Guernica* and may want to know more about World War II. The young person who studies *Washington Crossing the Delaware* might be interested in factual errors in the painting and become a better historical researcher. Children who imagine the lives of the people in van Gogh's *Potato Eaters* will be able to see the world of leisure shown in Renoir's *Luncheon of the Boating Party* from a different viewpoint. Read some of the picture book *The Fantastic Journey of Pieter Brueghel* as you introduce the painting *The Land of Cockaigne,* and your students will want to study maps of Belgium and Holland. Young people will naturally tell their own stories about these paintings, keep art journals, and write scripts to tell stories, such as that of Harriet Tubman. And they may just want to read and write fairy tales after studying the fanciful paintings of Marc Chagall.

While students look at and study the paintings, they practice skills they need for all kinds of learning. The skills of observing details, comparing and contrasting different paintings, making inferences from objects in pictures, and drawing conclusions about what is happening can be applied to any area of study. Not only are these skills useful to children as they advance in school, but most jobs in the twenty-first century require constantly acquiring new knowledge based on reasoning, exploring the world creatively, and thinking in new ways.

The books in this chapter's bibliography represent a small but exciting variety of titles about art and story. Some span great periods of art history, and others focus on paintings by a single artist. The texts of some books are lyrical and poetic. Some novels and fictional journals of artists appear. Some books tell the story behind famous paintings, and others guide the teacher or librarian in using art with children. Two titles not included in the bibliography deserve special comment. Françoise Barbe-Gall's *How to Talk to Children about Art* (Chicago Review Press, 2005) contains questions and answers about taking children to museums and finding the kinds of art they will enjoy, in addition to thirty full-color paintings with a discussion of each. Marianne Saccardi's encyclopedic *Art in Story: Teaching Art History to Elementary School Children* (2d ed., Teacher Ideas Press, 2007) covers world art from ancient days to the present, with impressive bibliographies, stories behind artworks, and suggestions for art projects.

The programs in this chapter involve close observation of selected paintings with prompt questions and games to evoke children's responses to the stories told in the pictures. "Story Art," the school program, includes detailed information about pairs of narrative paintings, with handouts for student use. Art and language arts projects are also suggested. "Art Quest and Café," the public library program, shows you how to create a kid-friendly place for playing art games while they snack and create "Dream a World" pictures inspired by the fantasy paintings of Chagall. Children will have so much fun that they'll forget that they are learning.

Bibliography

Balliett, Blue. *Chasing Vermeer.* Scholastic, 2004.
(Reading Level: Accelerated Reader, 5.4)
    Two sixth graders discover their mutual passion about art as they embark on an art mystery and try to recover a Vermeer painting that has been stolen en route to Chicago. The plot becomes fairly complex, but kids of this age will enjoy the sleuthing along with the main characters.

Chagall, Marc, and Britta Hoepler. *Life Is a Dream: Marc Chagall.* Prestel, 1998.
(Reading Level: Flesch-Kincaid, 9.7)
    Part of the Adventures in Art series, this brief picture book uses a lyrical text with fanciful type-faces and full-color prints of Chagall's paintings to motivate readers to interact with art. Information is given, but the major value of the book is its creative approach to looking at and thinking about the paintings. This source will inspire creative writing.

Duggleby, John. *Artist in Overalls: The Life of Grant Wood.* Chronicle Books, 1996.
(Reading Level: Flesch-Kincaid, 7.4)
    This lively biography was the first book written for young readers about the Iowa artist. It chronicles his life and discusses many of his paintings and artworks, so kids will gain a greater appreciation for the images and stories behind his works.

Duggleby, John. *Story Painter: The Life of Jacob Lawrence.* Chronicle, 1998.
(Reading Level: Flesch-Kincaid, 8.5)
    Full-color reproductions and an informative text convey the story of this famous African American artist. Historical details of the Depression, the Harlem Renaissance, and the civil rights movement extends the reader's knowledge of the stories behind Lawrence's art.

Hoving, Thomas. *American Gothic.* Chamberlain Bros., Penguin, 2005.
(Reading Level: Flesch-Kincaid, 6.3)
    This biography of Grant Wood's *American Gothic* tells the story behind this famous painting along with details of the artist's life. Further, it trains the viewer to look for details and gain insights into viewing art and appreciating narrative qualities of other paintings.

Hoving, Thomas. *Master Pieces.* W.W. Norton, 2006.
(Reading Level: Flesch-Kincaid, 9.8)
    Based on art games played by curators, Hoving challenges the reader to look at details from selected famous paintings and guess the name and artist of each work. Verbal clues are also given, and the viewer can check the catalogue of full-color reproductions and information in the second half of the book. This fascinating resource will keep readers looking and guessing for hours.

Howard, Nancy Shroyer. *Jacob Lawrence: American Scenes, American Struggles.* Davis Publications, 1996.
(Reading Level: Flesch-Kincaid, 9.8)
    One of the Closer Look Activity Books, this well-organized book of Lawrence's life and paintings takes young readers into the world of the artist to learn about his subjects and how he executed his paintings. Numerous full-color illustrations and bullet points encourage kids to look at details and create their own art projects inspired by this noted artist.

Janson, H. W., and Anthony F. Janson. *History of Art for Young People.* 4th ed. Abrahms, 1992.
(Reading Level: Flesch-Kincaid, 10.4)
    This encyclopedic history of art will be useful to good readers at the middle school and high school levels. It is well recognized as the definitive art history text and is a good reference tool for libraries.

Koningsburg, E. L. *From the Mixed Up Files of Mrs. Basil E. Frankweiler.* Atheneum, 1967.
(Reading Level: Accelerated Reader, 4.7)

In this popular and award-winning book, two children run away from home to live in the Metropolitan Museum of Art in New York. While they inhabit the museum, the kids solve an art mystery involving a statue by Michelangelo.

Lawrence, Jacob. *Harriet and the Promised Land.* Aladdin Paperbacks, 1997.
(Reading Level: Flesch-Kincaid, 4.5)

In a series of stunning narrative paintings and with a sparse, poetic text, Jacob Lawrence captures the power of Harriet Tubman, who led her people to liberty by way of the Underground Railroad during the American Civil War.

Reichold, Klaus, and Bernhard Graf. *Paintings That Changed the World.* Prestel, n.d.
(Reading Level: Flesch-Kincaid, 12.0)

This compelling introduction to world art examines ninety masterpieces with full-color reproductions and one-page essays that discuss the cultural, historical, and artistic importance of each work. This is highly recommended for teachers and for good readers in middle school and higher grades.

Seillier, Marie. *Chagall from A to Z.* Peter Bedrick, 1996.
(Reading Level: Flesch-Kincaid, 7.5)

This short picture book, arranged alphabetically, tells the story of Marc Chagall's life and work. It introduces major themes in his paintings, discusses common images, and gives background to some of the paintings so that the viewer will gain insight into the art. Lyrical text and layout will attract readers in elementary and middle grades.

Shafer, Anders C. *The Fantastic Journey of Pieter Brueghel.* Dutton Children's Books, 2002.
(Reading Level: Accelerated Reader, 4.6)

Based on known information, Shafer has created a fictional diary with richly detailed illustrations, as if the artist Brueghel had left this treasure for modern readers. The story begins when the young artist is challenged to take a trip to Rome by his mentor, Hieronymous Cock. Some of the entries and illustrations can be directly compared to Brueghel's paintings, such as *Hunters in the Snow.* A catalogue of select paintings by the artist appears in the back of the book.

Selected Web Sites

Goya Website: http://eeweems.com/goya/3rd-of-may.html

Erik Weems, art expert on Goya, provides biographical information, a discussion of Goya's paintings, and resources for students.

Mood Book: www.moodbook.com/history/postimpressionism/vincent-van-gogh-works.html

A free Windows utility with links to many artists, their paintings, and lengthy information about these works.

National Public Radio Features: www.npr.org/programs/morning/features/patc/georgewashington/ and www.npr.org/programs/morning/features/patc/nighthawks

These two sites on *George Washington Crossing the Delaware* and *Nighthawks* discuss the artists and the works cited in this chapter. Texts to the feature stories on National Public Radio.

The Van Gogh Gallery: www.vangoghgallery.com/painting/potatoindex.html

Online Web site of the Van Gogh Gallery (not to be confused with The Van Gogh Museum), with information about his life, specific paintings, lesson plans, and free downloads. This link focuses on *The Potato Eaters.*

Web Museum, Paris: www.ibiblio.org/wm/paint/auth/delacroix/liberte/ and www.ibiblio.org/wm/paint/auth/bruegel

Links to numerous paintings. Excellent discussion of Delacroix's painting. Another link to Brueghel contains basic information about his *Peasant Wedding* painting.

Wikipedia: http://en.wikipedia.org/wikipedia.org/wiki/The_Arnolfini_portrait

The free online community-built organization has an extensive discussion of van Eyck's *Arnolfini Portrait*.

Story Art: A School Program

This program unit develops students' skills of observation and recall of detail by learning to look carefully at paintings. This practice not only makes art more pleasurable but enhances all learning. Several exercises are provided, along with specific paintings to study, with background information. Further opportunities to interact with art are suggested by the creative activities in this unit.

Materials Needed

Posters of paintings (most are available from the Internet site www.allposters.com) or large art prints—ten to twelve prints if possible.

Copies of handouts in this chapter (pp. 8, 14).

Art supplies for student murals in the projects list, such as three or four sets of poster paints, two or three sets of oil pastels, and two or three sets of colored markers (or have kids use their own art supplies), plus several yards of white paper purchased from teacher supply stores or art stores.

Procedure

Before You Begin

1. Order posters of paintings to study and set up a large display of art books to encourage students to look at many paintings and works of art.

2. Gather art supplies and/or inform those who have registered to bring their own art supplies.

First Meeting

1. Read aloud portions from the book *The Fantastic Journey of Pieter Brueghel* in preparation for looking at some of this artist's paintings.

2. Tell students they will be testing their own skills of looking at the world of art carefully.

3. Use "Introducing Pictures That Tell Stories" (pp. 6–7) to discuss van Eyck's *The Arnolfini Portrait* and Brueghel's *Wedding Feast*. Locate these paintings in books listed in this chapter's bibliography or purchase prints from the online store AllPosters.com. Try the warm-up exercise (on pp. 7–8) to record details of paintings in groups of twos with your students.

Second Meeting

1. Distribute the paired paintings (found on pages 9–13) to small groups and ask students to use the look, learn, and like (LLL) section and "Are YOU an Art Sleuth?" handout (p. 8) to write about the paintings. (After students have written about the paired paintings, you may wish to

share the background comparisons provided in this chapter or simply discuss some of the points with your class.)

Third Meeting

1. Divide the class into two or three larger groups to make story murals or perform stories based on select paintings from the art project list found on page 14.

2. As a bonus assignment, some students may want to write poems about their favorite paintings. An excellent resource book of "ekphrastic poems" (poems that describe or respond to art) is *Heart to Heart: New Poems Inspired by Twentieth-Century American Art,* edited by Jan Greenberg (Abrams, 2001).

Fourth Meeting

1. Continue work on murals, dramatic presentations, and poems.

Fifth Meeting

1. Present art dramatizations and have students read the poems they have written. If time permits, read some of the poems from Greenberg's book *Heart to Heart.*

Introducing Pictures That Tell Stories:
The Arnolfini Portrait by Jan van Eyck and
Wedding Feast by Pieter Brueghel

Before photography, artists were the source for recording pictorial accounts of important events. The paired pictures students will study in this project focus on themes of war, daily life, and moral questions. To introduce the idea of looking at paintings from a storyteller's view, use the paintings by Jan van Eyck and Pieter Brueghel for general class discussion. They center on another important event in people's lives—weddings and marriages. The following information provides background for the teacher or librarian.

The van Eyck portrait of Giovanni Arnolfini and his wife shows the wedding couple in a room of their home in Bruges, Belgium. Some scholars believe this is the couple's betrothal picture rather than their wedding portrait, but it does record an event associated with a particular marriage. The couple is richly dressed in velvet and silk damask with fur trimmings. Other details in the room suggest wealth—the elaborate bed with red curtains, the ornate brass chandelier, the fancy mirror with its brass frame on the wall. The couple is holding hands affectionately, but their faces are solemn, underscoring the idea that marriage is a sacred sacrament. Everything in the picture is painted in clear, careful detail, but there is more than meets the eye on first glance.

Ask students to point out objects in the picture. Everything in this painting has a symbolic meaning to the educated eye. Notice that the man has shed his sandals, and the woman's clogs rest near the bed. Their stocking feet tell us that they are standing on sacred ground. The green dress of the woman symbolizes hope; her white cap signifies purity. The red bed curtains suggest the passion of love and the marriage act. The little dog is a symbol of fidelity, and the oranges on the chest by the window may refer to fertility or remind us of the Garden of Eden, a state of innocence. One lighted candle in the chandelier stands for the presence of God in their lives, especially at this sacred event. Much has been made of the reflection of the artist and other witnesses in the mirror on the wall. Students may wish to give their own interpretation of why they are here. Point out the elaborate signature of the artist on the wall above the mirror. It clearly documents that van Eyck himself was present, because the writing translates, "Jan van Eyck was here. 1434."

The scene in the painting has been set with characters and furnishings. We know the couple is about to be married. Full details are not given about the event, but students can tell their own stories given this much information. To help them elaborate on the story, interested students may want to read *Catherine Called Birdy,* a modern novel by Karen Cushman, set in the Middle Ages, in which the main character frets about her future as a bride.

The people in Pieter Brueghel's wedding painting are not as wealthy; they are peasants enjoying a big wedding feast nonetheless. Unlike the van Eyck portrait, we do not know who the couple is, nor do we know very much about them. The bride is clearly indicated by the decoration hanging on the wall above her head. She is also wearing a crown. We are not certain who is the groom. Some think he is the man pouring wine. Others suggest he is the man seated two people away from the bride. The setting may be the inside of a barn that has been cleaned out, with a long table and simple benches provided for the guests. The wedding guests are busy talking, eating, asking for more drink, helping themselves to pies, and generally enjoying a good time. At the end of the table sits a gentlemen who is more elaborately dressed, and some scholars think he is the artist Brueghel. Look for other details in the picture. Someone wears a spoon in his hat. Someone is licking a pan. Musicians are on hand to add music to the gathering. Perhaps people will go outside to dance. Brueghel uses color to call attention to people in the picture and to make a pleasing composition rather than using color symbolically as van Eyck does.

Ask students what story Brueghel is telling in his painting. Given the information provided here, the teacher or librarian may wish to have students prepare a script or write an account of the wedding activities.

Looking at, Learning about, and Liking Art

Prepare students to look closely at several paintings in posters and in art books that are on display in the library. Point out obvious details in pictures, then guide students to look for the less obvious things that may be hidden in corners or the background of a painting.

Then try this exercise. Divide the class into groups of two. Give each group a picture to study for five minutes. Give each student five minutes to write down as many details from the pictures as possible. Have students share their lists to make a more complete list. If there is time, repeat this exercise with another set of pictures. Generally, people improve their skills of observation when given more opportunities to look and think about pictures.

Introduce students to paintings with many details such as Pieter Brueghel's crowded compositions of village life or a mural by Thomas Hart Benton or a large painting by Jacob Lawrence. Ask "guide questions" such as, "What characters are in the foreground of this picture?" "What kind of animals do you see in the picture?" "Are there any tools or machines in the painting? What kinds?" The complexity of Brueghel's, Benton's, and Lawrence's paintings challenges our skills of concentration and observation.

As students study paintings in this unit, ask them to use the following points to record what they see and what is happening in artworks. The handout "Are YOU an Art Sleuth?" (p. 8) uses the LLL approach to understanding art. First we must "look" carefully at pictures. Next we need to "learn" all we can about the picture and how it was created. Then we can "like" much more about the picture than we would from casual observation.

Are YOU an Art Sleuth?
Discovering Clues in Paintings

I. Look at the painting.

- Write down concrete details of things in the painting.

- Be specific. Don't just say "people" but give physical descriptions. Itemize how many objects (three trees, four dogs, one orange) are in the picture.

- Tell where objects appear (the couple who are talking are on the left side of the painting).

- Describe the setting as clearly as you can.

- What action is occurring, if any?

II. Learn about the painting.

- When and where is the painting set?

- What did the artist tell us about this painting (perhaps in written sources)?

- What other paintings by this artist show similar subjects?

- Describe exactly what is going on in the painting in one paragraph. (Do not add your own judgment at this point.)

III. What I like about the painting.

- In your own words, tell the full story of the painting. Here you are free to add your own evaluation and impressions. Describe the emotional content and meaning behind the painting, if you can.

- Tell what parts of the painting are particularly memorable to you.

Painting Pair I: Revolution!

Paintings: *The Third of May, 1808* by Francisco de Goya and *Guernica* by Pablo Picasso

Background for these paintings:

Art history is filled with art objects and paintings of famous battle scenes and war. A chest found in King Tut's tomb in ancient Egypt is decorated with pictures of the young king standing in a chariot as he aims an arrow at enemy Nubian warriors. Two thousand years later, another famous battle scene was embroidered on an enormous linen piece that is known as the Bayeaux Tapestry. In this battle William of Normandy successfully fought Harold of Hastings in England to become William the Conqueror.

The two paintings in our study are from the modern world. They are dramatic scenes of revolutions fought in Spain. Goya's *The Third of May* dates to 1803, and Picasso's *Guernica* depicts the horrors of another war more than 130 years later. Share this brief background with students to give them a context within which to discuss the stories.

The Spanish artist Goya was living in Madrid on May 2, 1808, when he witnessed an uprising of Spanish citizens against King Joseph Bonaparte (who was placed on the Spanish throne by his brother, Napoleon Bonaparte). Because the Spanish men were greatly outnumbered, their revolt was quickly suppressed, and 400 citizens were arrested within the day. The military tribunal arrested many people who were completely innocent. Early the next morning a French firing squad shot forty-five men before dawn.

This painting is said to be the first to put victims of war in the center stage of a painting. It is a deeply moving picture of war, especially from the expressions on the men's faces, but it is not so specific in its details that it is simply a recording of this one revolution. Goya's painting has become a statement of the injustices and horrors of war itself. Some say this is a powerful antiwar painting.

Pablo Picasso, also a Spanish artist, painted his *Guernica* in the twentieth century as a protest against war based on disturbing events during the Spanish Civil War in the 1930s. A fascist group led by Francisco Franco, who promised peace and prosperity, attacked the newly elected Spanish government. In April 1937 dreadful atrocities were committed against the civilian population of Guernica, in northern Spain, by Franco's men. Bombs pounded the town for three days as its citizens ran in horror from crumbling buildings. Picasso was living in Paris at the time, but the newspaper photographs of this event reached him, and the famous artist was moved to paint this unforgettable work.

Although the themes of these paintings are similar, the artists' treatments of their subjects are very different. Goya's painting uses color, chiaroscuro (light and dark contrasts), and a strong composition to dramatize his realistic picture of revolution. Picasso purposely chose to not represent the realistic details of war. He abstracted significant details—a woman with outstretched arms, human skulls, a dead horse, a bull, a naked light bulb—to symbolize the world gone mad in the midst of a devastating war.

Painting Pair II: The Fight for Liberty

Paintings: *Liberty Leading the People* by Eugene Delacroix and *Washington Crossing the Delaware* by Emanuel Leutze

Background for these paintings:

These two paintings tell dramatic stories of people fighting for liberty in two different countries in two different eras. The scene of the America Revolution in Leutze's picture dates to December 1776, although the painting was done almost one hundred years later. The scene in Delacroix's painting dates to 1830, and the artist executed his work contemporaneously with the event. Neither painting was meant to be a realistic depiction of actual events; rather, each work has become iconic. They are representations of the fight for liberty itself. Delacroix's painting was even used as a war poster. Leutze's painting has become one of the most memorable symbols of the American Revolution. This painting, along with the Statue of Liberty and the Liberty Bell, symbolizes liberty itself to generations of Americans.

In Delacroix's painting the fighters are a mixture of different social classes who rose up to dethrone the Bourbon king of France on July 28, 1830. The figure of Liberty is a half-draped woman wearing a cap of Liberty, holding a gun in one hand and the tricolor flag of the new republic in her other hand. Many slain warriors on the ground show the sacrifice of the French people, but the young boy and the man with the top hat (supposedly the artist himself) reign triumphant along with Liberty in leading the people. This is obviously a highly sentimentalized painting, but it has inspired other works of art, including the modern stage musical *Les Miserables.*

Washington's crossing of the Delaware River was actually a minor event in the Revolutionary War, but it gave the patriots a huge moral boost. In December 1776 the British army under the command of General Howe was confident of victory. They settled in for the winter in New York. The little band of patriots navigated the icy river on Christmas Eve and made a surprise attack on Hessian soldiers, the British mercenaries, and captured 900 of them. Although the war went on for five years after the event, this victory was symbolically crucial for the young country. The artist of this picture was obviously not alive at the time of the war, nor was he concerned about realistically showing the actual details of event. For example, the "Stars and Stripes" flag shown in the painting was not used at the time. Washington could not have been standing up in the boat, or he would have been thrown into the icy water. The sky is bright in the painting, rather than pitch black as it would have been at the time Washington made his midnight crossing. Despite these historical inaccuracies, Leutze painted a picture that so dramatically captures the spirit of the event that it probably tells a better story than a more realistic depiction could have done.

Painting Pair III: Sharing a Meal

Paintings: *Luncheon of the Boating Party* by Pierre-Auguste Renoir and *The Potato Eaters* by Vincent van Gogh

Background for these pictures:

Since the subject of food is universal, the history of art quite naturally has incorporated pictures of food and people eating since ancient days. Egyptian tomb paintings show lavish feasts so that pharaohs might enjoy food in the afterlife. Medieval tapestries depict elaborate meals. Seventeenth-century Dutch paintings not only focus on elaborate still life food arrangements, but genre paintings of the day show middle class citizens enjoying the delights of the table. The two paintings for this study focus on people sharing a meal, but they are very different from one another. Interestingly, the two paintings were created within five years of one another.

Renoir, a successful French painter of the late nineteenth century, is known for his charming portraits of upper middle class life, lovely women, and children. He was an Impressionist painter who enjoyed using outdoor scenery and light in his work. His pictures show an artist who was engaged with life and who socialized with a wide circle of friends. *The Luncheon of the Boating Party* captures Renoir's world. Here a group of Parisians gather at the Masion Fournaise, a retreat on the Seine River, to enjoy boating, food in a good restaurant, and a restful night at the inn.

This painting shows a group of Renoir's friends (who can be identified from reference sources). Among the guests are Jules Laforgue, a poet; Ellen Andree, an actress; Gustave Calliebotte, an artist and boatman; and Aline Charigot, a seamstress, who would later marry Renoir. The people are dressed casually but wear jaunty hats. Bottles of wine and the remains of what must have been a delicious lunch are spread upon the white clothed table under the canopy of the open-air restaurant. The composition and expressions of the people suggest an atmosphere of conviviality in which conversation and a good repast mark the sharing of a good meal.

Vincent van Gogh, the prolific Dutch painter, was a contemporary of Renoir, but he never achieved success in his own lifetime. His life was vastly different from Renoir's. He struggled mentally and financially to survive in the world. Always an iconoclast, he ventured beyond the light-filled world of the Impressionists to show a deeply felt Expressionistic scene. *The Potato Eaters* was one of van Gogh's early paintings. It pictures a family of dirt-poor farmers crowded around their dinner table lit by a single light. The five figures share a common bowl of meager potatoes in dim light. No one is identified, but these simple peasants seem to symbolize the status of those who eke out a living from the soil, surviving as well as they can. This is not a meal for socializing and conviviality. The potato eaters simply eat to live.

Painting Pair IV: A Slice of Life, City and Country Styles

Paintings: *Nighthawks* by Edward Hopper and *Dinner for Threshers* by Grant Wood

Background for these paintings:

Although both of these paintings are realistic in style, created by American artists within ten years of each other, and show people engaged in eating or drinking, they are almost completely different in setting and mood. Hopper's city scene, with its isolated street, makes a dramatic statement of loneliness, while Wood's rural setting, filled with bright light and a crowd of people, is the picture of hospitality. Both pictures share an important artistic element in their compositions. Hopper frames the glass-front café with the strong black outline of the building and an adjacent red store across the street. Wood shows a cutaway dining room in the farmhouse, framed by the porch and roofline of the house itself with an adjacent red barn. Thus, the people in each picture almost look like actors in stage settings that we, the viewers, can study at our leisure.

Nighthawks has become Hopper's most famous painting. The setting is a café located in Greenwich Village, and it seems to be an oasis with its fluorescent lighting amid the dark night outside. Most of the canvas is filled with the buildings and open space. The people are small in relation to the size of the picture. The three diners in the café are seated at a counter, where a man dressed like a short order cook waits on them. One man and the woman seem to be a couple, but they do not look at each other. No one seems to be talking or even relating to anyone else. The people look isolated, bored, perhaps even trapped. Note that there are no doors into the restaurant. *Nighthawks* was painted in 1942, not long after the Japanese bombed Pearl Harbor, a time when people felt afraid and vulnerable. This mood is captured in Hopper's painting. Even though the scene evokes silence, we may be tempted to add our own dialogue or create a story about the scene we have just observed.

Dinner for Threshers looks like a scene from Grant Wood's childhood, when farmers from the area came to help thresh each family's oat crop. The men worked from sun up to noon. Then they washed up, trudged into the dining room, and sat down to a long table set with a big dinner of fried chicken, ham, mashed potatoes, vegetables, pie, and cake. The men sit at the table in Wood's painting with two women serving them. More men wait outside to join them as two other women work at the stove in the kitchen. Unlike the lack of detail in Hopper's café, Wood's painting is filled with detail—patterned wallpaper, a checked tablecloth, neatly stacked dishes in a kitchen cupboard, lace curtains at the windows, print dresses on the women. The people in *Dinner for Threshers* eat, drink coffee, look at one another, and appear to carry on pleasant conversation. Wood painted his work in 1934 during the Great Depression, but the people in this picture are enjoying the generous bounty before them.

Painting Pair V: Pictures of Folly

Paintings: *Beware of Luxury* by Jan Steen and *The Fight Between Carnival and Lent* by Pieter Brueghel or *The Land of Cockaigne* by Pieter Brueghel

Background of these paintings:

In ages past, artists imparted moral truths in their paintings by showing the ugly effects of people's follies or foolish actions. The Dutch and Flemish painters of the sixteenth and seventeenth centuries were especially concerned with these matters. The English artist William Hogarth painted a series of pictures about domestic intemperance. The paintings in this study combine realistic detail and didactic advice of the day, and they show us clothing, behavior, and activities from a colorful past time.

Jan Steen's *Beware of Luxury* shows a Dutch wife fallen asleep at the table. She is surrounded by a serving girl, several children, and other people wasting time and acting carelessly. The servant invites the advances of one gentleman. A fiddler turns to laugh at a child who takes things from a cupboard. An old woman and a man sit gossiping. The floor is littered with food and overturned drinking vessels. Other objects foreshadow what will come of these foolish actions—there is a basket with crutches, and a sword hangs from the wall. Steen underscores his message by a slate in the far right-hand corner of the picture. The message translates, "At a time of good living, beware."

Several of Pieter Brueghel's paintings communicate a similar warning. *The Land of Cockaigne* clearly shows three dissolute people sprawled on the ground under a gnarled tree stump that supports an odd table of food and dishes. The men look like they're in a stupor from overeating and drinking, but we can imagine when they awake, they will repeat their foolish actions. More food lies about—a cactus plant made of bread grows nearby, an egg on legs has been opened by a knife, a roast pig ready to be sliced also has a knife in its side, and a chicken lays its neck on a plate so that it might be eaten. A curious rooftop in the left-hand corner of the painting is covered with pies that seem to be guarded by a knight. Is he also tempted to indulge? This is a land of earthly delights guaranteed to tempt men into indulgence.

Brueghel's more complex painting, *The Fight Between Carnival and Lent,* gives us a panoply of village life at a festival just before Lent begins. In the foreground of the painting a fat fellow, who symbolizes Carnival, sits astride a beer barrel and turns a pig on a spit. He is pitted against a lean man, who symbolizes Lent and is pulled along on a cart. This pair is surrounded by dozens of people engaged in indulging themselves by eating pancakes, dancing, gambling, and playing pranks. A play is being performed outside an inn. A few people are coming out of the church, but they don't seem much better than the other folk. Everyone is ignoring the group of crippled men in the middle of the painting. Everything in this busy and highly detailed painting reflects the artist's message that, in the end, we are all fools in one way or the other.

Art Projects List for Telling Stories

1. Study Jacob Lawrence's paintings in the Harriet Tubman series of art, and create your own story mural about another famous African American hero in one large painted mural for the library or classroom. Write out the story so that it can be read or told to the class when your group finishes its mural.

2. Scan and print some of Jacob Lawrence's paintings in the Harriet Tubman series to make an art display on poster board or on display boards for the library. You may want to create pictures of your own in Lawrence's style to tell the story of Tubman's life. Make this a multimedia show by adding gospel and jazz music, poetry, and dance. Write your own poems or find the one about Tubman by Eloise Greenfield.

3. Borrow or create simple peasant costumes to re-create scenes from one of Pieter Brueghel's paintings. Write a script for your scene so that each character in the painting will have several lines to speak, and add a narrator's part to introduce what is going on in this story.

4. Create a script for a proposed television documentary on a historical event shown in a painting such as Goya's *The Third of May* or Leutze's *Washington Crossing the Delaware.* You might have several television reporters interview the people in each painting about what is happening at the time the paintings were created. For example, interview the people from Spain just before they are arrested in the Goya painting, or talk to the men just before they board Washington's little boat that will cross the Delaware.

5. Re-create Grant Wood's dinner meal of the threshers from his painting of the same name. Set up a table with people at it and conduct an extemporaneous conversation between the threshers and the women serving them.

From *Story Celebrations: A Program Guide for Schools and Libraries* by Jan Irving.
Westport, CT: Libraries Unlimited. Copyright © 2008.

Art Quest and Café: A Public Library Program

Older kids love the idea of sleuthing, going on a quest to solve a mystery. They also love to do art and enjoy the atmosphere of a café for kids their own age. Combine these interests in a program at your public library. Consider advertising the program with reproductions of famous paintings displayed around town or in schools, with intriguing questions such as, "What's wrong with this picture?" or "Is this a fake painting?" Invite kids to come dressed in an "artsy" way, and have plenty of yummy food and games ready for a festive occasion. For wider participation, ask teen volunteers to cover the café tables, assemble the food, and decorate the room.

This program involves a one-hour session before the program for kids to decorate the room. The program itself is planned for one session approximately 1½ hours long.

Materials Needed

Art posters and prints that can be cut into pieces and used for games. Other posters for display. (Check the Web site www.allposters.com for a wide variety of art prints and posters.)

Plenty of art books from the library for a display. Use the books listed in this chapter's bibliography and titles from the Time-Life Library of Art, which many public libraries own.

Bright-colored paper for collages and art projects, about six sheets of different colors for every program participant.

Colored pencils, markers, and tempera paint (if you are willing to deal with something more complicated).

Plain white watercolor paper, or a good grade of bond paper, about two sheets of cover weight stock per student, for drawings

Butcher paper or large sheets of white paper to cover tables, allow about 3 yards of paper per table

One gallon of lemonade for every sixteen participants, and a recipe of party mix for every twenty-four participants. (Use the original recipe on the Web site www.chex.com.)

Fruit and cheese tray, purchased from discount grocery stores or created by kids who help plan this event, about one twelve-inch tray for every twelve participants.

Paper napkins and cups, one cup and two napkins per participant.

Gel pens for prizes in the Art Quiz game, one per participant.

Procedure

Before You Begin

1. Order posters and set up a display of art books for the program. Choose both "how to" books and books of paintings. Check the bibliography on pages 3–4.

2. Set up the room café style, with small tables and chairs. Cover tables with plain paper and jars of colored pencils and pens.

3. Invite teens to decorate the room with other "jazzy" touches such as colored paper pinwheels, balloons, confetti, and posters.

4. Purchase and assemble food to serve (bowls of party mix, cups of punch and lemonade, platters of fruit and cheese arranged attractively as a work of art).

5.   Before participants arrive for the program, cut one of the posters into six or eight pieces (enough so that every table will have one piece of the "puzzle") and place them around the room. These paintings would be good choices: *Sunday on La Grande Jatte, The Village and I,* or *The Fight Between Carnival and Lent.*

The Day of the Program

1.   As participants arrive, invite them to make drawings on their paper table coverings in the style of a famous artist or with "artistic shapes." Serve bowls of party mix and punch at the beginning of the program.

2.   Play jazzy music before the program begins, then lower the music to welcome your art sleuths.

At the Program

1.   Booktalk or read portions from *From the Mixed Up Files of Mrs. Basil E. Frankweiler* or *Chasing Vermeer* to introduce the idea of kids becoming art detectives.

2.   Ask children what they see in the puzzle piece on their table. Then invite each table to place their puzzle pieces on a larger table or the floor.

3.   When all puzzle pieces have been gathered, ask for three volunteers to put the painting back together again. Remind them that careful observation is important for good sleuthing. Ask the group what the entire painting seems to be telling them. What is the story in the picture?

4.   Pass around art prints and art books with the following paintings in them. You may select other paintings, but these examples have plenty of details to study: Chagall's *The Village and I,* Chagall's *The Juggler,* Chagall's *The Lovers,* Seurat's *Sunday on La Grande Jatte,* Brueghel's *The Fight Between Carnival and Lent,* Brueghel's *The Land of Cockaigne,* van Eyck's *The Arnolfini Portrait.* (All of these paintings are available as posters or prints from www.allposters.com.)

5.   Give kids about ten minutes to look quickly but carefully at all the pictures. Then gather up the books and ask questions from the art quiz in this chapter (pp. 17–18). To help students as they answer questions, give each table a handout that lists the names of the paintings and the artists for all artworks they have seen. Award points for correct answers to questions. Those sitting at the table with the largest number of points each receive a gel pen as a prize.

6.   Show Chagall's paintings *The Village and I, The Juggler, The Lovers,* and *Birthday.* Ask kids what objects they see in the pictures. You may need to point out details that are missed. Explain that this artist repeatedly used images of farm animals, fiddlers, circus people, his wife, flowers, and birds to tell his dreamlike stories. These objects and places were important parts of his world.

7.   Distribute art materials and invite students to make pictures of things important to them. Some may want to draw a large circle on their art paper to frame their "Dream a World" pictures. Point out that Chagall's *The Village and I* resembles the pattern of a kaleidoscope. If you turn the painting, different objects can be seen from various angles.

8.   Invite participants to enjoy snacks as they complete their projects.

Art Quiz for Young Sleuths

Note: This is an oral quiz.

1.   Someone is making pancakes in this picture. What is the picture?
     (Answer: *The Fight Between Carnival and Lent*)

2.   A bride is swinging from a trapeze in this picture. In which painting is this happening?
     (Answer: *The Juggler*)

3.   A man is over a barrel in this painting. Which one?
     (Answer: *Fight Between Carnival and Lent*)

4.   Which painting shows a woman with a pet monkey?
     (Answer: *Sunday on La Grande Jatte*)

5.   In which painting do we see a pig with a knife in its side?
     (Answer: *The Land of Cockaigne*)

6.   In which painting do we see a lighted candle?
     (Answer: *The Arnolfini Portrait*)

7.   In which painting do we see a little girl in a white hat?
     (Answer: *Sunday on La Grande Jatte*)

8.   In which painting do we see a fiddler?
     (Answer: *The Lovers* or *The Juggler*)

9.   A man with a green face appears in which picture?
     (Answer: *The Village and I*)

10. A man is asleep under a tree in this picture. Which picture fits this description?
     (Answer: *The Land of Cockaigne*)

11. In which picture do we see a sailboat?
     (Answer: *Sunday on La Grand Jatte*)

12. In which painting do we see someone milking a cow?
     (Answer: *The Village and I*)

13. In which painting has a man taken off his shoes?
     (Answer: *The Arnolfini Portrait*)

14. In which painting do we see crippled people?
     (Answer: *Fight Between Carnival and Lent*)

15.   In which painting do we see a bird man?
      (Answer: *The Juggler*)

16.   In which painting do we see a mirror?
      (Answer: *The Arnolfini Portrait*)

17.   A little dog appears in which painting?
      (Answer: *The Arnolfini Portrait* and *Sunday on La Grande Jatte*)

18.   A woman is riding a horse in which painting?
      (Answer: *The Juggler*)

19.   In which painting do we see a bed?
      (Answer: *The Arnolfini Portrait*)

20.   In which picture is a roof covered with pies?
      (Answer: *The Land of Cockaigne*)

21.   In which painting is a woman carrying a black umbrella?
      (Answer: *Sunday on La Grande Jatte*)

22.   In which picture is a couple getting married?
      (Answer: *The Lovers*; will also accept *The Arnolfini Portrait*)

2

Puns of Fun:
Wordplay for Kids

Instead of prescribing an apple a day to keep the doctor away, psychologists now suggest that laughing on a daily basis can keep us healthy. Actually, scientists tell us we need to laugh at least fifteen times a day for our health. If this sounds contrived, remember that the laughing produces healing chemicals beneficial to the body, according to numerous scientists and natural healers. The Sunstone Cancer Support Center in Arizona even sponsors a retreat "Laughter: Your Inner Pharmacy." This reason alone justifies including a chapter on humorous wordplay in this book, but in addition, wordplay stretches mental abilities and is just plain fun. Chapter 7, "Barrel of Fun," in my book *Stories NeverEnding* (Libraries Unlimited 2004) introduced simple wordplay for a younger audience, kids in kindergarten through grade six. This chapter extends the fun through more sophisticated use of puns and humorous wordplay.

Very young children have not yet developed the verbal skills to appreciate much more than obvious incongruent situations such as a picture of a fish wearing glasses. Very silly words will also cause young children to laugh. In a preschool storytime I once told a story about a woman whose name was "Madame Poofapuff," to the delight of one young boy who couldn't stop repeating that name over and over again with hearty laughs. Preschoolers engage in their own wordplay as they are acquiring language but mixing up parts of words. My daughter made up the word "tilenheart" for "valentine" when she was a preschooler. This kind of whimsical wordplay is easy for young children.

As they mature, children begin to see discrepancies between what is said and what is meant. We call this "irony," and older students with rich language skills must understand how irony works to appreciate the more complex forms of humor such as satire, puns, and political cartoons. Upper elementary and middle school students generally have a better grasp of spelling and word sounds; therefore, they enjoy manipulating language for humorous effects.

Some studies on the nature of creativity tell us that creative people demonstrate high degrees of flexibility, originality, elaboration (formulating ideas), and redefinition, or the capacity to view problems in a new light. All of these components are facets of understanding and creating puns. Rigid educational practices do not always reward creative answers, but enlightened teachers and schools give students time to take divergent routes and encourage curiosity.

One of the best ways to encourage creativity is through wordplay and puns. Some people tend to denigrate puns as the lowest form of humor, when, in fact, the act of punning is an act of creativity. One must be able to play with sounds of words that have different meanings in order to pun.

Although not comprehensive in the treatment of wordplay, this chapter includes some basic knock-knock jokes, riddles, and idioms as well as homonyms, visual puns, spoonerisms, and shaggy dog stories that use puns for punch lines. Here the creative teacher can find activities to build on kids' natural curiosity about words. Librarians in public libraries might enjoy planning a "Pun-der-ful" party at which kids play pun games, "noodle around," and tell knock-knock jokes. The bibliography includes a variety of materials, from joke and pun books to stories, that use plenty of wordplay. Since students today may not have read Norman Juster's classic *The Phantom Tollbooth,* you might want to read to them the chapter in which Milo visits the Kingdom of Dictionopolis and serve a banquet at which people eat their words. Daniel Pinkwater's *Attila the Pun* and Andrew Clements's *Frindle* will also delight kids. Finally, explore some of the Web sites listed for a wealth of material to tickle the funny bones (or should we say "punny" bones?) of children.

Bibliography

Clements, Andrew. *Frindle.* Simon & Schuster, 1996.
(Reading Level: Accelerated Reader, 5.4)

   Nicholas Allen, a fifth grader, challenges his teacher, who has a fixation about using the dictionary. Nick decides to test his teacher on her own ground and win by inventing a new word (*frindle*), then getting everyone in his class to use the word as a substitution for the word "pen." Nick's idea grows to huge proportions, and this book will inspire clever students to try their hands at a similar game.

Gordon, Harvey C. *PUNdemonium.* The Punster's Press, 1983.
(Reading Level: Spache, 4.7)

   Filled with one-sentence puns and numerous quizzes, this little book of wordplay includes collections of puns about professions, food, sports, and Americana. Special sections involve pun use in advertisements and business.

Juster, Norman. *The Phantom Tollbooth.* Random House, 1961, 1989.
(Reading Level: Accelerated Reader, 6.7)

   This classic children's novel about Milo and his strange adventures through quirky places such as Dictionopolis and the Island of Conclusions plays with logic, irony, nonsense, and all manner of wordplay. Here you will meet Tock, the watchdog, and enjoy a royal banquet at which everyone says delicious words because one has to eat his words. People dine on synonym buns and square meals.

Lederer, Richard. *Crazy English.* Pocket Books, 1989.
(Reading Level: Spache, 6.7)

   One of numerous books by master wordsmith Lederer; introduces words for various phobias, irregular verbs, sound wordplay, and other quirks of the English language.

Lederer, Richard. *Get Thee to a Punnery: An Anthology of Intentional Assaults upon the English Language.* Revised, expanded, and updated. Wyrick, 2006.
(Reading Level: Fleisch-Kincaid, 12.0)

   This popular book proves "the pun is mightier than the sword" with its numerous quips, quotes, puns, and jokes. Young and old will pour over the quizzes (and perhaps need to check the answers if they are stuck) but be encouraged to make up their own puns, for as Phyllis McGinley reminds us "Strike while the irony is hot!"

Lederer, Richard. *The Play of Words.* Pocket Books, 1990.
(Reading Level: Spache, 6.6)

   The popular linguist plays with words through metaphors, clichés, rhymes, proverbs, logic, and odd names for things. Numerous games and quizzes will inspire teachers, librarians, and students to create their own examples of wordplay.

Lederer, Richard. *Pun and Games.* Chicago Review Press, 1996.
(Reading Level: Spache, 5.59)

This funny book croaks with humor, from the frog and fly quote on the front ("Times fun when you're having flies") to the contents list of jokes, riddles daffynitions, tairy fales, rhymes, and more wordplay for kids. Goofy games and opportunities to pun and create wacky jokes make this an indispensable source for teachers, librarians, and kids who love words.

Leedy, Loreen, and Pat Street. *There's a Frog in My Throat: 440 Animal Sayings a Little Bird Told Me.* Holiday House, 2003.
(Reading Level: Spache, 3.30)

Grouped in categories, this picture book provides visual puns for many animal expressions, many of them idioms. Younger and older students will enjoy the whimsical illustrations and become inspired to draw their own visual puns.

Pinkwater, Daniel. *Attila the Pun.* Four Winds Press, 1981.
(Reading Level: Spache, 4.46)

The employees of the Magic Moscow, an ice cream parlor, summon a ghost and get a punster, who possesses a collection of ancient puns. Some favorite old puns involve eating "spookghetti" at an Italian restaurant; crossing a cat with lemon to make a sourpuss; and making an elephant float from ice cream, root beer, and one elephant.

Shulman, Mark. *Mom and Dad Are Palindromes.* Chronicle, 2006.
(Reading Level: Fleisch Kincaid, 4.3)

In this clever frenzied story, Bob and his family are plagued by palindromes. Kids will enjoy finding the 101 palindromes in this book.

Terban, Marvin. *Scholastic Dictionary of Idioms.* Scholastic, 1996.
(Reading Level: Spache, 5.02)

This invaluable resource defines hundreds of idioms and provides the quirky origin of each term. Teachers and students curious about words and their history will pour over the humor in this resource book. Librarians will want copies for reference and for circulation.

Selected Web Sites

AVKO Educational Research Foundation: www.spelling.org/free/puns.htm

A nonprofit organization for teachers and parents provides numerous jokes and anecdotes using puns.

Humanities through Brigham Young University: http://humanities.byu.edu/elc/student/idioms/proverbs/best_advice.html

The English Language Center, designed for ELC students, provides numerous proverbs along with student art to illustrate the meanings.

Read Write Think: www.readwritethink.org/lessons/lesson_view.asp?id=254

Web site of the International Reading Association provides lesson plans, activities, standards, student objectives, and resources for teaching idioms.

The Shaggy Dog: www.theshaggydog.org/detail.asp?ID=18

Advertised as providing "good, clean, pun" appeals to a wide variety of people. Jokes and shaggy dog stories are provided, and students can submit their own shaggy dog stories to share.

The Vol Web Project: http://volweb.utk.edu/Schools/bedford/harrisms/lesson6htm

Sponsored by the University of Tennessee's Virtual K–12 Learning Community Web Site. Provides lesson plans on the subject of puns.

The Worsley School: www.worsleyschool.net/socialarts/puns/pun.html
    An online Canadian school defines all kinds of wordplay, from puns to palindromes and spoonerisms, and gives numerous examples of these.

For the Pun of It: A School Program on Wordplay

This program introduces kids to puns and other forms of wordplay. The activities may be planned for a one- or two-week unit or dispersed throughout the school year. The activities for each meeting are planned for approximately forty-five to fifty-five minutes. Teachers and media specialists can adjust according to their own time frame. These lighthearted exercises lend themselves to times before school holidays or at the end of a testing period when students need a change of pace.

Materials Needed

Soup pot from home or a purchased plastic pot.

Piece of foam core or display board if needed.

Grocery bag and paper lunch bags.

Procedure

Before You Begin

1. In preparation for this humorous program, make a riddle display board, fill a soup pot with spoonerisms, and fill a grocery bag with shaggy dog bags. The dog bags are filled with shaggy dog stories, and the bags may be decorated with dog faces.

2. Riddles may be found in Richard Lederer's *Pun and Games* (see bibliography), and spoonerisms may be found at http://library.thinkquest.org/J0111282/spoonerisms.htm.

3. Shaggy dog stories for the dog bags may be found at www.theshaggydog.org.

4. Consult the bibliography of this chapter and gather books for a display on this topic.

5. Before each meeting, review directions carefully and prepare any required handouts.

First Meeting

1. Begin this program by reading aloud several short books that use wordplay. Revisit the Amelia Bedelia books, or one of Jon Scieszka's titles. Older students might prefer hearing several chapters from the classic novel of wordplay, *The Phantom Tollbooth,* by Norman Juster.

2. After reading one of these books, ask students to recall their favorite jokes or humorous parts of the story.

3. If there is time, you might also begin to read the short novel *Frindle,* by Clements (listed in the bibliography), continuing the reading over several class periods. After completing the book, ask students to submit their own "frindle" (a made-up word with its "real" word association). Suggest that each student use his or her own word instead of the real word throughout the week. Students can keep a log of the results of this word substitution.

Second Meeting

1. Tell students they will "beat time" with this next activity. This is a timed exercise in which students are instructed to find a book with riddles or jokes in the library to read aloud to the class. Set a timer for approximately three minutes. If some students are still looking for books, reset the timer until everyone is ready. At the end of the time, students are called upon to read aloud two riddles or jokes from the books they have found.

2. Introduce the term *idiom* and distribute the "Idiom's Delight" handout (p. 25) for student homework. Tell students to draw pictures that illustrate the expressions on the sheet, so they can share them during the next class period.

Third Meeting

1. Let students share the visual idiom pictures that they created as homework, and give them time to begin writing an idiom story. (See handout on p. 26.)

Fourth Meeting

1. Introduce the words *pun, spoonerism,* and *homonym. Note:* A spoonerism switches the first sounds in a pair of words ("funny bone" becomes "bunny phone") . A homonym is a word that sounds the same as another but has a different meaning (whole/hole). A pun is humorous wordplay that suggests different meanings or applications of words. It incorporates homonyms but actually substitutes one word for another. (Example: A donut ad might read "I can't believe I ate the hole thing.")

2. Set out the "Pot of Spoonerisms" (see pp. 27–28 for complete instructions) and select a few students to spoon out one of the expressions to read to the class. Give students an opportunity to turn the expression or words into a spoonerism. If everyone is stumped, read the answer inside the folded slip of paper.

3. Pass out the "Pun of It All" sheets (pp. 29–30) and group students into small groups to solve the humorous puzzles. Provide time for groups to work and ask for volunteers to provide the answers.

Fifth Meeting

1. Ask students to add their favorite riddles to the riddle board. The riddle board is created by the teacher or media specialist in preparation for the program. (See this on page 24.)

2. Ask for student volunteers to select a shaggy dog bag (found on page 28) to read to the class.

3. Have students turn in the Frindle Logs they began after the first session, and ask them to share experiences if time permits.

4. End this pun unit with an "Eat Your Words" banquet. (See the menu on page 28.)

Red Hot Riddle Board Ideas

Cover a bulletin board with red fabric or stretch a length of red wrapping paper around the room as a background for riddles. To make the riddles especially appealing, write them with large felt-tipped markers on different colors of construction paper or print in a large and playful typeface. Don't include the answers with the riddles, but have them hidden in another part of the room so curious students are motivated to find them.

Encourage students to add their own riddles to the riddle board throughout the week. On the last day of this program unit, each student needs to bring at least one new riddle for the display.

Since this program focuses on wordplay, select riddles that use this element for humorous effect. Here are a few examples (with answers):

Why shouldn't you iron a four leaf clover?
(Answer: You don't want to press your luck!)

What did the horse say when he fell down?
(Answer: I can't giddy up!)

How do pigs get to the hospital?
(Answer: By Ham-bulance!)

Why did the pig block traffic!
(Answer: He was a road hog!)

Why can't you trust the king of the beasts?
(Answer: Because he is a lion!)

How do you change a pumpkin into another vegetable?
(Answer: Throw it up and it comes down squash!)

Why wouldn't the dachshund wear his Christmas sweater?
(Answer: Because he was a hot dog!)

What is a duck's favorite snack?
(Answer: Cheese and quackers!)

Idioms Delight

This activity is wordplay based on the title of a play by Robert Sherwood, *Idiot's Delight.* The same title was used in a radio show and in a musical film. Begin this activity by introducing students to the term *idiom.* An idiom is an expression that has a meaning beyond the literal use of the words in the phrase. Idioms are particularly confusing to young children and to people beginning to learn a new language. The expression "a bed of roses" might confuse a young child when her aunt says, "Hey, my life is just a bed of roses." The meaning of this idiom is that "a bed of roses" is something that is easy. So, the aunt means her life is easy.

Provide students with several idioms and ask them to illustrate the idioms in pictures for the next class period. Some examples are provided in the handout on page 25.

Idiom's Delight

Pie in the sky

Under the weather

Bed of roses

Cat got your tongue

Raining cats and dogs

Story Idioms

Test your students' knowledge of common idioms using one of the books of idioms listed in the bibliography (pp. 20–21). Then challenge students to write a story that tells about the improbable origin of this idiom. Make it clear that you are not asking students to research the actual origin of the idiom, but to complete a creative writing assignment in which they make up their own story about the idiom. If students are interested in the "real stories" behind common idioms, have them consult Marvin Terban's *Dictionary of Idioms,* which is listed in the bibliography.

The following story draft of "Raining Cats and Dogs" provides a sample for student work. You may wish to read the story aloud before having children complete their assignment.

The Raining Cats and Dogs Story

In the old days when early men and women saw things in nature like rain, snow, thunder, or lightning, they didn't know what to think. There weren't any weather forecasters. Early humans were just making up words to call "rain" rain and "snow" snow. Men were especially challenged in trying to communicate with women. This story explains the situation.

One day a man and woman were having a little fight about "whether" or not the "weather" was going to change. Man pointed to a dark cloud in the sky. He yelled out "Rain!"

Woman asked, "What do you mean?"

Man repeated, "Rain!"

Woman asked again, "What do you MEAN?"

Man shouted, "I said RAIN!"

After that, woman started shouting and man shouted even louder. Their pet dog and cat looked up.

The wind started blowing wildly. Lightning flashed. Thunder crashed. Dog chased cat. Cat hissed at dog. Dog and cat ran around and around the family cave and made so much noise that all the dogs and all the cats of the world began fighting. Man and woman looked outside their cave to see what was going on.

Soon Siamese cats blew in from Siam. Irish wolfhounds blew in from Ireland. Sphinx cats flew in from Egypt. And Norwegian elkhounds flew in from Norway. The ground was covered with wet cats and dogs, and more animals were coming down from the sky.

"Husband," said Woman, "It's raining cats and dogs out there!"

Man just shook his head. Very quietly he said, "Woman, that's what I've been trying to tell you."

So after that when the sky got very dark, Man didn't have to say anything. He just shook his head. And Woman said, "I know, it's going to rain cats and dogs out there. I don't have to look."

Pot of Spoonerisms or Tips of the Slung
(Slips of the Tongue)

The term *spoonerism* refers to the practice of switching the first sounds in a pair of words. The handout on page 27 provides good examples for your pot of spoonerisms. To create the pot of spoonerisms, prepare three-inch squares of paper folded in half. Write the word or phrase on the outside of the folded square. Then open up the square and write what the phrase sounds like as a spoonerism. Place all the paper squares in a soup pot or kettle and add a large serving spoon for humorous effect.

Spoonerisms for Your Pot

funny bone
(Spoonerism: bunny phone)

pack of lies
(Spoonerism: lack of pies)

take a shower
(Spoonerism: shake a tower)

lighting a fire
(Spoonerism: fighting a liar)

Is the dean busy?
(Spoonerism: Is the bean dizzy?)

toe nail
(Spoonerisms: no tail)

Cinderella and the Prince
(Spoonerism: Prinderella and the Since)

jelly beans
(Spoonerism: belly jeans)

For more fun, give students proverbs and ask them to substitute a word or two to change the meaning. A good source for proverbs is the Web site *Commonly Used Proverbs,* prepared for ESL students (www.manythings.org/proverbs). This doesn't have to be a complete spoonerism, simply change the first letter in one or more words of the proverb. (Examples: "You can't judge a book by its cover" can become "You can't judge a crook by his mother." "Time flies" can become "flies rhyme." "You can lead a horse to water but you can't make him drink" can become "You can lead a dinosaur to college but you can't make him think."

Pun of It All Worksheets

A large part of the fun of puns is "getting it." Students who pun easily have an edge over other students who think more literally and would be left out of the fun. To prevent embarrassment and show kids that true humor is really kind, group students together to unlock and understand the puns and wordplay in the handout (pp. 29–30). Answers to the fill-in-the-blanks section appear right after it.

Shaggy Dog Bags

Shaggy dog stories can draw groans from audiences who are "in the know" about the punch lines, usually a pun or wordplay that is commonly known. Older students can be introduced to these clever uses of language if the teacher or media specialist sets up the story in advance.

First, the shaggy dog story is usually a long-winded tale featuring many, many details. The story tends to go on and on. The reader (or teller) "sets up" the audience to listen to an almost excruciatingly long story, then ends it quickly with a pun or twist at the end.

Write out a shaggy dog story on a sheet of paper and put it into a lunch bag marked "shaggy doggy bag" for a student to read. Make several of these doggy bags and place them in a large grocery bag for sharing with students.

Locate shaggy dog stories at *The Shaggy Dog* (www.theshaggydog.org).

Eat Your Words Banquet

A world of puns and wordplay revolves around the subject of food. Think of expressions such as "eat your words," "eat your heart out," "pie in the sky," "egg on your face," "lettuce go . . ." "in a pickle," "finger in every pie," that's the way the cookie crumbles," "easy as pie," and "sand-witch."

Use these expressions to plan a menu of linguistic food dishes for an "eat your words" banquet. For example, serve heart-shaped cookies (eat your heart out), an assortment of pickles (in a pickle), a plate of cookie crumbs ("that's the way the cookie crumbles"), or "sand-witches." (See examples in my books *Mudluscious* [Libraries Unlimited, 1986] and *Second Helpings* [Teacher Ideas Press, 1994]. These books include many activities to use with elementary schoolchildren.)

Ask students to bring their favorite food treats based on wordplay. They may choose to create traditional foods and just give them silly names. Here are a few examples: green eggs (from Dr. Seuss's *Green Eggs and Ham*), square-shaped sandwiches (based on the idea of a "square meal"), or a bag of gummy worms (inspired by the book *How to Eat Fried Worms* or the expression "just go eat worms!").

Pun of It All "Work" for Fun

A. Fill in an appropriate word or words to complete these "punny" sentences.

1. Frogs have it easy. They can eat what _____ them.

2. One thing you can give and still keep is your _____ .

3. I'm tired of working in this coffee house. It's just a _____.

4. Sportswriters in Chicago go to Wrigley Field first because they are _____ reporters.

5. A carpenter's favorite dessert is _____ cake.

6. Cinderpiggy's fairy godmother _____ her three wishes.

7. Kermit's swinish girlfriend wears her hair in _____ .

8. The Thanksgiving bird's favorite dance is the _____ _____.

Answers:

1. bugs

2. word

3. grind

4. cub

5. pound

6. grunted

7. pigtails

8. turkey trot

II. Make a list of homophones (homonyms): words that sound the same but are spelled differently. Now from your list create an ad based on the pun. For example: steak and stake. Your ad might read: "Enjoy a stake in our restaurant!" Another example: pear and pair. Your ad might read: "Stanley's Fruit Stand: Don't buy just one Bartlett. We only sell pairs!" One more example: lion and lyin' Your ad could read: "Honest George's Law Office: We're not about to be lion to you!"

III. Valentine greetings: Express your affection for your pet or friend with one of these sayings. Draw it and write it out in beautiful writing:

From *Story Celebrations: A Program Guide for Schools and Libraries* by Jan Irving. Westport, CT: Libraries Unlimited. Copyright © 2008.

Pun of It All "Work" for Fun (*Continued*)

"You are my friend, and I'm not lion."

"Wooden shoe be my valentine?"

"My heart beets for you!"

"You are the apple of my eye."

A Pun-der-ful Party: A Program for Public Libraries

This program is planned for approximately 1½ hours. The first three activities should each take about ten to fifteen minutes. Allow about thirty to forty minutes for the final pun games. Refreshments may be served as kids arrive and leave the event.

Students in upper elementary and middle school are verbally sharp enough to understand wordplay and create their own riddles, jokes, and puns. Introduce these punny games, and they will create their own versions for a fun afternoon. Invite children who regularly come to the library to create humorous ads and posters to advertise the program outside the library in places where kids congregate in your community.

Materials Needed

Note: Exact quantities will depend on the size of your group.

White paper tablecloths or rolls of brown paper; allow a small roll of brown craft paper per table.

One dozen colored markers per table of eight.

Small wooden box, about the size of a shoe box. (Wood is important for this game since jokesters will want to actually knock on the box as they begin telling these jokes.)

Several empty noodle boxes (such as spaghetti or lasagna noodle boxes).

Vanilla ice cream (one gallon serves about sixteen, allowing one cup per child).

Root beer, cola, and orange drink enough for the crowd, approximately six to eight ounces per person.

Popcorn (pickles and pizza too, if you wish). *Note:* One bag of microwave popcorn will serve two to three people; allow one twelve-inch pizza for 12 kids (cut pizza in small squares); one gallon of pickles will be plenty if you cut the pickles in small pieces and serve them on toothpicks.

Six or more paperback joke and riddle books for door prizes Two fun titles are *The Everything Kids' Joke Book: Side Splitting, Rib-Tickling Fun*, by Michael Dahl, and *1,000 Knock Knock Jokes for Kids,* by Michael Kilgarriff.

Seven or eight plastic Slinkies™, silly pencils (pencil with silly designs purchased from discount stores), bags of jelly beans, or containers of Silly Putty™; several small plastic brains purchased from a novelty or game store.

A large bowl for your door prize raffle.

Procedure

Before You Begin

1. A few weeks before the program, if you wish to have a guest jester, arrange to have a stand-up comic or drama student come and tell jokes.

2. Collect paperback joke books for door prizes and resources.

3. Purchase or gather materials on the materials list.

4. Print knock-knock jokes (p. 33) and cut them into strips.

5. Fill your wooden box with knock-knock jokes.

6. Make large signs for each noodle box reading, "Noodling Around." Glue or tape these signs to noodle boxes. Fill the boxes with riddles written or typed on paper slips. You may wish to just write the riddles without answers to challenge program attendees.

On the Day of the Program

1. Set up tables and cover them with brown paper or white paper tablecloths. Place a can or cup of colored markers on each table so that kids can write or draw their own jokes all over the paper. You might wish to write "Knock Knock" "Who's There?" in a silly script or lettering on each table to get things started. Place several paperback joke books on the tables for use during the program and to give away as door prizes at the end.

2. Set up a juice bar with bright-colored plastic glasses or cups, with punch bowls or large plastic bowls filled with root beer floats and orange floats. You could simply have large gallons of vanilla ice cream with large spoons and soft drinks and juice for kids to make their own concoctions. To expedite the juice bar, ask several teens to serve as juice bar hops and make the drinks.

3. When children arrive, invite them to get a drink at the juice bar and take a seat at one of the tables. Each child should draw a number from a box upon arriving. These numbers determine who wins a door prize at the end of the program.

4. Begin the program with a stand-up comic or have a high school or college drama student tell funny stories. Or you can tell a few shaggy dog stories of your own.

5. Ask for seven or eight volunteers to participate in the Knock-Knock Box Game. To encourage participation, tell kids that those who agree to tell one of the knock-knock jokes selected from your box will receive a prize. Consult the knock-knock jokes listed on page 33, or select others from the books and Web sites listed. Ask each volunteer to choose a knock-knock joke and tell it to the audience. You might want to have several rounds of play, with the audience voting for the best three jokes they hear. Use plastic Slinkies, Silly Putty, silly pencils, or bags of jelly beans as prizes.

6. The librarian or a master of ceremonies now acts as a jester or "noodler." Wear a jester's hat or a silly hat of some kind and show the "Noodling Around" box to the audience. Draw riddles (written on lasagna-shaped paper noodles or long, skinny paper slips) from the box and read each one slowly to the audience. Each table acts as a team to answer the riddles. The answers given on page 33 may be used, or alternative answers may be accepted. Give prizes to the team with the most inventive answers.

7. Choose one or two of the pun games described on pages 33–34 for the final activity. If time permits, have students do them both. One game asks kids to concoct their own puns or wordplay, and the other game asks them to draw a visual pun for one of the expressions on the visual pun sheet.

8. Serve pretzels, pizza, pickles, and popcorn for treats at your Punderful Party. (What could be sillier for a humorous wordplay program?)

9. Draw numbers to give away door prizes.

Knock-Knock Joke Box

Use these knock-knock jokes to fill your wooden box, but don't restrict yourself to this short list. Ask children to contribute their favorites, and check some Web sites, such as www.knock-knock-joke. com/.

Have participants select a knock-knock joke from the box and share it with the audience. Encourage kids to engage in a lively exchange as if they are stand-up comics. Give prizes such as jelly beans, Silly Putty, silly pencils, or plastic Slinkies to participants.

Knock knock	Who's there?	Lionel	Lionel who?	Lionel get you nowhere!
Knock knock	Who's there?	Thatcher	Thatcher who?	Thatcher could get away with it!
Knock knock	Who's there?	Ivan	Ivan who?	Ivan to suck your blood!
Knock knock	Who's there?	José	José who?	José can you see by the dawn's early light
Knock knock	Who's there?	Orange	Orange who?	Orange you going to open the door?
Knock knock	Who's there?	Police	Police who?	Police stop telling those awful knock knock jokes!

Riddles for Noodling Around

Write out these riddles on lasagna-shaped paper "noodles" or on skinny slips of paper and place them in an empty lasagna box with the sign "Noodling Around" on the outside. Read these aloud to kids, who will provide answers to the riddles. I suggest children work in teams to answer riddles, and the "riddler" may accept alternative answers to those given here.

Why was baby ant confused?

(All his uncles were ants.)

What gets wetter the more it dries?

(A towel)

What grows down when it grows up?

(A goose)

When can you put pickles in a door?

(When it's ajar)

Why did the turkey cross the road twice?

(To prove it's not a chicken)

The Punnery Game

This game is best played in groups, so many minds can come up with the puns and stories inspired by the puns. For those unfamiliar with making puns, explain that this punnery game substitutes similar-sounding words for one or more words in an expression. For example, the expression "in the pink" can be changed to "win with a wink" for a successful pun in this game. Give each team one or more expressions (consult a dictionary of idioms such as *Scholastic Dictionary of Idioms,* by Marvin Terban, listed in this chapter's bibliography) and give them four or five minutes to make up several puns. Each team reads and acts out its puns with great exaggeration. Assign two points for each pun created.

Then, if students are interested, challenge them to make up a story using the newly created puns for punch lines. Note that shaggy dog stories do this. Read the following story to kids to demonstrate a shaggy dog story ending in a pun. Tell students to remember the expression "Up a creek with no paddle" before you share the story.

Once there was a man who found that every time he bent over to pick up the paddle to his canoe, he got a terrible crick in his back. He went to the doctor, who told him if it happened again he should shove the paddle into the ground and pull himself up. The next day when the man tried to pick up his paddle, sure enough, his got a crick in his back. He shoved the paddle in the ground and slowly worked himself up. He was delighted to find himself up a paddle with no crick.

When you read the story, be certain to pause briefly before you read the pun "up a paddle with no crick" slowly, so that the audience will savor the humor of the pun.

Following are some expressions, with puns that students might create from them. If students choose to create a shaggy dog story with a pun, award that team five points. The team that wins might receive a small silly prize such as plastic brains purchased at novelty shops or from catalogues.

Barking dogs seldom bite. (Pun: Barking frogs seldom fight.)

Crime doesn't pay. (Pun: Grime doesn't stay.)

Let sleeping dogs lie. (Pun: Creeping frogs spy.)

As the crow flies. (Pun: As the flies know.)

Fly by the seat of your pants. (Pun: You can tell who's sly by the feet that dance.)

Bed of roses. (Pun: Red of noses.)

Beat a dead horse. (Pun: Heat a bed if you're hoarse.)

Is That a Pun I See? (Visual Pun Game)

In this game the teacher or librarian introduces students to the term *idiom,* which refers to an expression that has a meaning different from what is literally said. Perhaps at one time the expression meant something literally, but today the meaning is not a literal one. For example, the expression "let the cat out of the bag" means to give away a secret. Hundreds of years ago in England people bought expensive pigs at farmer's markets. Sometimes dishonest merchants would slip a worthless old cat into the bag, and the duped farmer would not know this until he got home and opened the bag.

Provide kids with drawing paper and pens to illustrate one or more of these idioms. The drawings, of course, should be literal interpretations of the expressions.

Kick the bucket.

Pie in the sky.

Eat your words.

People who live in glass houses shouldn't throw stones.

Raining cats and dogs.

Family Roots

"Did you really wear that weird hat when you got married, Mom?" "Dad, is that you under all that hair?" "Did you fight in the Civil War, Grandpa?" Children ask questions about their families, from the brutally honest to the totally unpredictable. Kids are eternally curious, curious about who they are and where they came from. We might recall the old joke about parents fretting over the answer to, "Where did I come from?" Thinking that the child is asking about sex, the parent hesitates, only for his child to say, "Jimmy's family came from Cleveland. I just wondered where we came from." Persistent questions may only require simple answers.

Children like to know about their families and enjoy hearing stories about them. Many families share stories daily as a part of their lives growing up together. Children may cringe at hearing the "cute baby" stories about them repeated at every family gathering, but these retellings become part of the family ritual that creates a sense of belonging. Some families are not as communicative or close, and children may be left to wonder how they fit into a larger family and what makes them grow up with the gifts that they have. Did anyone else in the family have musical talent? Am I the only one who writes with his left hand? If our family didn't come to this country on the *Mayflower,* when did they immigrate? Was our family name always the same as it is today?

Because children may not live in the same neighborhood or town as their parents did when they grew up, extended families may not be geographically close enough to share family stories or even answer questions. Children in past generations may have even lived in the same house with their parents and grandparents. Children from newly immigrated families may or may not even live in the same country as their aunts and uncles.

During the latter half of the twentieth century, many families moved from family farms into large cities. In recent decades many parents have divorced, with each parent moving to a different city to start a new life. Adults lose jobs and are forced to move long distances to find employment. Other parents move to accept better opportunities. Whatever the reason for a family's mobility, children usually experience mild to more extreme feelings of disorientation and disconnection. With this growing trend in our society, exploring family history becomes a positive experience for many children. Keeping in touch with far-flung friends and family can ease a child's loss.

Genealogy, the study of family history, has become a wildly popular hobby with adults in the United States, and it is a perfect way for families to learn together. Some adults become so obsessed with minute details, chronologies, and research that kids can feel overwhelmed. Smart parents look for child-appropriate activities to share on a different level. Younger children enjoy simply visiting grandparents on summer vacation, and older kids can e-mail extended family members to find out more about their family history. They can fill out their own pedigree charts and may like to explore a family home, especially if it has an attic stuffed with old family albums and keepsakes. Some of us remember finding great grandma's dresses and grandpa's tools in an old trunk and have even kept these heirlooms to pass on to our children.

Visiting one-room schoolhouses that grandparents attended or exploring a local history museum or a historic battlefield along with visiting relatives help kids place their own families in a larger historical context. Not all families will be able to make such visits, but most can look through family photo albums and make time to tell stories from the past.

School programs and projects on genealogy can open doors to student research that enliven social studies so that students participate not just willingly, but enthusiastically. Along with learning reference skills, children can engage in oral history projects and learn skills that range from conducting interviews to storytelling. Creating timelines and studying maps extend historical and geographical knowledge. Natural links to the topic include exploring arts and crafts from different cultures, introducing words from different countries, and preparing favorite recipes from various places around the world.

Of course, educators may face challenges regarding this subject. Children of newer immigrants may not be able to complete family tree assignments. Other children may find their parents are uncomfortable talking about family history. Eleven-year-old Tyler in Katherine Ayres's book *Family Tree* faces her father's anger and hurt when she asks questions about his Amish family to complete a school genealogy project. The girl's teacher ends up helping Tyler handle the sensitive situation and it ends on a hopeful note. Children with African American backgrounds may be uncomfortable or unable to talk about ancestors brought to this country as slaves. Even kids whose families immigrated to America from Northern Europe may uncover painful stories of oppression or discrimination.

Attitudes regarding ethnic diversity reflect our society's lingering reluctance to fully accept people who do not share similar values and backgrounds. Adoptees are another special group who usually know little about their biological backgrounds. Insightful teachers might suggest alternative possibilities such as studying the backgrounds of adoptive parents who share a new history with their adopted children. Children living in foster families and children in single-parent homes will have incomplete stories to share, but they can be encouraged to build on even fragments of what they know.

As an educator or librarian, you can make a difference in this world of changing family patterns and multicultural understanding. Public library food fairs, ethnic arts and crafts workshops, and storytelling events featuring tellers from different cultures are just a few winning programs on this topic. Book displays on genealogy combined with offerings of family tree workshops for different generations extend the library's traditional programs of storytimes and reading programs targeted at one narrow age group.

This chapter only scratches the surface for beginning genealogists. The bibliography includes nonfiction and a few fiction titles on the subject, and there is a sampling of Web sites. Some collections of stories and cookbooks from a few cultures have been selected as examples to introduce a much larger body of multicultural literature. Adapt this list to your particular community. Children in southern Colorado, for example, may need more sources from Mexico and Latin America. Kids in New Mexico need materials on the many native groups living in their state. Savvy educators know their communities and can use these suggestions to explore the topic appropriately to the children they serve.

Bibliography

Ayres, Katherine. *Family Tree*. Delacorte, 1996.
(Reading Level: Accelerated Reader, 3.7)
Eleven-year-old Tyler Stoudt struggles with a sixth-grade school project to research her family tree. Her father becomes angry and hurt when she asks questions, but the determined girl perseveres in finding out about family secrets in her ancestry. Moving story for all kids who feel isolated from their peers and their family background.

Bunting, Eve. *The Memory String*. Clarion, 2000.
(Reading Level: Accelerated Reader, 2.9)
Although the reading level of this book is much lower than others in this list, it is a good read-aloud story to introduce the idea of keeping family memories with different kinds of materials.

Cowley, Joy. *Big Moon Tortilla.* Boyds Mills, 1998.
(Reading Level: Accelerated Reader, 3.8)
   In the Papago Indian Reservation of Arizona, a young girl faces several setbacks but is comforted by her grandmother's family stories and a serving of homemade tortillas.

Dooley, Norah. *Everybody Cooks Rice.* Carolrhoda, 1991.
(Reading Level: Accelerated Reader, 3.8)
   In scouting the neighborhood to find her brother, a girl discovers that all kinds of cultures eat rice in her multicultural city block. She samples delicious dishes, from Chinese fried rice to Indian biryani. Recipes are included.

Douglas, Ann. *The Family Tree Detective: Cracking the Case of Your Family's Story.* Owl Books, 1999.
(Reading level: Flesch-Kincaid, 7.0)
   This valuable sourcebook clearly explains family relationships, family trees, and how to conduct interviews with family members, and has many exciting activities to interest kids in genealogy.

Goldin, Barbara Diamond. *A Mountain of Blintzes.* Gulliver Books, Harcourt, 2001.
(Reading Level: Accelerated Reader, 3.1)
   This picture book can be used as an introduction to telling family stories and collecting recipes. It is loosely based on a traditional Chelm or Polish story. Mama and Papa have foolishly squandered their money needed to buy ingredients for blintzes, a special food eaten on the Jewish holiday of Shavuot. Their resourceful children save the day.

Hirsch, Marilyn. *Potato Pancakes All Around.* Jewish Publication Society, 1982.
(Reading Level: Spache, 3.6)
   This engaging Hanukkah story is a Jewish variant of the traditional "Stone Soup" tale and makes a wonderful read-aloud story to introduce a wide audience to telling family stories and collecting family recipes.

Jacobs, William Jay. *Ellis Island: New Hope in a New Land.* Scribner, 1990.
(Reading Level: Spache, 5.3)
   This well-illustrated book gives the history of Ellis Island and immigration into the United States at this famous location. Old photographs are especially helpful, as they show close-ups of immigrants waiting in lines, enduring physical examinations, and eating meals in the island's dining halls.

Nixon, Joan Lowery. *Land of Hope.* Bantam, 1992.
(Reading Level: Accelerated Reader, 5.5)
   One of the Ellis Island series of fiction books, this story introduces a young woman, Rebekah Levinsky, and her family, who travel to America on a big ship en route to Ellis Island. The gripping story tells of the illness and hardships in steerage class and the family's worries upon landing and beginning their lives again.

Perl, Lila. *The Great Ancestor Hunt: The Fun of Finding Out Who You Are.* Clarion, 1989.
(Reading Level: Accelerated Reader, 8.3)
   This well-respected nonfiction writer has compiled a wealth of information about genealogy, family names, and how to write family histories.

Rocklin, Joanne. *Strudel Stories.* Random House, 1999.
(Reading Level: Fleisch-Kincaid, 4.5)
   Warm recollections of Jewish family stories from the author's background span several generations. Willy and Jessica's apple strudel recipe and a family tree are included. This is a perfect book to use in oral history units.

Rosenberg, Liz. *Roots & Flowers: Poets and Poems on Family.* Henry Holt, 2001.
(Reading Level: Flesch-Kincaid, 8.2)
　　This rich collection of family stories, told by well-known poets, includes one or more poems by each writer. The poems are funny, sad, and deeply felt.

Soto, Gary. *Too Many Tamales.* Putnam, 1993.
(Reading Level: Accelerated Reader, 3.4)
　　Although the reading level of this picture book is lower than most books in this bibliography, it is a delightful read-aloud story to introduce family stories about food. A Hispanic family enjoys tamales on Christmas Eve, but a diamond ring is lost in making this special food. The resolution involves laughter and tears in a well-told tale kids of many ages will enjoy.

Taylor, Maureen. *Through the Eyes of Your Ancestors: A Step-by-Step Guide to Uncovering Your Family History.* Houghton Mifflin, 1999.
(Reading Level: Accelerated Reader, 8.3)
　　Besides providing a basic background about researching family history, this fascinating guide points out pitfalls in doing family interviews, how to plan a family history project sequentially, and working with old family photographs, and describes places to look for esoteric information.

Wolfman, Ira. *Do People Grow on Family Trees?: Genealogy for Kids and Other Beginners.* Workman, 1991.
(Reading Level: Accelerated Reader, 7.3)
　　This official Ellis Island handbook should be purchased for any school or public library genealogy collection. The reading style is lively, and kids will discover all kinds of information about planning research for family histories, a list of questions new immigrants were asked in coming through Ellis Island, interviewing family members, and understanding census records and other forms of vital information.

Woodruff, Elvira. *The Orphan of Ellis Island.* Scholastic, 1997.
(Reading Level: Accelerated Reader, 4.9)
　　This time-travel novel of an Italian American boy involves an exciting venture into the past, where he discovers his family roots in Italy in the early 1900s.

Zimmerman, Bill. *My Paper Memory Quilt: A Family History Pack.* Chronicle, 2004.
(Reading level: Flesh Kincaid, 8.6)
　　This unique family history pack contains a handbook to guide kids in expressing ideas about their family through paper quilt collages and a series of paper quilt blocks to render their visual presentations.

Selected Web Sites

Ancestry Home Town: www.ancestry.com
　　Many records available, such as access to the Federal Census reports, phone directories, immigration passenger lists, and more.

Family Tree Research: www.familytreemagazine.com/articles/oct01/kidsprojects.html
　　Sponsored by the popular *Family Tree Magazine.* You can do free genealogy searches online, use their templates to create family trees, and go to other genealogy sites. It has an article on family history projects for the whole family, a large bibliography for kids, and links to finding scrapbooking materials for kids' projects.

The National Archives: www.nara.gov

   Called "The Nation's Attic," this place in Washington, D.C., is a treasure house of records, though most actual records are not available online. However, this site lists resources and records that can be ordered and has links to many other resources.

The National Genealogical Society: www.ngsgenealogy.org

   Must join ($55, individual membership) to use the online searches. Many libraries belong as institutional members. With membership, you can search ancestry charts, conduct global searches, and search databases of marriage and death records.

Tell Me Your Stories: www.tellmeyourstories.org/curriculum/class10.htm

   A complete curriculum on oral history for middle school and older students. Lessons include how to interview family members and do research, and it lists many final projects in all curricular areas.

The Worcester Family Kids Only Page: www.worcesterfamily.com/kidspage.htm

   Includes lots of family projects, such as making a family tree or a family mobile and using genealogy in the classroom. Links to other genealogy sites.

The Family Story Tree: A School Program

   This program resembles a patchwork quilt in that students select from among a variety of projects. Several projects have a visual component—collections of family photographs, quilt blocks made of paper or collages of fabrics and objects, or family treasure boxes created by students and their families. Other projects involve oral histories, interviews, pedigree charts, or creative writing based on life stories. A multimedia project that tells the story of a culture has been included for those students who may have difficulty telling their own family story.

   This program unit is planned for five class meetings, with each meeting lasting approximately fifty to sixty minutes. You may choose to give students more than two days to complete their projects so that the two days for presentations occur about a week after the assignment is made.

Materials Needed

   Students will provide most of their own materials unless you determine there is a financial problem. In this case, consider providing a few disposable cameras, folders with brad fasteners, construction paper, and photo corners. You can also prepare pedigree charts for students to complete.

   A long length of art or mural paper to hang on the wall for the second meeting.

   You will need computer access for student research, as well as print sources for genealogy work.

Procedure

Before You Begin

1. In preparation for this unit, photocopy the sample handouts included on pages 44–48 and 55 for student use (e.g., interview page, pedigree chart, quilt block page).

2. Review passages that you will read aloud ("My Family Is a River" and a closing selection of your choice) (see note at the end of the instructions for the first meeting).

3. Write up notes for a simple story about your family that you will share with students.

4. Assemble a few old photographs to go with your story.

First Meeting

1. Introduce the program by reading "My Family Is a River" (below). Ask students to discuss how all families are like rivers. What do they know about different branches of their families?

2. Who is the oldest ancestor they have heard about? What is the connection or difference between stories from rivers and stories we hear from people?

3. Tell students a story from your family and illustrate the story with photographs. This exercise is a model for the class assignment that will be shared in the next class session.

4. Telling family stories through pictures: Ask students to remember a family event such as a holiday gathering, a reunion, or a vacation and find a family photograph that tells a story about that event. The stories will be told in class during the next meeting. Each story will be told in three or four minutes. (See the "Stories from Family Photographs" handout [p. 45] to guide students.)

5. Give students packets of family roots activities and handouts (pp. 42–48).

6. Read a chapter or selection from one of the books in the bibliography such as *Family Tree*.

7. Have students begin researching the library to decide on their projects. (**Note:** The specific projects are described in the handout "Your Family Story Project" on pp. 42–43.)

8. As a homework assignment, have students write a paragraph describing what project they will complete and a plan of how they will proceed.

9. Also, tell students to bring family photos, memorabilia (e.g., postcards, tickets), and family quotes or short family stories to the next meeting.

My Family Is a River

My family is a river—
flows from branch to branch
picks up streams
climbs mountains
rolls over ridges
spills down hills
waters farm land
gathers up lakes
drops rain
sucks up ponds
pours them
over cities
splashes down streets
running
gushing
flooding
ebbing away

Where did we start

Where will we go
I'd like to ask the river
What stories it knows.

Poem by Jan Irving Duncan-O'Neal

Second Meeting

1. Before class, tape a long length of art paper or colored mural paper to walls with a large sign reading, "Discovering Our Family Roots—Telling Our Stories." Add some of the facts from the Ellis Island handout (p. 49) and a picture of this historic place printed from the Internet.

2. Students retell their family stories based on photographs (assigned during the previous class session).

3. Work with students on their projects for this class session and provide a schedule for the class presentations.

4. Each student contributes a few pictures, quotations, stories, and objects such as tickets, postcards, or letters to be attached to the mural paper.

5. Give students time to research their family history in the library, and on computers.

6. As homework, have students work on their family story projects.

Third Meeting

1. Students continue to work on their projects.

Fourth and Fifth Meetings

1. Students present their projects.

Your Family Story Project

Choose one of the projects described below for your project.

1. Interviewing a Family Member: An Oral History Project

    - Use the interview form to talk with a family member about your family history.

    - A face-to-face interview usually works best, but a telephone, e-mail, or written interview could be used if the personal contact is too difficult.

    - The final presentation may be presented in several ways—inviting your relative to talk to the class, interviewing your relative in class, preparing a talk about the interview to present in class, or even writing a short story based on the interview and reading it to the class.

2. The Family Photo Album with Stories

    - Use the "Stories from Family Photographs" handout (p. 45) to plan this project. You will need to find old family photos and talk with your family about these pictures.

    - Arrange your collection of photos and stories in one of the ways suggested on the handout and put them in an album to submit on the due date for this assignment.

    - You will show the photo album to the class at the final meeting.

3. From the Family Trunk

    - Use the "From My Family Trunk" (p. 46) handout to plan this project.

    - Collect family heirlooms and objects to bring to school along with descriptions and stories about these items.

    - For class presentation, put items in a cardboard trunk or suitcase along with accompanying stories collected in a notebook.

4. Family Scrapbook

    - Consult the handout "Scrapbooking Your Family" (p. 47) for this project. It contains some of the elements of numbers 2 and 3 above. The focus is visual creativity.

    - You may wish to use the quilt block page on page 48 in the scrapbook.

    - Begin your scrapbook with a two- to three-page summary of the purpose of the scrapbook, list your family members, and explain how the scrapbook tells the story of what your family is like.

    - You will show and discuss the scrapbook to the class at the final meeting.

5. Pedigree Charts and Stories

    - Complete the pedigree chart. Perhaps your mom or dad has already done one of these for your baby book. If not, you will need to contact aunts, uncles, grandparents, and other relatives to help you complete as much information as you can.

    - Put your pedigree chart on a poster board along with short summaries of as many people on your chart as you can complete. (Instead of using a poster board, you may wish to place the chart and accompanying stories in a scrapbook.)

    - You will show and discuss your pedigree chart with the class at the final meeting.

Your Family Story Project (*Continued*)

6. Stories from the World's Families: Tell the story of a culture such as "The Story of Mexican Americans," using books such as *The Great Ancestor Hunt*. This can be an oral presentation lasting about five to eight minutes or a written four- or five-page report. You might include these parts:

- Location of country.

- A few major historical events that give us an insight about the country.

- Major festivals and holidays celebrated in the country and in America.

- Favorite foods (provide a recipe or food sample if you wish).

- Contributions in the arts, business or industry, or sports (famous or noteworthy people from this culture).

- Language: share a few words of the language of this country.

- Briefly tell a legend from the country if this is an oral presentation.

Interviewing a Family Member: An Oral History Project

Use this form to find out about your family from one or more relatives. You may add other questions of your own. If you are interviewing the person face-to-face, allow opportunities for the relative to go in other directions. The face-to-face interview usually works best, but if this is not possible, you may telephone, e-mail, or send the questions by mail. Use additional pages to record stories and longer responses.

1. Name of person and date of interview

2. How I am related to this person

3. Date and place of interviewee's birth

4. Other family members (father, mother, sisters, brothers, cousins, aunts, uncles, children)

5. Occupation (s) or professions of person and his or her husband or wife

6. Favorite family memory

7. Schools attended

8. Favorite subjects in school

9. Favorite hobbies and interests as a child and as an adult

10. Special vacations or adventures

(What surprises happened during the interview and what I learned from this conversation.)

Stories from Family Photographs

Collect ten to twenty photographs from someone in your family and talk with him or her about the photos. The following list will give you some ideas of the kinds of photos to look for in making an interesting collection for this project:

- Holiday events—Christmas or Hanukkah, Thanksgiving, St. Patrick's Day, Fourth of July, Halloween

- Family reunions

- Birthdays

- Family vacations

- New births

- Events such as losing front teeth, wearing a cast, first communions, graduations, weddings, leaving for military service, first day of school

- Favorite adventures and pastimes—fishing, camping, participating in athletic events, winning contests, dance recitals, acting in plays

- Family pets

- Humorous situations

Look carefully at your pictures and include this information in the description of each photo: Who is in the photo? When was the picture taken? Who took the photo and why? Try to be more specific than just saying, "This is a picture of my grandma and me at Christmas." Give a little more background so the situation becomes alive. For example: "I was three years old when this picture was taken on Christmas in 1945. My grandma is wearing her Sunday suit and I am wearing a ruffled dress my mother made for me. The tree in the background was decorated in hopes that my father would be with us at the end of World War II. He had been stationed in France, but his army outfit did not return until February 1946. That tree stood in our living room for a whole month before Mother said we had to take it down. It was so dry she was afraid it would catch fire."

Other questions to think about in writing your descriptions include: What are people wearing and doing in the photo? What story does the picture suggest? What are the people feeling? Do they look sad? Excited? Shy? Thoughtful? Serious?

Arrange your photos (or copies of the photos) either chronologically (in time order from early pictures to later ones) or by theme (look at the list above).

Put your photographs and stories in a scrapbook or album to submit on the due date.

From *Story Celebrations: A Program Guide for Schools and Libraries* by Jan Irving.
Westport, CT: Libraries Unlimited. Copyright © 2008.

From My Family Trunk

Gather together family heirlooms and treasures to tell your family's story. Does your grandma have an attic filled with old boxes and trunks of goodies? Maybe your great aunt has a basement cedar chest filled with old clothes or your uncle has a workshop with tools passed down from his father's tool shop. Ask your mother or father for little keepsakes of their childhood that you could borrow. The following list may help you think of the kinds of items for this project:

- Old letters and picture postcards
- Baby books
- Newspaper clippings
- Old hats or antique clothes (perhaps christening gowns, gloves, ties)
- Old toys—teddy bears, trains, model cars, dolls, board games, marbles
- Children's books
- Old records, videos, home movies, sheet music
- Theater or athletic programs, graduation programs
- Passports and train tickets
- Travel journals
- Pocket watches, jewelry
- Handkerchiefs
- Samplers or needlework
- Tools
- Family recipe boxes, cookbooks
- Baby cups

Try to date each item, tell who it belonged to, and explain the significance of the item, such as: "This baby cup belonged to my great grandma, who was born in 1918. It was the gift of her grandmother, Anna Gowdy. Anna bought the cup in Canada when she was on a family trip."

Put your items in a cardboard box or suitcase with labels tied to the objects. If possible, learn a story about the people associated with the item so that you can collect these stories in a notebook placed in your trunk.

Scrapbooking Your Family

The focus of a family scrapbook tends to be more visually creative than the family photo album or the family trunk. If you like to draw or do collages, this may be the project you choose.

Collect photos and memorabilia from different family members. Think of trips you or your family have taken and special events and happy memories your family has shared: your parents' wedding day, fishing with your grandpa, a picnic lunch at your grandma's on the Fourth of July, books you and your parents read together, favorite family quotes, favorite toys or hobbies of different family members, favorite family dishes and recipes, pets, babies and cute kids in the family, or best vacations and adventures.

Think of overall themes to organize your scrapbook. Some themes are "My Family as a Patchwork Quilt" (reproduce several pages of the quilt block on page 48 to use for each page of the scrapbook) or "My Rainbow Family Scrapbook" (use different colored pages for each subject—green for summer photos and events, blue for baby pictures and baby stories, creamy white for recipes, or red for holiday drawings and pictures).

Consult *My Paper Memory Quilt* by Zimmerman for ideas if you are interested in the patchwork quilt idea.

Your scrapbook should have a two- to three-page summary explaining who is in your family and how your scrapbook tells the story of what your family is like.

Consider combining your visuals with "story pages" in which you tell little incidents or story happenings along with the pictures and drawings.

Keep these tips in mind to write lively stories:

- Zero in on lively ways to grab attention from the beginning instead of the traditional, "My favorite pet was a dog. His name was Sandy. He was brown and white and we all loved him."

    Isn't this more interesting? *My dad said we couldn't have a dog. One night Dad came home with something inside his coat. He said, "Close your eyes! Don't open them until I say 'open'!" When we opened them, my brother Sam and I saw a skinny little brown dog sliding around on the kitchen floor.*

- Focus on scenes as in a movie or action events.

- Give specifics that help tell your story through sensory details, such as, "I can still smell the sugar cookies we made for Christmas and the pine tree we decorated on Christmas Eve when I was in first grade. Grandma came to visit and wrapped us in fuzzy blankets on the sofa but we all fell asleep by the fire. Early Christmas morning I think I heard Santa's sleigh go 'thud' on the rooftop."

- Think of a "punch line" or satisfying conclusion to the story.

From *Story Celebrations: A Program Guide for Schools and Libraries* by Jan Irving.
Westport, CT: Libraries Unlimited. Copyright © 2008.

My Quilt Block Page

Thoughts and Quotations for Mural

DID YOU KNOW THAT?

- Most people traveling on ships to Ellis Island were in third class or steerage accommodations.

- Men were separated from women and children on these trips.

- Women and children traveling alone were detained upon arrival to America until a male relative came to get them.

- Doctors had to inspect all of these passengers before they could enter the United States.

- Most people immigrating to America during the heyday of Ellis Island did not speak English, had little formal education, but hoped for a better life.

- Most immigrants coming through Ellis Island were not from Eastern Europe, as is commonly believed. They were from Northern Europe or Italy.

- Many people's names were changed at Ellis Island.

- The first person to emigrate through Ellis Island was a fifteen-year-old Irish girl, Annie Moore, on January 1, 1892. She was given a ten dollar gold piece.

- The year of the most immigration was 1907, when over one million people came through Ellis Island.

- The single most memorable site new emigrants saw was the Statue of Liberty, erected in 1886 on Bedloe's Island (now Liberty Island).

Tidbits and Quote from the Ellis Island Experience

- "I was always glad my father brought us to the United States in 1920 because our home in Sicily was bombed during World War II."

- One Irishman who emigrated at age twenty-five came to America with a $20 bill in his shoe. He later became a manager of several electronics stores in the United States.

- Many new immigrants from Europe tasted their first bananas soon after arriving in the United States. They often didn't know the bananas had to be peeled before eating them!

- Many Irish immigrants remembered dancing on the ship decks during the voyage.

- "In a way, traveling is a lesson in tolerance. We learn by traveling and by immigrating." Issac Bashevis Singer, well-known author.

From *Story Celebrations: A Program Guide for Schools and Libraries* by Jan Irving.
Westport, CT: Libraries Unlimited. Copyright © 2008.

Celebrating Family Roots:
A Public Library Program Series

This series of programs can be offered individually or as a series over a period of weeks or even months, with staff members from youth services and adult services cooperating to plan the programs. Several programs utilize guest speakers rather than presentations from staff. You may choose to offer a one-day or evening program, as this plan is flexible. In order to test the popularity of this topic, you may wish to plan one program in a season, evaluate its success, then offer another program the following year at a different time.

A Family Food Celebration from Around the World

In this program you invite participants to bring a recipe (or e-mail it prior to the program) and sample of the food to the library from their family or representing their ethnic background or ancestral culture. Young adults can help—they can help plan the program, do the publicity, set up the room, and call a core group of families to get the program going. If a teen group sponsors the program with a library coordinator, the young people should bring a recipe and food. The public is invited to enjoy the event whether or not they are active participants. This program will last about 1½ hours.

Materials Needed

Plenty of tables, with paper plates, napkins, and plastic spoons and forks.

Refrigerator space, electric outlets, and a kitchen, if possible.

Copying facilities to copy recipes that participants bring. (The library may request that people bring multiple copies of recipes or submit the recipes ahead of time so the library can make copies.)

A head table that can be set with table runners or several lengths of fabric from different countries or a length of white butcher paper with pictures of food on it.

Library cookbooks and duplicated recipes (for display on the table).

Procedure

Before You Begin

1. Gather cookbooks for display and duplicate any recipes you wish to display or distribute.

2. Review selections to be read aloud at the first meeting, to open and close the meeting.

3. Arrange for a guest speaker, if you wish to have one—a local chef or food expert, who will give a demonstration at the first meeting. Cooks from local restaurants or food cooperatives are good choices.

4. Promote the event by posting details on the library's Web site or in the library newsletter. You may wish to publish one of the sample recipes (pp. 57–58) along with your announcement. Ask interested participants to RSVP, leaving their e-mail addresses or phone numbers.

5. Send e-mail instructions or call participants and ask them to send you a recipe of the dishes they will bring.

6. Create folders of recipes based on the recipes participants e-mail to you.

On the Day of the Program

1. Welcome guests and give everyone a folder of recipes that have been contributed, along with food provided by young adults, library staff members, and volunteers. Read aloud a story about families and food, such as *Everybody Cooks Rice, A Mountain of Blintzes,* or *Big Moon Tortilla.* The poem "Grandma's Irish Cabbage" (below) is another short introduction to food and a family experience.

2. Ask each family group to introduce themselves and tell something about the food they brought. Encourage participants to tell a short story or incident that is associated with the food.

3. Invite the group to take a paper plate to sample foods and talk with one another about the recipes.

4. End the program with a song or story or have a cooking expert to do a cooking demonstration.

Grandma's Irish Cabbage

January, Ma cut
worm green cabbage
thick wedged for the pot
poured water to the rim
boiled and boiled
'til our noses wrinkled up.

Kitchen smelled ugly like skunk
March, Grandma came
with hugs and her knife
cabbage,
two heads.

Uh oh! Grandma's makin' skunk cabbage.
She sliced her cabbages
crossways thin
layered in the pan
covered with onions
bacon fat
peppercorns
water, one flick,
simmered gently *not too long.*

Kitchen smelled happy,
Spring in the air.

Poem by Jan Irving Duncan-O'Neal

Recipe Card for _____

Recipe from _____

Ingredients:

Directions:

Serves:

The Family Trunk

This program can be offered as a follow-up to the previous program, or it can be offered separately. It combines family artifacts and heirlooms with family storytelling. Publicize the program for families and ask participants to bring an object passed down to them from another generation. Consult the list under the school program on family trunks (p. 46). Encourage guests to come prepared to talk about their objects and why they are invested with special meaning in their families. Since this sharing may not take much time, invite a guest speaker from a local history museum or an antique expert to talk about unusual household items that families collect. Allow about 1 to 1½ hours for this program.

Materials Needed

A large old trunk, such as a steamer trunk or an antique trunk borrowed from a member of the community.

A display table draped in a tablecloth or covered in maps from around the world.

Refreshments, if you wish.

Display of books on family history and family stories (consult the bibliography on pages 36–38).

Procedure

Before You Begin

1. Arrange to have several families with preteen and teenage kids act as co-hosts with the library, so you will have a core group of participants. Ask one or two of these families to speak to the entire group about their objects and tell a story. Plan to speak about some of your own family objects as well.

2. Gather books about family history (see bibliography on pages 36–38 for some ideas) and set up in a display.

First Meeting

1. Ask each family group to introduce themselves, describe the objects they brought, and tell a story or share a memory about it.

2. Guest speaker or speakers do their presentation(s).

3. Refreshments are served.

4. The family trunk may be left at the library for display in a secured area (such as a locked display case).

Family Scrapbooks and Family Stories

This program relies on good guest speakers and can be organized in several different ways. Larger communities and cities have scrapbooking departments in craft and hobby shops as well as scrapbooking stores. This hobby is so popular that even in smaller cities many people could be invited to share tips with the audience. You might choose to use a combination of businesspeople and private individuals as your speakers.

This program combines a few tips from an expert and a short hands-on workshop, with the public bringing family items (pictures, mementos, etc.) to incorporate in a page or two of a scrapbook of their own. Allow about 1 to 1½ hours for this program. If many people are interested in this workshop, you might consider having a second program for completing the scrapbooks.

Materials Needed

Plenty of tables and chairs, especially for the guest speaker(s) and for the public to work on their scrapbooks.

Scrapbooking supplies that the guest speaker suggests, such as paper, glue, scissors, a selection of stickers, or clip art.

Ask participants to bring their own scrapbooks, with a few items they may want to include during the work session portion of the program.

Procedure

1. Introduce the program about keeping family treasures and keepsakes in albums and scrapbooks with a family story from a guest storyteller or library staff.

2. Read a family story such as Eve Bunting's *The Memory String*.

3. Introduce a guest speaker, who will give participants a few tips about making attractive scrapbooks, then give participants most of the program time to work on a sample page or two with help from the speaker and library staff.

Exploring Your Family Roots: A Genealogy Workshop

This program relies on guest speakers either from the library's genealogy department or from a local genealogy group. State associations may also be contacted to set up this program. If your library is small and you intend the program to be a simple introduction to this topic, you can briefly talk about what resources the library and community have in terms of genealogy records and reference books. Reproduce the bibliography on pages 36–38 for handouts and create a display of books and magazines on the topic.

If your library does not subscribe to a specific genealogy magazine, work together on this program with other librarians and write for sample copies of the journals mentioned in the bibliography, such as *Family Tree Magazine*.

Materials Needed

Books and bibliography handouts.

Computers and electronic equipment for genealogist to show useful Web sites to audience.

Copies of the Pedigree Chart (p. 55).

My Pedigree Chart

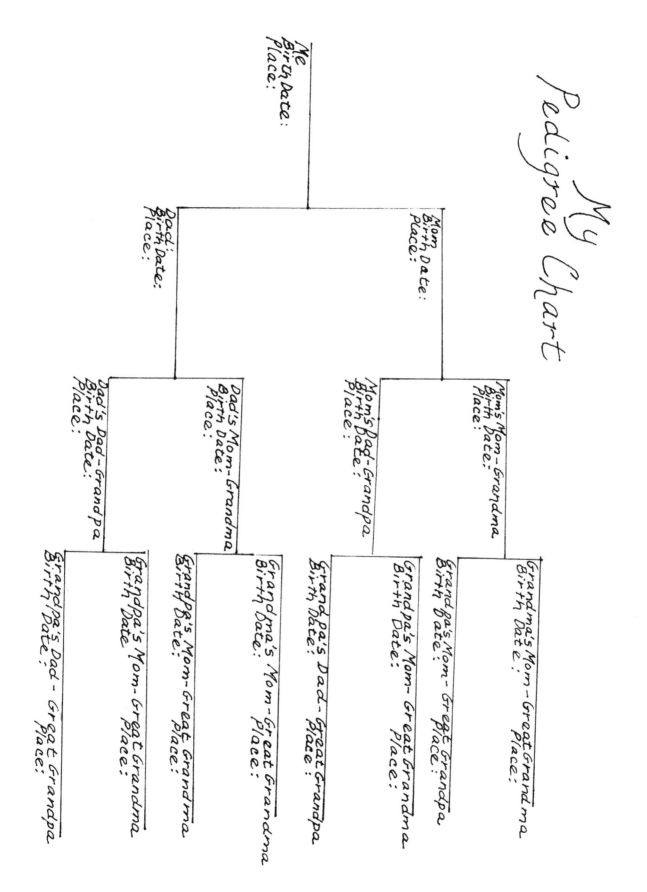

Me
Birth Date:
Place:

Mom
Birth Date:
Place:

Dad
Birth Date:
Place:

Mom's Dad – Grandpa
Birth Date:
Place:

Mom's Mom – Grandma
Birth Date:
Place:

Dad's Mom – Grandma
Birth Date:
Place:

Dad's Dad – Grandpa
Birth Date:
Place:

Grandma's Mom – Great Grandma
Birth Date: Place:

Grandpa's Mom – Great Grandma
Birth Date: Place:

Grandpa's Dad – Great Grandpa
Birth Date: Place:

Grandma's Mom – Great Grandma
Birth Date: Place:

Grandpa's Mom – Great Grandma
Birth Date: Place:

Grandpa's Dad – Great Grandpa
Birth Date: Place:

Procedure

Before You Begin

1. Set up a book display of genealogy resources (see bibliography).

2. Reproduce any handouts you wish to distribute to participants.

3. Arrange for a genealogy expert from your library or elsewhere to be a guest speaker.

4. Purchase refreshments, if desired.

On the Day of the Program

1. Booktalk some of the more interesting and useful sources on this topic. Lila Perl's *The Great Ancestor Hunt: The Fun of Finding Out Who You Are* and Ira Wolfman's *Do People Grow on Family Trees?* are two good choices. Also show copies of *Family Tree Magazine.* If your library does not already subscribe to this periodical, consider getting one before the program.

2. Introduce your guest speaker and have him or her give tips to the audience about how to trace family roots and do pedigree charts.

3. Have the expert or a librarian show selected Web sites that will be helpful. The list of Web sites in this chapter (pp. 38–39) are good choices, and you can add others specific to your own state.

4. Set aside plenty of time for questions, and serve refreshments if desired.

Fusion: Family Recipes from Different Cultures

The family recipes on pages 57–58 represent some of my family's Irish food traditions and other recipes I have collected and adapted for my own family's enjoyment over the years. Like many other cooks, I love food from all over the world. Some of these recipes have been passed on to me from friends, or I have found them in children's books and cookbooks from all over the world.

Grandma O'Neal's Irish Cabbage

Ingredients

1 small or medium-sized cabbage
1 small or medium-sized white onion
6 or more slices of bacon
coarse ground pepper

Directions

1. Slice cabbage very thinly across the grain. Place in large frying pan or electric skillet (not a deep pot).

2. Slice onion very thin and place on top of cabbage.

3. Cut bacon in 3- or 4-inch pieces and lay on top of onion. Sprinkle 3 or 4 drops of water on top of cabbage and onions. (Cabbage has a lot of water, so you will need only a very small amount of additional water.)

4. Grind plenty of fresh pepper across top of cabbage mixture or add about ½ tsp of coarse ground pepper. The amount depends on your taste.

5. Cover the skillet and cook mixture on medium heat for 10 to 15 minutes so it is soft but not overdone. (My grandma used to cook cabbage for an hour, but I prefer it much less done.)

English Trifle Several Ways

The English call it "trifle," and colonial Americans adapted it. Italians make their own version, called "Zuppa Inglese" (soup of the English). Here is a delicious recipe that can be made many different ways, combining what you have on your pantry shelf and in the refrigerator. Although this sounds and looks fancy, it's just a cake, custard, cream, and fruit concoction.

Ingredients

custard powder such as Birds (an English import available at British tea shops or in grocery stores) or an American-style mix (milk and eggs are often needed also)

commercial pound cake (frozen or store made, or homemade if you are adventurous)

pint of whipping cream (much better than a frozen whipped topping)

fresh or frozen berries—strawberries, blueberries, or raspberries

sliced almonds if desired

Directions

1. Prepare custard and whip cream in separate bowls. Tear the cake into chunks.

2. Put a small amount of custard in the bottom of a deep bowl or casserole. A glass container is best so you can see the layers.

3. Add a layer of cake chunks, then some of the fruit. Add a few spoonfuls of the custard.

4. Repeat layers.

5. Whip the cream and top with the whipped cream and sliced almonds.

Potato Latkes (Pancakes)

"A little touch of heaven for potato lovers and people everywhere who love food from the Jewish tradition."

Ingredients

4–6 medium potatoes

1 small onion

2 eggs

several tbsp commercial bread crumbs

½–1 tsp salt

½ tsp pepper

¼ cup (or more) cooking oil

Directions

1. Peel potatoes and grate into a bowl. Add a little water if potatoes will sit for any length of time, since raw potatoes discolor quickly.

2. Peel and grate onions into another bowl.

3. Break eggs into a clean bowl.

4. Drain potatoes and combine with eggs and onions. Add bread crumbs to give the mixture a "bind." Add salt and pepper to taste.

5. Heat oil in skillet until it is hot enough for a drop of water to sizzle in the oil. Carefully add a ladleful (several tablespoons) of batter to the hot oil. Allow plenty of space between pancakes so you can turn them easily.

6. Let pancakes cook several minutes before turning. Fry on both sides until latkes are golden brown on both sides. Drain on paper towels.

7. Place pancakes on an ovenproof platter. Serve with sour cream and applesauce.

This is a traditional Hanukkah treat, but I love them with beef brisket for dinner or for a brunch. Baked apples or apple and orange fruit salad are good sides.

From *Story Celebrations: A Program Guide for Schools and Libraries* by Jan Irving. Westport, CT: Libraries Unlimited. Copyright © 2008.

4

Going Dutch: Exploring Holland and Its Culture

The tiny country of the Netherlands, less than the size of Vermont and New Hampshire combined, demands far more attention than its mere size might suggest. Historically speaking, it was a world power during the "Golden Age" of the seventeenth century. It held enormous wealth, had colonies all over the globe, and produced some of the greatest art the world has ever known. Today it stands as a model for the rest of the world in water engineering and land reclamation. Imagine! Over two-fifths of Holland was once below the sea, but its dykes and canals, developed over the past 600 years, have literally made this proud land. Egypt consulted with Dutch engineers when the Aswan Dam was built. The United States could well have profited from studying Dutch accomplishments in water engineering before Hurricane Katrina destroyed thousands of miles of America's coastlands. Look to the Dutch for practical solutions in the future!

The Netherlands, or Holland, as the country is often called, is equally famous as the "world's flower shop," known for a thriving chemical industry, the world's busiest seaport (Rotterdam), and its high standard of living. Because of its political and economic stability, many companies find Holland an attractive place to do business. It is a nearly classless society whose royalty take "real" jobs and work among the people to improve conditions for all citizens. The Netherlands has a long tradition of caring for the less fortunate. For more than 400 years, Dutch almshouses, small attractive dwellings arranged around secluded gardens, have housed the poor and elderly. Americans might envy the good pensions senior citizens receive today in Holland.

Dutch people are well educated, and American tourists are often pleasantly surprised to discover most people they talk with speak English fluently. Excellence in the arts draws thousands of visitors to Holland's world-class museums (over 1,000 of them). Food, flower, and cheese markets attract shoppers, and spectacular views inspire observant travelers.

Certainly Holland has its contradictions. Its city populations tend to be liberal and open-minded, but in more rural towns, a more conservative approach is taken. Manners are important, but the onslaught of thousands of bicyclists moving full speed ahead without using warning bells sometimes seems rude to visitors on foot. While Dutch people are helpful, they can also sound brusque and overly frank to some tourists. The country has a reputation for cleanliness (street washing is a major event in Dutch festivals in the United States), but Amsterdam in recent years has become less than spotless.

Here is a complex, varied, and fascinating culture that affords many opportunities for learning and entertainment. Because fewer books have been written about this place, and many existing resources may not be found in libraries due to their paper formats and limited distribution from small presses, the bibliography of this chapter lists some obscure sources. Web sites supplement the print materials.

The school program "Dutch Spectrum" explores five different curricular topics—art, history, literature, food and customs, and science/invention/business. Classroom teachers work with the school media specialist, and students are given opportunities to study Dutch history and science, create poems, write letters and diaries, cook Dutch food and explore customs, and evaluate Dutch art.

The public library program "Celebrate Holland!" can be an indoor event with different activity centers on storytelling, food tasting and preparation, as well as arts and crafts activities. Suggestions for outside community fairs are given. Recipes, story suggestions, and art ideas are given.

This chapter provides other information about Dutch cities and festivals in the United States. Young people may want to explore these and learn more about the Dutch culture through travel and through the hands-on activities in this chapter.

Bibliography

Bowman, Crystal. *Windmills and Wooden Shoes.* Cygnet Publishing Company, 1995.
(Reading Level: Spache, 6.4)
   Published in cooperation with the tulip festival in Holland, Michigan, this story of a boy who visits his grandmother relates the events during this exciting time of year. Colin sees the *klompen* dancers, visits the windmill brought from Holland, enjoys the street scrubbing and parade, and eats traditional Dutch food. This book will inspire students to visit a Dutch community or plan a simplified festival in their school or library.

Braaij, C. P. *Windmills of Holland.* Distributed by Kooijman Souvenirs and Gifts, n.d. Available at www.woodenshoe-workshop.nl.
(Reading Level: not readily available)
   Through extensive photographs and diagrams, this invaluable resource provides a history of windmills and how they work. This book is published in Holland, and it provides information not readily found in other sources. Order from the address above or purchase in gift shops in Dutch communities in the United States, such as Pella, Iowa.

Davis, Kevin. *Look What Came from the Netherlands.* Franklin Watts, 2002.
(Reading Level: Flesch-Kincaid, 6.4)
   Organized by ten topics from inventions to language, this brief nonfiction picture book will grab young readers' attention with the fun information and presentation.

Fleming, Candace. *Boxes for Katje.* Farrar, Straus & Giroux, 2003.
(Reading Level: Accelerated Reader: 3.5)
   Just after World War II in a small Dutch town, Katje's family, like most Dutch people at the time, has few basic supplies. One day she receives a goodwill package as well as a letter from a girl in Indiana. More boxes arrive with goodies that help the Dutch as they recover from war's devastation. This book is based on a true story.

Frank, Anne, et al. *Diary of a Young Girl: The Definitive Edition.* Bantam, 1997.
(Reading Level: Accelerated Reader, 6.5)
   This newly revised edition tells the complete story of this remarkable teen whose diary is internationally known and loved. She and her family lived in hiding from the Nazis for over two years in a makeshift apartment above her father's warehouse in Amsterdam.

Heusinkveld, Holly Flame, and Jean Caris-Osland. *Dutch Proverbs.* Penfield Press, 1996. Available at www.penfield-press.com.
(Reading Level: not applicable)
Essentially a gift book of Dutch proverbs, this inspiring little volume is decorated with Hindeloopen designs and includes a history of this folk art style developed in northwest Holland.

Hort, Lenny. *The Boy Who Held Back the Sea.* Dial Books, 1987.
(Reading Level: Flesch-Kincaid, 6.6)
This fictional retelling of an "invented" folktale relates the story of a boy who sticks his finger in a hole of a leaking dam in Holland. His effort works just in time for adults to rescue the stalwart lad. This short book has been praised for its glowing illustrations by Thomas Locker, reminiscent of seventeenth-century Dutch painting.

Noyes, Deborah. *Hana in the Time of the Tulips.* Walker, 2004.
(Reading Level: Spache, 8.5)
This picture storybook tells about a girl's concern over her father's growing sadness because he has lost his fortune during the tulip market craze in the 1630s in Holland. This story is exquisitely illustrated with paintings reminiscent of Dutch art of the day, and the author's note about this economic disaster will fascinate young readers.

Van Klompenburg, Carol, and Dorothy Crum. *Dutch Touches.* Penfield Press, 1996. Available at www.penfield-press.com.
(Reading Level: Flesch-Kincaid, 7.37)
This collection of essays covers such topics as Dutch in America, modern Dutch history, tulip festivals, windmills, Dutch arts and crafts, holidays, and family stories. A large selection of traditional Dutch recipes and garden recipes makes this book invaluable for class projects and library programs.

Wiedijk, Fr. M. *Wooden Shoes of Holland.* Distributed by Kooijman Souvenirs and Gifts, n.d. Available at www.woodenshoe-workshop.nl
This history of wooden shoes and clogs includes an explanation of how the clog maker carries out his craft and how clogs are made by machine. A selection of wooden shoes is also available at the Web site.

Woelfle, Gretchen. *Katje the Windmill Cat.* Walker Books, 2001.
(Reading Level: Accelerated Reader, 3.1)
Katje, the beloved cat of a Dutch couple, leads an easy life until a baby is born. Then she is ignored and cast aside, until she comes to the rescue of the baby during a fierce storm. This fictional story is based on an actual storm in south Holland in 1421. Nicola Bayley's soft illustrations and decorative Dutch tiles make a perfect complement to the gentle text.

Woelfle, Gretchen. *The Wind at Work: An Activity Guide to Windmills.* Chicago Review Press, 1997.
(Reading Level: Flesch-Kincaid, 8.6)
This comprehensive guide to wind power and windmills has explanations of how windmills work, a history and location of windmills around the world, extensive photographs and diagrams, and instructions for student projects. In addition to the main text, many sources for further information are provided.

Selected Web Sites

American Folklore Web Site: www.americanfolklore.net/folktales/ny.html
   Gives several folktales of Dutch origin from New York (New Amsterdam).

The Holland Ring: www.thehollandring.com/dutchculture.shtml
   Web site created by an American who is a Dutch enthusiast; provides an insight into Dutch customs and culture.

Kennedy Center: http://artsedge.kennedy-center.org/content/2219
   Provides a lesson plan on writing fables.

Pella Iowa Web Site: www.pellatuliptime.com
   This active chamber of commerce promotes the Dutch sites and Tulip Time festival held every May in Pella, Iowa.

Rabbel Information Site: www.rabbel.info/corleisure.html
   Commercial site has links about the Netherlands, its language, and its food.

Ristenbatt Genealogy: www.ristenbatt.com/genealogy/dutch._bi.htm
   Provides information about Dutch customs.

The Van Gogh Museum: www3.vangoghmuseum.nl/vgm
   Web site of this popular Amsterdam museum gives a wealth of information about the artist and his works.

Dutch in the United States

The Dutch have migrated to the United States since 1613, and it is estimated that between eight and ten million Dutch immigrants and their descendents currently live in America. Some of the places where Dutch people have settled are Sheboygan, Wisconsin; Milwaukee, Wisconsin; Albany, New York; New York, New York; Tarrytown, New York; Kinderhook, New York; Schenectady, New York; Staten Island, New York; Fulton, Illinois; Cedar Grove, Wisconsin; Holland, Michigan, Grand Rapids, Michigan; Orange City, Iowa; Pella, Iowa; Oak Harbor, Washington; Nederland, Texas; and Denver, Colorado.

Note that the "Pennsylvania Dutch" are of German ancestry, not Dutch.

Three well-known Dutch festivals in the United States are held annually in Holland, Michigan (www.tuliptime.com or www.holland.org); Orange City, Iowa (www.octulipfestival.com); and Pella, Iowa (www.pellatuliptime.com).

Dutch Spectrum: A School Program

This program presents a spectrum or broad range of varied but related ideas with Holland as their central focus. Students may explore one or more of the five areas of this spectrum: literature; art; history; food and customs; and science/invention/ business. Since the spectrum represents cross-curricular topics, the school media center is a perfect place to research and present this program, with teachers from different subject areas contributing to the success of this project.

Five class meetings of approximately fifty minutes are suggested for this program.

Materials Needed

Colored paper for colored spectrum packets: one sheet each of five different colors of paper such as yellow, blue, pale green, peach, and hot pink for every student.

Art reproductions of van Gogh's paintings, available as postcards from museums or larger prints from www.allposters.com; seven or eight reproductions of your choice from those categories suggested on page 65, "Spectrum One: Dutch Art."

Food, as indicated in recipes in this chapter, or have students supply food as part of their projects. A sample list for "The Dutch Table" includes three loaves of Dutch bread (rye, honey bread, onion), three pounds of bologna, one to two wheels of Gouda or Edam cheese, three dozen Dutch spice cookies. For a sample from a *rijstaffel* make Gado Gado: two bags of fresh spinach, one box of yellow rice, one large bunch of fresh broccoli, one pound of fresh green beans, one pound of fresh bean sprouts, and six hard-boiled eggs. *Note:* These quantities will serve about thirty-five students with a sample.

Procedure

Before You Begin

1. Prior to beginning the first unit, prepare a mural of the Netherlands, with pictures of sights and scenes of the country. Include quotations that introduce the culture. Use the list of "What to Know about Holland" on page 64 to make notes on the map.

2. Gather books for display (see bibliography on pp. 60–61).

3. Arrange to have a dance instructor or music or art teacher attend the second meeting, to teach participants Dutch folk dances, or talk about Dutch art during the Golden Age.

First Meeting

1. Read portions from *The Diary of Anne Frank* or the entire picture storybook *Boxes for Katje,* by Candace Fleming. Both of these stories are set during or just after World War II in Holland. Class should discuss both the content and questions these stories raise.

2. Distribute Dutch spectrum packets for students to read later. Tell students to be prepared to select their topics by the next meeting. If desired, set up a book and research station in the school library for students to browse in making their selections.

Second Meeting

1. Introduce Holland, its history, and its culture, through various Web sites, such as www.thehollandring.com/index.html, www.annefrank.org, and www3.vangoghmuseum.nl.

2. Discuss questions presented in "What to Know about Holland" (p. 64).

3. Read another section from Anne Frank's diary or the picture storybook *Hana in the Time of the Tulips,* by Deborah Noyes. The latter book, based on real events in seventeenth-century Holland, introduces a fascinating story of the tulip trade and the economic consequences of speculative trade. Although historical, this example could lead to student projects about the economy of a nation.

4. Have students begin their research for projects from the spectrum packet. The projects may be individual or small group work.

Third Meeting

1. A music teacher leads the group in learning a Dutch folk dance, or an art teacher gives an overview of Dutch painting during the Golden Age. (These presentations do not replace student projects, but rather serve as springboards for whole class interest.)

2. Have students continue their research for the spectrum project.

Fourth Meeting

1. Have students present their projects in the areas of science/invention/ business and history.

Fifth Meeting

1. Have students present their projects in food and customs, art, and literature.

Note: Adjust the schedule as needed. Two class sessions may not be enough to complete the unit.

What to Know about Holland

Use the ideas and questions in the following box for your mural or display on the Netherlands to introduce the unit "Dutch Spectrum."

- Print quotations from Van Gogh and small reproductions of his art from the Web site www3.vangoghmuseum.nl. Find other Dutch prints to display.
- Display maps of the Netherlands using the Web site www.embassyworld.com/maps/Maps_ of_Netherlands.html.
- Display pictures of tulips, windmills, and Dutch shoes. Use Internet sites listed in this chapter.
- What Dutch folklore character is popular at Christmas?
- Dutch proverb: Silence and thinking never hurt anyone.
- Did you know that the practice of holding bridal showers came from the Dutch?
- Did you know that tulips did not originally come from Holland? Where did they come from? (They came from Turkey!)
- What is the difference between "Holland" and "the Netherlands?"
- Did you ever think that today's Crocs™ are similar to Dutch wooden shoes?
- Why is the sea referred to as "Waterwolf" by the Dutch?
- What famous diary written by a Dutch person has sold more than 22 million copies?
- Do you "Dutch treat" when you are with friends?
- Did you know that Holland is one of the most crowded countries in the world?
- What kind of vehicle is owned by most people in Holland?

Dutch Spectrum Packets

Note: Print each of the spectrum handouts (pp. 65–70) on a different color of paper and place sheets in a nine-by-twelve-inch envelope or a pocket portfolio, so that students can add their own research and materials to the packet. The idea of a spectrum is used in two ways. First, a color spectrum contains a series of different colors, and Holland is famous for its art contributions to the world. Second, a spectrum is a collection of varied but similar ideas. This unit gives students different themes to study as they explore the Netherlands.

Spectrum One: Dutch Art

1. Appreciating Dutch Art during the Golden Age

    Some art historians believe that seventeenth-century Dutch art is unparalleled. Others believe the Italian Renaissance would surpass it, but most agree that Dutch art during the Golden Age is amazing.

    For this project, select one Dutch artist from this period. Prepare a brief biography of the artist, written as an encyclopedia article or as interview. Find three to five paintings by that artist to show to the class. (Find inexpensive art reproductions from Internet sources or postcards of the works at an art store or museum, if possible.)

    Assume the role of a museum guide or an art dealer and tell the class why this artist is important and what the appeal of his art is today. (What specific qualities do you admire in the artist's work? The color? Subject matter? Hidden messages? The way it shows typical life in Holland?)

    Two of the most popular artists from this period are Rembrandt and Jan Vermeer but other good choices are Jan Steen, Pieter Brueghel, and Avercamp.

2. Van Gogh (the Great)

    Many people today agree that Vincent van Gogh was one of the greatest painters in the world. Choose one or two paintings from van Gogh's early works (such as *The Potato Eaters*), two paintings of flowers, two paintings of landscapes, and one painting of your own choosing (such as an interior, a person, or a self-portrait).

    Bring reproductions of these works (found in books, or postcard reproductions) to class. Tell van Gogh's art biography through these paintings. This kind of biography may give details from Vincent's life, but the focus should be on why he chose these subjects, how they reveal his feelings about the world and himself, and what makes this painting important to the world.

3. Architecture in the Netherlands: Past or Present

    Dutch houses and buildings dating to the Golden Age (1550 to 1700) remain timeless reminders of the wealth and beauty of Holland. Study fine examples of these buildings in art books and travel guides (note the *Michelin Guidebook*). Select examples of different styles of gable roofs or photographs and paintings of town halls and historic houses to share with the class. Bring these to class or make your own sketchbook of examples.

    Assume the role of a travel guide or an anonymous architect of the day to make your presentation lively for the class.

    You could focus instead on modern Dutch architecture through studying buildings of Cuypers and Berlage. Show examples of modern buildings in The Hague, Rotterdam, or Amsterdam and explain important features of this art form.

Spectrum Two: Food and Customs

1. Traditional Dutch Cooking

    Have students study the history and menus of Dutch cuisine of the past. Two Web sites are particularly helpful: *On the Trail of our Ancestors* (www.ristenbatt.com/genealogy/dutch) and *The Holland Ring: Dutch Food and Eating Habits* (www.thehollandring.com/food.shtml). Many of these dishes are still enjoyed in Holland and in Dutch communities in the United States. For their reports, students might show pictures of Dutch still life paintings or scenes of Dutch people selling and eating foods such as cheese, potatoes, bread, and fish. Include stories of Dutch *hutspot* (important in Leiden's history), cheese markets, and Dutch pastries. Make samples of some Dutch recipes to share with the class and compile a short cookbook. See this chapter's bibliography and recipe pages for ideas.

2. *Rijsttafel*

    Indonesian cooking has become popular today in the Netherlands because Indonesia was formerly occupied by the Dutch. This spicy and exciting meal may include dozens of different side dishes based around rice. (The word *rijsttafel*, pronounced "rye-sh-toffel," means "rice table.")

    Have students study cookbooks and menus for their reports and prepare a few dishes to share with the class. Children can make their own cookbooks based on recipes they find in cookbooks and on the Internet. Consult with teachers, Indonesian restaurants, and local cooking classes for availability of ingredients and for guidance in finding dishes the class might enjoy. Make a glossary of terms and ingredients that are unfamiliar to you. The recipe for Gado Gado (p. 76) is easy to prepare.

3. Dutch Customs, Manners, and Values

    Study the Dutch way of life, traditional manners, and customs as if you are preparing your class for a trip to Holland or a Dutch community in the United States. Consult Web sites and books listed in this chapter for this topic. Explore the following questions to understand Dutch culture and the people of Holland:

    - What words best describe Dutch character (such as "thrifty" or "cleanliness") ? Explain how the Dutch demonstrate these qualities in their lives.

    - What tips might you give your classmates so they will be considered thoughtful guests in this country? (Discuss Dutch table manners, for example.)

    - What Dutch proverbs give insight into Dutch culture, and what do they mean? (Make a poster of these to display in the library.)

    For an alternative project, choose a proverb from the "Dutch Proverbs and Quotations" (p. 67). Write a fable (a story with a moral) and use the proverb itself as the moral to your story. The following Web site will help you write a fable: http://artsedge.kennedy-center.org/content/2219.

Dutch Proverbs and Quotations

Crumbs, too, are bread.

For the concert of life, no one receives a program.

Hunger is the best sauce.

He who is not careful with little is not worthy of lots.

Hasty questions require slow answers.

There's clean and then there's Dutch clean.

Better alone than in bad company.

Don't throw away your old shoes until you have new ones.

Silence and thinking never hurt anyone.

Spectrum Three: Dutch History

1. Holland before the Golden Age

    Early Dutch history is a story of battles, tribal disputes, and occupation by many different countries. Have students write reports giving an overview of this exciting past and illustrating it with pictures of artifacts and paintings. Students may choose to highlight a particular area (such as the Frisian region and its resistance against the Romans) and create a script or news report of the time.

2. The Golden Age of Holland

    Have students create a Dutch newspaper of the seventeenth century with articles that describe events of the day. They can include several news stories about big events (such as the Treaty of Utrecht, struggles with Spain beginning in 1568, a Dutch voyage by a famous explorer), ads for goods produced by local guilds, an announcement of an art show, or a feature article about life in an almshouse.

    If a small group works on this project, have different class members report on their articles in class. They might dress in character or show examples of clothing worn by people of the day in different regions of the country.

3. Holland during World War II

    Ask students to research this dark period of Holland's history and prepare a ten- to fifteen-minute documentary report for class. If children are working in small groups, assign subtopics to different class members. One student could cover the events leading up to the Nazi occupation. Another could discuss the life of the royal family preceding the occupation. Another might report on the bombing of Rotterdam. Topics that are especially important include the Dutch resistance movement, the Battle of Arnhem, and Operation Manna (the dangerous Allied air mission to deliver food to starving Dutch people during the last days of the war.)

Spectrum Four:
Literature and Writing about Holland

Although the Netherlands does not possess a large body of literature compared to England, France, Italy, and some of the other European countries, two notable examples of Dutch writing are the letters of Vincent van Gogh and *The Diary of Anne Frank*. Scenery, art, and Dutch culture may inspire students to create poems and stories of their own. The following projects are based on these ideas.

1. In Holland wind has been a major force of destruction, inspiration, and triumph in overcoming its power. Write a poem or series of poems from the point of view of the wind, from the point of view of a sailor or a windmill, or through the eyes of a child.

2. Create a wind or water legend about the origin of these forces in nature. Some legends begin with a tall tale hero or heroine who has captured or tamed nature. Other legends tell of the origin of the force itself. Student legends might tell the story of the battle between Peter (an invented character) and Waterwolf (the term the Dutch use to describe the sea). The origin of Dutch storms could begin as a "chain reaction" tale. The first action in the story could be how a strong sun danced so wildly on the sea that it sent the water spinning in violent circles. From there, birds above the water began flapping their wings, which caused dogs to chase their tails, cats to chase dogs, rats to run to the sea, and an enormous storm to blow over the land. In the end, the vicious cycle ends when a sailor sings a ballad to stop the raging storm. Each action in the story then reverses, leaving the sun to set in peace over the quiet water.

3. Van Gogh's letters reveal his love of color and the sounds of words, his inspiration from reading French literature, his close observation of nature (trees, the sun, wheat fields), and his love of Japanese art. Read several of van Gogh's letters and write a response to him as if you had received the letters.

4. Visit the van Gogh museum's Web site (www3vangoghmuseum.nl/vgm/) and read portions of his letters found there that describe specific paintings such as *The Sunflowers*. Select two other van Gogh paintings and write letters as if you were van Gogh writing to his brother Theo about a scene in nature that inspired those works of art.

5. Anne Frank wrote her diary in the form of letters to Kitty, an imaginary friend. Write letters to Anne as if you were Kitty and had received several of these letters. Comment on her observations and view of life in Holland during the 1940s.

Spectrum Five:
Science/Invention/Business

1. Have students research one of Holland's inventions and its history. In a report they should describe the invention and how it has proved useful to the world. A few of these inventions are the compound microscope by Zacharias Janssen, the precision microscope by Anton van Leeuwenhoek, and the telescope by Hans Lippershey. Other inventions are a dredger, submarine, thermostat, pocket watch, audiocassette tape recorder, and windmill. Have students give an oral report as if they were the inventor, with a three-dimensional model or drawings of this invention. An alternative project would be to write an inventor's diary, explaining the new invention with illustrations to show how the idea works. The "new" invention should be one made by a Dutch person the student has researched.

2. Have students make posters or models of various kinds of Dutch windmills, accompanied by oral reports explaining how a windmill works. Students can show how windmills have been useful in controlling the wind, pumping water, and grinding grain.

3. Ask students to research agricultural contributions of the Dutch and report on one important kind of this agribusiness. If this is a group project, some class members might report on "tulipmania" during the Golden Age; other class members could report about the Dutch flower industry today. Encourage them to use stories, scripts, and news articles for business magazines to give lively accounts to the class, rather than giving just straight factual accounts.

From *Story Celebrations: A Program Guide for Schools and Libraries* by Jan Irving. Westport, CT: Libraries Unlimited. Copyright © 2008.

Proverbs in Pieter Brueghel's Paintings

Brueghel's painting *The Blue Cloak* (*Netherlandish Proverbs*) visually depicts dozens of Dutch proverbs. For example, a man is shearing sheep in the foreground of the painting. Another man with shears holds a pig producing no wool. This is a visual explanation for the proverb "Pig shearing yields no wool." Following are other proverbs among seventy-five maxims the insightful observer can discover in this painting:

- Don't count your chickens before they are hatched.

- He speaks out of two mouths.

- A man must stoop low if he wishes to go through the world.

- He opens the door with his backside (he doesn't know if he's coming or going).

- He who spills his gruel can't get it all up (no use crying over spilled milk).

Celebrate Holland!: A Public Library Program

In the spirit of a Dutch tulip festival or a traditional *kermis* (fair), create a Dutch celebration in your library. This program has been designed as an indoor event staged in a separate program room, or in different corners of the library if space is limited, with the help of volunteers (student or adult). It can also be held outdoors during pleasant weather. If you wish to involve many volunteers or plan this event cooperatively with other community agencies, consider holding a parade or setting up stalls and tents with banners and ribbons for making crafts and sampling food. This outdoor fair could take on an international flair, with activities planned from many cultures.

The program described here is planned for about two hours, with different stations set up around the library so that children and their families can participate in one or more of the centers. Quantities of supplies given in the materials list anticipate a crowd of fifty to eighty people. Adjust these quantities for your situation. The program could be for just young people or be a multigenerational event, with older kids helping library staff execute the program.

Materials Needed

Boxes of oven bake clay. *Note:* Della Robbia brand clay comes in four-pound boxes that will make about eight ½-inch tiles. Have teen volunteers make tiles and bake them in a home oven prior to the program. If you plan to have one hundred tiles available, purchase twelve bags. The cost will be about $6.50 per bag. Purchase in art or craft stores.

Four to eight sixteen-ounce bottles or jars of acrylic paint in red, blue, green, and yellow or light orange, to paint the tiles.

Fifty to one hundred sheets of red and green cardstock for making tulip stencils, and at least twelve pairs of scissors.

Fifty to one hundred sheets of white card stock and four dozen felt tipped markers for making the Hindeloopen designs.

Food for "The Dutch Table." (Adjust this as you wish.)

- 6–8 loaves of rye bread, onion bread, and honey bread

- 5 pounds of sliced bologna or ham

- 5 pounds of Gouda or Edam cheese

• 8 dozen Dutch spice cookies (purchased)

Or, to make a large Dutch stew (*hutspot*), quadruple the recipe on page 75:

• 4 pounds ground chuck

• 4 pounds ground pork

• 12 pounds potatoes

• 8 pounds carrots

• 4 pounds onions

• salt and pepper

Decorations, such as Dutch flags, tulips or other flowers (real or silk), wooden shoes, or Delftware—gathered or made by student volunteers, based on designs found in books on Dutch culture and folk art. Blue and white is a traditional color combination for the Dutch.

Procedure

Before You Begin

1. Before the event, invite student volunteers or your student board to make decorations for the library. Before students meet, select books about Holland and Dutch culture using those listed in this chapter's bibliography. Ambitious kids may want to make banners painted in Dutch folk art style and gather collections of Dutch memorabilia from people in the community,

2. Prepare a program guide for participants, listing the different activities and providing directions on where to find them.

3. Find a storyteller (a librarian or professional storyteller) who can perform at your event, telling Dutch folktales. Alternatively, arrange for a group of folkdancers to perform the *klompen* dance at your festival.

4. Purchase and prepare foods for the tasting stations (see pp. 73–77 for details).

5. Purchase craft supplies and make Dutch tiles as described in the materials list. The tiles should be shaped and baked so they will be ready for program participants to paint them.

6. Set up event areas around the library: storytelling, food tasting, Dutch arts and crafts, and so on.

On the Day of the Event

1. Station student volunteers, librarians, and adult guides in each of the activity areas. Use the activity pages (79–81) to implement the activities. Identify the "official" library program staff (children, adult guides, librarians) with a Dutch hat or cap or a red, white, and blue ribbon tied horizontally from shoulder to waist. Set up activity tables and supplies for program participants to enjoy each experience.

2. Have an adult volunteer or librarian greet the public and show them to the program centers, or simply have a volunteer pass out a program guide with a list of events.

3. If desired, begin the event more formally, with a costumed librarian, a professional storyteller, or a group of folk dancers performing in a meeting room.

4. After the opening, lead program participants to designated activity areas. Costumed librarians or volunteers could take the role of travel guide from one of Holland's regions or wear a T-shirt decorated with windmills and tulips to welcome people to the library's "Holland for the Day" event.

Storytelling Center

Teen storytellers and librarians tell stories alternately in the storytelling corner of the library. Picture books with stunning illustrations can be shown after the stories are told orally. The illustrations are too small to use with a group, but the books can be made available for checkout later. The two books recommended for a wide audience are *The Boy Who Held Back the Sea,* retold by Thomas Locker, and *Katjke, the Windmill Cat,* by Gretchen Woelfle. The pictures in these books beautifully capture the light in famous Dutch paintings, and the settings make readers feel as if they have taken a trip to Holland in days past.

The Locker book is similar to the "legend" that appears in Mary Mapes Dodge's *Hans Brinker,* in which an otherwise untrustworthy lad known for skipping school and avoiding tasks one day notices that there is a small leak in the village dyke. Because he knows that even a small leak will quickly let in the sea and cause a flood, the boy sticks his finger in the hole. The child waits a long time for help to come and becomes a hero in his village. This "legend" is not actually Dutch, but because of its popularity, many adults have retold the tale as if it were. This story captures the imagination of young and old, and after the storyteller has related it, the truth can be told.

Other popular legends of the Dutch in America include Washington Irving's *The Legend of Sleepy Hollow* and *Rip Van Winkle.* Read portions of Irving's *The Legend of Sleepy Hollow* (Boyds Mills Press, 1992) or retell the story in your own words.

The Dutch Table

Traditional Dutch fare consists of plenty of meat, potatoes, cabbage, apples, cheese, and pastries. This hearty food gave industrious Dutchmen the energy to work hard and survive during harsh winters and flood times. The cookbooks listed in the bibliography on pages 60–61 contain authentic recipes. The ones given on the recipe pages in this chapter (75–77) are adaptations.

Give program participants samples of some of these foods for a tasting table of Dutch cuisine. Remember that Dutch food does not include Pennsylvania Dutch dishes, as this culture is German in origin rather than Dutch.

Sample Dutch Menu for Tasting

Salads

- Coleslaw (The name of this dish is Dutch: since *kool* means cabbage and *sla* means salad.)
- Dutch lettuce (Leaf lettuce is combined with hard-cooked eggs, bacon, and a boiled dressing.)
- Dutch potato salad (Similar to the dish above, with the eggs, lettuce, bacon, and boiled dressing, but diced cooked potatoes are added.)

Breads

- Choose a sampling of Dutch rye and onion rye, as well as sweet breads with orange peel and Dutch honey bread.

Meats

- Ham or bologna
- Baked fish
- Chicken croquettes

- Meatloaf or meatballs
- *Hutspot* (stew

Cheeses

- Gouda
- Edam

Pastries and Sweets

- *Pofferjes* (mini pancakes)
- Sand cookies
- Spice cookies
- Dutch apple cake
- Fried donuts
- Windmill cookies

Dutch *Rijstaffel* or Rice Table

This kind of lavish feast based on Indonesian recipes is actually Dutch in origin. Holland occupied Indonesia for 350 years and began the practice of serving many small side dishes to accompany the main staple, rice. Today, "rice table" is not popular in Indonesia, but it is enjoyed in the Netherlands. Typically dozens of dishes are served at a meal, but the menu may consist of fewer side dishes, thus becoming a "mini *rijstaffel*."

The Web site www.indonesiancooking.com/recipes.html will be helpful for finding authentic recipes of a tasting table. Some of the ingredients are not easy to find if local grocery stores and food shops stock limited food varieties. Ingredients such as chili paste tend to be very spicy and do not always appeal to less adventuresome eaters. The following menu lists some choices that would appear on a *rijstaffel*. The recipes on pages 76–77 include modified dishes.

Sample Rijstaffel for Tasting

- Cucumber bean salad
- Vegetable appetizer
- Sweet Indonesian soy sauce
- Chicken satay with peanut sauce
- Curried lentils
- Gado Gado
- Vegetable curry
- Sambals (spicy side dishes such as cabbage *sambal goring*)
- Yellow vegetable relish
- Fried bananas

Dutch Recipe Pages

The Dutch Kitchen (Traditional Dutch Recipes)

Note: Hutspot is served annually in Leiden, Holland, to commemorate a sixteenth-century event when the Spanish were besieging the town. The Spaniards made such a hasty retreat one night that they left their beef stew dinner behind. The starved Dutch enjoyed the meal and have celebrated this dish ever since.

Dutch *Hutspot* (Stew) Adapted

Ingredients

- 1 lb ground chuck
- 1 lb ground pork
- 3 lbs potatoes, peeled, sliced ¼-inch thick
- 2 lbs carrots, sliced ¼-inch thick
- 1 lb onions, cut in chunks or sliced
- salt and pepper to taste

Directions

1. Sauté meats in a Dutch oven or large electric frying pan until lightly browned.

2. Add potatoes, carrots, and onions and enough water to just cover the vegetables.

3. Cover tightly and cook until the vegetables are tender.

4. Mash lightly (if you like).

5. Season and serve hot.

This recipe makes about 10 dinner-sized servings. Since this dish is intended for just a sampling per person, it would probably serve about 15–20 people. For this program you may wish to have several Dutch ovens and electric frying pans (or a warming tray) filled for the crowd.

Sand Cookies

Ingredients

> 1 cup butter (two sticks)
> ⅔ cup brown sugar
> ⅔ cup white sugar
> 1 egg
> 2 cups flour
> ½ tsp baking soda
> 2 tsp vanilla

Directions

1. Cream butter and sugars, add egg, and mix.
2. Slowly add flour and baking soda, then vanilla.
3. Drop teaspoonfuls of the batter into small muffin tins. (Authentic cookies are larger, but this recipe is intended to make smaller servings for many people.)
4. Bake at 350 degrees F for 14–15 minutes or until done. Yields about 2 dozen small cookies.

Note: If the library does not have an oven, ask students to make this recipe at home and shop for spice or windmill cookies to serve with the *hutspot.*

Rijstaffel Recipe

Gado Gado

Arrange the ingredients on a very large platter and provide serving spoons for the public. You may wish to have a volunteer actually serve small portions of this delicious veggie dish to program attendees so the food is fairly distributed.

Ingredients

> several large bags of fresh spinach or several pounds, washed, picked over, and spun dry
> 4 cups yellow rice cooked in 6 cups water (white rice simmered with 1 tsp turmeric)
> 1 large bunch fresh broccoli, cut into small pieces and steamed
> 1 lb fresh green beans, lightly steamed
> 1 lb fresh carrots, thinly sliced and steamed, or raw
> 1 lb fresh bean sprouts
> 6 hard-boiled eggs
> fresh tofu, if desired

Directions

1. Make a bed of the fresh spinach, then add a layer of the rice.
2. On top of the rice add as many of the fresh or steamed veggies as you wish.
3. Top with the tofu and hard-boiled eggs.
4. Drizzle peanut sauce (recipe follows) on top.
5. Makes 12 to 15 servings.

Peanut Sauce

Ingredients

    1 cup creamy peanut butter

    1 tbsp grated fresh ginger root or 2 tsp ground ginger

    1 tbsp minced garlic

    3 tbsp brown sugar

    1½ cups hot water

    4 tbsp cider vinegar

    2 tbsp soy sauce

    1 tsp salt

    crushed red pepper to taste

Directions

1. Puree everything in a blender until smooth, adding a little more hot water if it is too thick to drizzle over the Gado Gado.

Dutch Arts and Crafts Station

Paper Chains

Use the pattern on page 79 to make a chain of tulips. Cut out the designs from construction paper or paper stock so the paper chains can stand, or use the designs as a decorative border in a room of your house. These chains can also be taped to windows and doorways. Paper cutouts are especially popular in Europe.

Decorative Tiles

Purchase plain clay tiles or have student volunteers make square tiles from purchased oven bake clay, as described in the materials list.

Decorate the tiles with craft paints purchased from craft, hobby, or discount stores. Students may use the designs found on page 80 or paint their own Dutch decorations. The windmill, decorated shoes, and bird are typical Dutch designs.

Hindeloopen Design Page

Use one of the borders on the Hindeloopen Design Page (p. 81) to make your own stationery, or decorate a border for your bedroom wall. Hindeloopen designs were named for a town in the Netherlands on the Zuider Zee. These designs were used in home interiors.

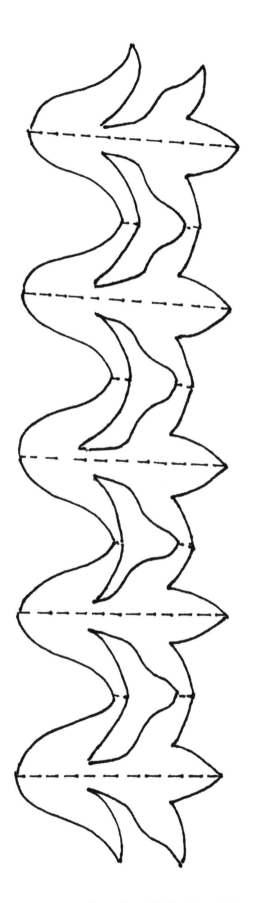

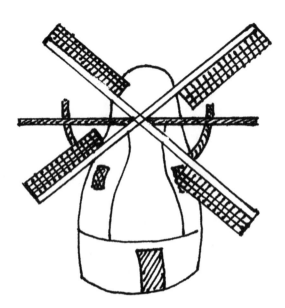

Welcome to Victorian London

Step back to the days of horse-drawn carriages, cries of street vendors, and puppet shows on the beach! Teachers and librarians can make this fascinating time come alive for today's students with the projects and ideas found in this chapter. Those concerned with children's lack of historical perspective need only look back to the Victorian era for parallels with our own day. Rapid growth, change in attitudes, technological and scientific advancements, and economic upheaval characterize our own times just as they did the nineteenth century. London continues to capture America's heart, from its hot trends in music to its sites and celebrities. And children are already familiar with many things from Victorian London. Build on their knowledge of *A Christmas Carol* and the musical *Oliver*. Ask them about favorite characters or scenes from *Alice in Wonderland*. Link this chapter to related ones in this book about diseases and gross science. And tell kids they will be going back in time to Harry Potter's hometown!

Almost 200 years ago, an eighteen-year-old princess named Victoria ascended to the throne of England. She was crowned at Westminster Abbey in London in 1837 in an elaborate ceremony based on customs dating back nearly 800 years. Victoria ruled for more than six decades. More than thirty British monarchs had ruled before her, many brilliant and capable kings and queens, but no monarch has ruled longer. The British Empire became a world power under her rule, and her name is given to this historical period. Thus, we refer to the nineteenth century as the Victorian era.

Because so much happened during the sixty-four years Victoria ruled, the scope of this chapter covers events and changes in England, and more specifically in London, from approximately 1837 until 1901, when Victoria died. What a lively era that was!

The word "change" best describes life in Victorian London. England had been largely an agricultural society until this time. Prices of farm crops plummeted, small farms closed, and people flooded into cities, especially London, to find work. Factories blossomed, workers learned new trades, and the Industrial Revolution was born. Inventions from steam locomotives to steam ships and railways transformed the country.

While many people found work in factories, working conditions were usually dreadful. People worked twelve-hour days, endured dangerous mishaps such as loss of limbs, and contracted disease. Less skilled workers took whatever work they could find, such as working in coal mines, sweeping chimneys, and hawking wares on the street. Life for the poor meant living in filthy slums, subsisting on bread, potatoes, and a little beer. When life became unbearable, some went to workhouses to survive. Those who fell into bankruptcy were sent to debtor's prisons until someone could pay their way out. Charles Dickens worked in a blacking warehouse as a boy to earn money so that his family could leave this miserable existence. Dickens reminds us of the desperate situation of the working poor in most of his novels, including the celebrated *A Christmas Carol*. Crime grew and people died young, but changes were underway.

Through social reforms and new laws, life improved. Ragged schools were set up for the poor. Sir Robert Peel brought about a new kind of law enforcement through carefully selecting and training police officers, who were named "bobbies" in his honor. The Coal Mines Act prohibited women and children from entering mines. Public health acts and advancements in medical research lessened diseases caused by water pollution.

A middle class emerged, as men became clerks and office workers who could give their families a better life. Their wives could even stay at home to raise children, and families looked forward to enjoying simple entertainment during leisure hours. Picnics at the beach, family games in the evening, and visiting museums and zoos became a reality.

Of course, the upper class in Victorian London lived in another world entirely. They lived in huge mansions and employed dozens of domestics, from scullery maids and porters to personal valets and governesses for their children. The Public Television Series *Upstairs, Downstairs* (available for purchase from various vendors) presents a vivid picture of life for the upper class and their "downstairs" staff.

Not all facets of Victorian life were grim. Fashion, parties, entertainment, and the arts flourished. Fashions for rich women ranged from wide skirts and puffy sleeves to elaborate crinoline petticoats, hoop skirts, and whalebone corsets. Fancy bonnets, plumes, and feathers adorned ladies' heads, and strict conventions even dictated how many plumes a woman should wear. Even men were dandies. They always wore waistcoats in addition to their suit coats and trousers. Silk ties and silk top hats were the rage. Clothes for working class people were not this elaborate, of course, but even middle class folk gave a great deal of attention to their dress.

All classes of people enjoyed music halls and theatrical entertainments. The upper class enjoyed opera. Some of London's finest museums and auditoriums were erected, with Royal Albert Hall and the British Museum taking center stage. But the most illustrious event of the century was the Great Exhibition that opened in 1851. Thousands visited the glittering Crystal Palace in London, built expressly for this "show of shows," which housed over 14,000 exhibits of new inventions and scientific achievements.

A major change in attitude toward children was taking place. In the past, children had been regarded as "little adults" who were not given much attention. They were expected to work along with adults as soon as they were able. During the Victorian era, children began to be treated differently. Yes, they were expected to be obedient and use proper manners, but children were finally treasured. The whole idea of childhood as a separate stage of life clearly changed society and the way people acted toward children. And with the publication of Lewis Carroll's *Alice in Wonderland*—a turning point in literature, since this book was written specifically for a little girl—a whole new genre we now call "children's literature" was born.

Victorian authors were prolific. Older children relishing a literary challenge will enjoy Sir Walter Scott's *Ivanhoe,* Mary Shelley's *Frankenstein,* and Sir Arthur Conan Doyle's Sherlock Holmes stories. (Scott's and Shelley's novels, written before Victoria became queen, were still popular in Victorian times.) Certainly Rudyard Kipling's *Just So Stories* and the *Jungle Book* are good choices for this age group. Some Victorian poetry may seem too old fashioned for today's youth, but consider using the rousing verse of Alfred Lord Tennyson and Edward Lear's limericks. Of course, the one author who best represents the Victorian era is Charles Dickens.

Through his short stories and novels, Dickens gave us such memorable characters as Oliver Twist, Fagin, and the ultimate grouch, Scrooge. Dickens painted gloomy scenes of mystery and mayhem in London. He exposed crime and described harsh work conditions in factories and the heartbreaking plight of the poor. Charles Dickens defines the Victorian era for readers, and young adults will find much to enjoy among his works. The bibliography in this chapter lists selected titles, some in adapted versions, as well as complete texts of others.

The school program unit "The Story of Victorian London" presents a variety of research topics and projects appropriate for grades six through eight. It is a model for studying other historical periods and involves literature, history, science, and the arts. Classroom teachers working with the media specialist guide students through their activities that can later be shared in a Victorian Fair.

The public library program "Look What You'll Find in Great Grandma's Attic" involves students in making Victorian crafts and preparing food for their own "Alice in Wonderland Mad Hatter's Tea Party," a humorous twist on traditional English teatime. You might even want to include a few Edward Lear limericks, play games, or stage a Punch and Judy show to round out the day.

Bibliography

Carroll, Lewis. *The Annotated Alice: The Definitive Edition.* W.W. Norton, 1999.
(Reading Level: Fleisch-Kincaid, 8.0)
  This volume contains both *Alice's Adventures in Wonderland* and *Through the Looking Glass,* as well as lengthy and informative sidebar notes by Martin Gardner and the original illustrations by John Tenniel. Shorter versions of this classic are available, but students will enjoy learning about various obscure references in the story. This version is well worth the extra money. These tales of nonsense mark the beginning of children's literature because they were written for a young girl and trace her fantastic adventures down a rabbit hole into the marvels of Wonderland and through a magic looking glass.

Dickens, Charles. *A Christmas Carol.* Margaret McElderry Books, 1995.
(Reading Level: Accelerated Reader: 6.7)
  This timeless classic, set in Victorian London, traces the transformation of Ebenezer Scrooge from miser to benefactor after he is visited by a series of Christmas ghosts. Many editions of this book are available, but this one, with illustrations by British artist Quentin Blake, captures the spirit of Dickens's beloved story.

Dickens, Charles. *Great Expectations.* Penguin Classics, 2002.
(Reading Level: Accelerated Reader, 7.6)
  The dark tale about seven-year-old Pip, a blacksmith's apprentice, who encounters an escaped convict in a churchyard, then becomes an educated gentleman through the help of an anonymous benefactor, can interest young readers who favor gothic novels. Some critics think it is too complex for today's young readers, although it used to be prescribed reading for ninth-grade English classes. Various adapted versions are available, but Dickens's writing begs to be read for a more authentic flavor of Victorian London.

Dickens, Charles. *Oliver Twist.* Signet Classics, 2005.
(Reading Level: Flesch Kincaid, 8.0)
  Dickens's suspenseful novel about the orphaned Oliver and his life in workhouses and among street hooligans gives mature young readers an unforgettable picture of harsh realities of Victorian London. Some of the most memorable characters in English literature, such as Fagin, appear in this novel, which many consider one of the best books of the time.

Hart, Robert. *English Life in the Nineteenth Century.* Putnam, 1971.
(Reading Level: Dale-Chall Index, 8.91)
  The major sections of this detailed text trace the changes from rural life to the Industrial Revolution in England, focusing on the laboring classes and social reforms. The final chapter on family life describes middle class entertainments.

Hibbert, Christopher. *Daily Life in Victorian England.* American Heritage, 1975.
(Reading Level: Dale-Chall, 8.19)
  This dense text is filled with excellent details about different classes of Victorian society, from wages, duties, fashions, and schooling, to rules of behavior. The effects of industrial change and the importance of religion are discussed. Numerous photographs, advertisements, paintings, and clippings bring this period alive.

Kipling, Rudyard. *The Jungle Book.* Viking, 1996.
(Reading Level: Accelerated Reader, 7.4)

These popular tales, set in India, have delighted many generations of children with rousing stories of wild animals and people. The most popular ones involve Mowgli, the human boy raised by wolves; Mowgli's adventures with Shere Khan, the Tiger; and Rikki-Tikki-Tavi, the mongoose who saves a human family from cobras. The stories were written as fables to teach moral values of proper human behavior, the laws of nature, and matters of survival. This edition, part of the Whole Story Series, combines the unabridged text with many nonfiction annotations about animals and history, with lavish illustrations that will increase the book's appeal to kids.

Kipling, Rudyard. *Just So Stories.* William Morrow, 1996.
(Reading Level: Accelerated Reader, 6.4)

Kipling's collection of imaginative stories that tell how animals came to have humps, spots, trunks, and scales continues to delight young people of all ages. These stories are excellent read-aloud tales, can be used as writing models, and contain rich language to delight the ear.

Kramer, Ann. *Eyewitness Victorians.* Dorling Kindersley, 2003.
(Reading Level: Fleisch-Kincaid, 9.4)

In this typically appealing DK-format book, readers are introduced to a range of topics, from cities, to social reform, to schools, to Queen Victoria and famous people of the age, through text and numerous illustrations.

Kraska, Edie. *Toys and Tales from Grandmother's Attic.* Houghton Mifflin, 1979.
(Reading Level: Dale-Chall, 7.8)

This workbook and history of folk art toys and crafts was developed with the Boston Children's Museum and is an invaluable resource for those interested in Victorian crafts.

Lear, Edward. *The Complete Verse and Other Nonsense.* Penguin, 2002.
(Reading Level: Flesch-Kincaid, 9.6)

Silly verses, nonsense songs, and limericks fill the pages of this book, along with stories and line drawings by the gifted Victorian writer. A great resource for teachers and librarians to use with young people.

Picard, Liza. *Victorian London: The Life of a City, 1840–1870.* St. Martin's Press, 2005.
(Reading Level: Dale-Chall, 8.1)

This exhaustive study of the topic looks daunting to young adults but is so well written that it is well worth using with good students. Life in Victorian times is described, from such unusual perspectives as the sickening smells of the sewers to the lively activities of fruit sellers in Covent Garden, crimes and misdemeanors on the street, and royal ceremonies. The meticulous organization of chapter headings, subtopic headings, and index directs researchers to specific parts of the book.

Steele, Philip. *Clothes and Crafts in Victorian Times.* Gareth Stevens, 2000.
(Reading Level: Accelerated Reader, 5.9)

This book, part of the Clothes and Crafts in History series, succinctly introduces Victorian times with numerous colored photographs and illustrations. Crafts range from factory-made items to William Morris's contributions to design, homemade quilts, women's and men's fashions, and holiday decorations. Several projects, a glossary, and a bibliography add to the brief text.

Yancey, Diane. *Life in Charles Dickens's England.* Lucent, 1999.
(Reading Level: Accelerated Reader, 9.8)

Although the reading level of this book tests higher than others in this bibliography, the concise text, with its numerous illustrations and sidebars, will be so appealing to young readers that it is an invaluable resource for this chapter. Yancy combines Dickens's life with topics of interest from Victorian history to create a fascinating account.

Selected Web Sites

BBC Page: Children in Victorian Britain: www.bbc.co.uk/schools/victorians
Sponsored by the BBC, an interactive site about children in Victorian Britain for children ages nine to eleven.

The Charles Dickens Museum, London: www.dickensmuseum.com
Official site of the famous museum in London, located in a house where Dickens lived. Basic information about the author's years in the house and description of events at the museum.

David Perdue's Charles Dickens Page: http://charlesdickenspage.com
Created by David Perue, this treasure trove of information includes timelines, biographical data, and background of London during Dickens's time as well as a beautiful map of Dickens sites.

Museum of Childhood: www.museumofchildhood.org.uk
Sponsored by the Museum of Childhood, a branch of the Victoria and Albert Museum, located in East London. The link "collections" has photos and descriptions of many Victorian toys and games.

Victorian London: www.victorianlondon.com
A huge Web site created by Lee Jackson from London. More than two dozen links, with each link connecting to dozens of specific essays, on topics ranging from education and health to markets, prisons, and science. A gold mine!

Victoriana: www.victoriana.com
An online magazine with links to subjects such as history, fashion, and Victorian Christmas.

World of Peter Rabbit: www.peterrabbit.com
Sponsored by the publisher of Beatrix Potter's books, Frederick Warne. Links to biographical information as well as reproducible activity pages for children.

The Story of Victorian London: A School Program

This program is designed for students in upper elementary or middle school (grades 6 through 8) during four class sessions, but it can be adapted to a shorter or longer time frame as you desire. The first meeting introduces students to the Victorian era and provides research guidelines for the various student projects. Students choose among the topics, then research and plan individual or group projects during two meetings. (Classroom teachers may allow further work sessions as needed.) Projects can be presented as part of the Victorian Fair for the entire school and parents or simply shared with classmates during the last two sessions of this program unit. Because of the broad scope of this topic, you may wish to involve teachers from social studies (history or economics, for example), language and literature, art, and science in planning and guiding students through their projects.

The school program in this chapter is reminiscent of chapter 1, "Welcome to the Middle Ages" in *Stories, Time and Again* (Libraries Unlimited, 2006). That chapter was written as a model for studying a broad historical period, just as this chapter builds on a large-scale topic. Obviously the themes and ideas are representative and selective, as a comprehensive approach would be impossible to achieve in a single chapter.

Materials Needed

Students will provide their own materials.

You will need computers for students to use in doing research.

Procedure

Before You Begin

1. Create a display with some books about Victorian London and by Victorian writers Charles Dickens, Lewis Carroll, and Rudyard Kipling.

2. Copy the map of Dickens's London from http://charlesdickenspage.com/dickens_london_map.html.

3. Make a photo montage of Victorian drawings that represents different facets of life during the Victorian era. (Use the bibliography in this chapter and the list of Web sites to find suitable illustrations.)

4. Photocopy and reproduce the Victorian glossary of terms (p. 89). Teachers can give this sheet as a handout or simply give children the terms to research and project list (pp. 92–94) for students.

5. Before the second meeting, photocopy and reproduce the research guide and tips sheets (pp. 90–91).

First Meeting

1. Since Charles Dickens's works describe life in Victorian London better than any other single author of his day, begin this program by reading from Dickens. Passages from *Oliver Twist, Great Expectations,* and *A Christmas Carol* are suggested. Portions from "Stave One: Marley's Ghost," the beginning of *A Christmas Carol,* set the tone for Scrooge's character. This is a favorite choice to read aloud, as is Chapter 8 from *Oliver Twist,* when Oliver meets Jack Dawkins and Fagin.

2. Also, read aloud the first chapter in Diane Yancey's *Life in Charles Dickens's England* to introduce this time period.

3. Distribute a Victorian glossary of terms to peak children's interest in the rich vocabulary of the times. Instead of providing the definitions, simply list words and terms for students to research on their own or in small groups. This can be a class exercise or a take home assignment.

4. At the end of this session, distribute the project list (pp. 92–94) included in this chapter (or your own adaptation of it) for students to select from. Let students know they need to choose a topic and that they will be researching it at the next meeting.

Second and Third Meetings

1. During the next two class sessions, students choose a topic and research it with your guidance.

2. Distribute to students the photocopied research guide and tips sheets.

Fourth Meeting

1. During the last session, have students share their projects with classmates.

2. Alternatively, you might want to help student organize a Victorian Fair with display boards and display tables, and prepare a schedule for students to present their projects orally to parents and other students.

Glossary of Victorian Terms

Bedlam: An institution in London for the insane. In the past this hospital was known for cruel treatment of the mentally ill.

Boarding school: Schools where children live and study. In Victorian times, upper class boys attended boarding schools to get their education.

Chimney sweep: Boys between five and ten years old hired to clean soot out of chimneys. Considered dangerous work, as many boys became maimed or ill from the close quarters and nature of the work.

Costermonger: A hawker of fruits and vegetables.

Covent Garden: A famous fruit and vegetable market during Victorian times, located in central London.

Dustman: A trash or garbage collector.

Footman: A male house servant who might perform all kinds of duties, from cleaning boots to waiting tables, caring for animals, and looking after the gardens.

Housemaid: A female house servant who either worked in the kitchen of a wealthy person's home or performed various household duties.

Macintosh: A lightweight, waterproof coat made from rubberized cotton material, named for its Victorian inventor, Charles Macintosh.

Newgate Prison: Notorious London prison dating to the Middle Ages that closed in 1902. Victorian social reformers successfully stopped public executions there in 1868.

The Old Lady of Threadneedle Street: The Bank of England.

Orange girl: A girl during Victorian times who sold oranges on the street.

Rag and bone man: A junk dealer who collected rags and bones (for making glue).

Ragged schools: Schools set up during Victorian times to provide basic education to poor children.

Rotten borough: A depopulated election district that retains its original representation.

Scullery: A "back kitchen" where pots were scrubbed and dishes washed.

Workhouse: Place where people who couldn't support themselves could go to live and work. Conditions were often harsh.

From *Story Celebrations: A Program Guide for Schools and Libraries* by Jan Irving. Westport, CT: Libraries Unlimited. Copyright © 2008.

Basic Research Strategies for Students: Sample Topic—Costermongers in Victorian London

This guide shows you how to research the topic of costermongers in Victorian London to help you conduct an interview or write a report for this unit. These workers were part of the lively marketplaces in London such as Covent Garden. This actual term may be unfamiliar to you, but you may already know about one fictional costermonger. Her name was Eliza Doolittle, and she as one of the main characters in the musical *My Fair Lady.* Follow these steps to research your topic.

1. Find the definition for the term *costermonger* in a dictionary and on the Internet.

    A useful online encyclopedia wiki, *Wikipedia* (www.wikipedia.org), first developed in 2001, explains that these street sellers of fruit and vegetables (also nuts and flowers) have existed in London since the sixteenth century. They were most numerous in Victorian London. *Note: Wikipedia* is an enormous online encyclopedia that may be edited by anyone. Students should be warned that it is not always well written or completely accurate, but it is a huge information source. Although *Wikipedia* is a good starting place for quick research, they should consult another source for confirmation of information.

2. Trace links in this short article in *Wikipedia* and read some background about "the Victorian Era" to understand the times.

3. Consult several books and Internet sources with specific references to costermongers in Victorian London.

    For example, Diane Yancey's book *Life in Charles Dickens's England* gives a brief introduction to this period as well as a short commentary on costermongers. Several Internet sites are also helpful. One that describes student work in England on costermongers is www.ncaction.org.uk/search/entry.htm?id=977. Another site, which provides an encyclopedic store of information about Victorian London, is www.victorianlondon.org. In the index, select the term "professions and trades," then proceed to the term "food and drink." You will discover four main links to costermongers that provide over twenty pages of information relevant to your topic.

4. Make an outline or list of subtopics covered in the articles.

    A typical list might be kinds of costermongers, specific foods they sold, description of marketplaces, "equipment" (barrows, baskets) used, prices of the food sold, income costermongers made, their living expenses, and conditions and concerns.

5. Prepare a list of questions you might ask a fruit costermonger. Give these questions to a classmate to read aloud to you. Assume the role of a costermonger and respond to the questions with answers based on your research. You could even record this exchange and then write it out as an interview for a daily newspaper.

    Sample questions:

    Could you describe the marketplace where we are? How many sellers come here each day? Do you use baskets or barrows? Don't people steal your fruit?

    What fruits do you sell in the summer? What do you sell during the winter?

    What price do you charge for the fruit you sell? Where do you get your produce?

    How many hours do you work a day?

    Are you married? Where do you live? What are your main worries about your life and your children?

Tip Sheet

Writing Book Reviews

1. Give complete publishing information about your book: author, title, publisher, date of publication, and number of pages.

2. Describe the category of the book: fiction, nonfiction, biography, novel, play, or collection of stories.

3. Identify the themes or topics of the book. For example, the theme of "good versus evil" is common, and Charles Dickens addressed it in many of his books, such as *Oliver Twist* and *Great Expectations.* Single words may also describe what a book is about, but most novels have several themes. Some of the themes in *Great Expectations* are abandonment, ambition, and guilt.

4. Provide a background for the book, such as the time period and setting for works of fiction.

5. For fiction, briefly summarize the story. State the plot line in a few sentences or a brief paragraph. For nonfiction, give an overview and mention the topics covered.

6. Explain what is especially interesting about the book and why you hold this view.

7. Relate this book to others you have read and how it compares to them.

Writing Fictional Journals or Diaries

1. Browse through several fictional diaries and journals, as well as real ones, to discover how to make a person and a historical period come alive for other readers. Karen Cushman's *Catherine Called Birdy* relates the feelings of a strong, independent young woman during the Middle Ages. The author gives many details of Catherine's everyday life: food, dress, and even the number of fleas she kills one night!

2. Research the topic you have selected. If you are writing a diary of a housemaid in Victorian England, read chapters in books about household workers of this time period. The Web site www.victorianlondon.org is invaluable. Search "Professions and Trades/servants/housemaids."

3. Make notes about food, dress, duties, income, and living conditions.

4. Describe a typical day or two in the life of this person, including basic information and his or her feelings. For example, describe Christmas Day as a housemaid in a large Victorian mansion in 1875.

Projects for School Program on "The Story of Victorian England"

As you study Victorian England, you will create a project on *one* of the following eight topics. Read through this handout, select a project, and do appropriate research to complete your assignment.

I. Inventions/Scientific Advances/The Industrial Revolution

London became the hub of the Industrial Revolution, a period spanning the late eighteenth and nineteenth centuries. Manual labor was replaced by the development of machinery and industry. Inventions such as steam-powered ships and railways and machines in factories and homes transformed life throughout Europe and the United States. Scientific advancements, especially in the medical field, reflected huge changes during this period.

Student projects in this area:

1. Assume the role of an engineer who helped plan the London Underground System and describe its early development as well as the various locations of the first lines. Use diagrams and charts to illustrate your written and oral account.

2. Using the first person, tell the story of Florence Nightingale and her accomplishments.

3. Describe five major inventions of Victorian times and how they changed life for people in London. Find drawings and illustrations of these inventions to accompany your description, or make your own.

4. Assume the role of a doctor or medical researcher who discovered the cause of a disease in London during this period.

II. Childhood/Education and Learning

The concept of "childhood" as a distinct age separated from the idea of children as "little adults" developed during the Victorian Age. This shift in thinking had broad implications in educating and entertaining children and in the area of social reform.

Education among social classes varied widely, as it did between the sexes. Poor children received little formal education until the last third of the century, when the Education Act of 1870 made elementary education compulsory. Schools ranged from the more elite "public" (private in American terms) schools to the minimal fare offered in "ragged" schools. Learning for girls often focused on domestic matters rather than academic subjects.

Student projects in the area:

5. Assume the role of an educational reformer such as the minister John Relly Bear during Victorian times. Describe the various education acts that led to more universal education.

6. Tell the story of a child enrolled in a "ragged" school in London. Describe classroom conditions, subjects taught, and what you like or dislike as a student in this kind of school.

7. Write an article for a children's magazine of today about childhood during Victorian times.

III. Social Classes

England has always been a "classed" society, with more rigid distinctions between the rich and poor than in the United States. While these differences between upper and lower classes were great during the Victorian age, a new middle class began to grow.

Student projects in this area:

"The Story of Victorian England" (*Continued*)

8. Write an interview as a newspaper article between a reporter and a working class person of the day, or an interview with a member of the middle class. Typical lower class workers are costermongers, carpenters, and housemaids. Middle class workers include bank clerks, coffee house merchants, and postal workers.

9. Write a newspaper editorial about living conditions in the slums or workhouses in London.

10. Write the diaries of three women in Victorian times. One diary might describe a day in the life of a middle class woman who takes care of her children at home. A second diary describes a typical day in the life of an upper class single woman living with her parents. A third diary describes a day in the life of a poor woman working in the coal mines.

11. Write an ad or job descriptions for a full household staff for an upper class London family in 1850.

IV. Historical Events/Reforms and Improvements

The reign of Queen Victoria (1837–1901) frames the Victorian era. During this time, life for people in London changed dramatically from the polluted air and water, the crime-ridden streets, and harsh work conditions for everyone except the very wealthy, because of many political reforms and scientific advances.

Student projects in this area:

12. Give a speech (as Londoners do in Hyde Park) about the danger of pollution from factories of the day.

13. Write a press release about the opening of the Crystal Palace.

14. Give a speech protesting child labor practices before child labor laws were passed.

15. Write a story about Queen Victoria's coronation or her marriage to Prince Albert.

V. Fashion

Fashion defined class differences during the Victorian era. Clothing was important for all classes, but the wealthy, who could afford large wardrobes, regularly changed their clothes several times throughout the day.

Student projects in this area:

16. Assume that you are a clothing designer in the 1850s in London. Create a fashion show for the public. Use illustrations, sketches, and sample materials to include in your talk to the audience of eager customers. Create an ad that might appear in a fashion magazine of the times or make a poster to display in the media center.

VI. Arts and Crafts

Interior design and furniture for much of the Victorian era was dark and heavy, with elaborate carvings and an excess of doodads in middle and upper class homes. Designers such as William Morris introduced a newer look later in the nineteenth century, with emphasis on lighter colors and motifs from nature. Crafts and art projects became popular as many people began to enjoy making things to decorate their homes and celebrate holidays.

Student projects in this area:

17. Tell the story of William Morris's designs and how he changed Victorian home decoration. If you write down the story, illustrate the text with illustrations and drawings. Many examples are available on the Internet. If you tell the story orally, bring illustrations to enhance your presentation.

From *Story Celebrations: A Program Guide for Schools and Libraries* by Jan Irving.
Westport, CT: Libraries Unlimited. Copyright © 2008.

"The Story of Victorian England" (*Continued*)

18. Choose an artist from Victorian era England to study. A few examples are John Waterhouse, William Holman Hunt, Kate Greenaway, and Beatrix Potter. Show examples of the artist's works and tell why you would purchase his or her pieces for an exhibition in London during this time period.

VII. The Literary Scene

With more education, people in London read more than ever before during this period. Books, newspapers, and magazines proliferated. Authors such as Charles Dickens were extremely popular, and children's literature developed as a separate category in the world of literature.

Student projects in this area;

19. Write a review of one of Charles Dickens's books, such as *Great Expectations* or *Oliver Twist*. You may want to see several filmed versions of some of his books as well as reading a Dickens novel or several short stories. Compare film and book versions.

20. Make a readers' theatre script based on one or two scenes from a Dickens novel or story. Two possible scripts are the scene in *Oliver Twist* in which the main character first meets Fagin and the scene in *Great Expectations* in which Pip first meets Miss Havisham.

21. Read Kipling's *Just So Stories* and select one story to tell to the class, or write your own "just so" story.

22. Write a readers' theatre script based on a chapter or scene from Lewis Carroll's *Alice in Wonderland*. Perform this scene with other students in your class.

23. Assume the role of Beatrix Potter and tell an audience of Victorian families about your work, especially how you studied fashions at the Victoria and Albert Museum in preparation for writing *The Tailor of Gloucester*. If you have seen the movie *Miss Potter* you may wish to tell about how you felt when your first book was published by Warne Publishing Company.

VIII. Entertainments

Victorian families enjoyed a wide range of leisure time activities, from outings to the beach, to picnics, to playing games at home, to viewing or participating in new sports invented during this time, to attending the theater and visiting museums erected during this era.

Student projects in this area:

24. Make a London travel guide for a middle class Victorian English family citing interesting places to visit and how to find them in different parts of the city.

25. Write a magazine article on the new sports, such as lawn tennis or polo (actually reinvented in the 1860s), developed from the mid to late nineteenth century. Bring pictures and sports equipment to enhance your report or talk. Tell the class how one of the new games is played.

26. Dollhouses and toy theaters were popular during Victorian times. Research *Benjamin Pollock's Toyshop and Museum* on the Internet and design your own toy theater with changeable scenes and players. Write your own script or order one from this museum to present to your class.

Look What You'll Find in Great Grandmother's Attic: A Public Library Program

Young people enjoy arts and crafts as well as planning their own parties. Finding treasures from the past holds great appeal, and there has been renewed interest in having tea parties. Combine these interests in this program of Victorian arts and crafts with an updated version of a Victorian tea party as kids become involved in the planning along with library staff. I have found many children's tea sets in stores and took a traveling tea party to my nieces, who were thrilled. They had recently bought a tea set of their own!

This program has been planned for about 1½ hours, with approximately forty young people attending. Adjust the schedule and materials to your own situation.

Materials Needed

Victorian papers and stamps or stickers purchased from craft stores, or use the sample sheet provided (p. 101). Allow about forty sheets of Victorian paper (either wrapping paper or paper from a craft store), and eight stamps with eight colored stamp pads should be sufficient.

Photocopied pages of the jumping jack (p. 99) on card stock, about forty pages.

Large box of brad fasteners for the jumping jack toy and string. Allow two brads per child or eighty total, and about eighty yards of string.

Forty assorted boxes (shoe boxes, old check boxes, stationery or jewelry boxes) to cover.

Card stock or lightweight poster board in white and pastel colors for fans, about forty sheets.

Silly hats, large crepe paper flowers, silly teapots, bright-colored paper napkins or balloons, and plastic tea cups and saucers.

Ingredients for tea party (see directions and menu ideas on pages 96–97 to make your own list).

Forty photocopies of moving picture handout on card stock (p. 100), string.

Forty photocopies of Victorian paper dolls (pp. 102–4).

Colored pencils or markers for dolls and toys, four dozen pencils, and four dozen markers.

A mad hatter hat for yourself (optional).

Procedure

Before You Begin

1. Make photocopies and assemble a cart full of supplies with instructions and patterns for making projects. Assemble recipes and cookbooks for planning tea parties (see bibliography, and directions on pp. 96–97).

2. Gather books with limericks by Edward Lear and several copies of *Alice in Wonderland* for the workshop.

3. Invite young people to come to the library about a week before the scheduled event so they can select the projects to make during the program. Several examples are included on page 98.

4. Plan the food for the tea party, and ask for volunteers to go on a shopping trip with you if you wish to have them more actively involved.

5. Ask for volunteers to make a sample project or two to display during the program.

6. About two hours before the scheduled time of this event, have several older children come to the library to set up the Mad Hatter Tea Party table with large sheets of craft paper and brightly colored napkins, paper hats, etc. See the "Mad Hatter Tea Party" (below) for ideas.

The Day of the Program

1. To begin the program, read or tell the story of the Mad Hatter Tea Party from *Alice in Wonderland.*

2. Invite guests to make their own party favors—jumping jack paper toys, collage boxes, moving picture toys, and paper dolls.

3. Tell participants that paper crafts, paper dolls, toy theaters, and moving picture toys began during Victorian days. Few children had toys before this time.

4. Have children read limericks by Edward Lear or read the silly poems from *Alice in Wonderland*: "Jabberwocky" and "The Walrus and the Carpenter."

5. Assume the role of the Mad Hatter and invite kids to make their own tea sandwiches and treats. Enjoy the treats and play one of the games suggested in this chapter.

The Mad Hatter Tea Party

This silly tea party diverges from the fancy and proper type of Victorian tea party that uses white tablecloths and china teacups, so it will draw a larger audience of young people of both sexes. Invite participants to wear silly hats to the party, such as white rabbit ears on headbands, tall stovepipe party hats, hats with pinwheels, and even Dr. Seuss style striped tall hats.

Decorations

Cover the food-serving table with paper tablecloths or white craft paper so kids can write riddles, jokes, and limericks on it. Before the event, you might write quotes from *Alice in Wonderland* to inspire the audience. Sample quotes are "Why is a raven like a writing desk?" and "I say what I mean is the same as I mean what I say."

Make a display of silly hats for the table and add large crepe paper flowers, silly teapots, and bright-colored paper napkins or balloons. Add plastic tea cups and saucers turned over and in messy piles to increase the lunacy of the day.

Food

Typical tea party treats include assortments of tea sandwiches, scones, teacakes and cookies, and tea, of course! This silly menu may not be as elegant, but young people will love it. Adapt the following recipes and ideas as you like.

The Mad Hatter Cake

This cake should resemble a black top hat similar to the one worn by the Mad Hatter. You will need two white or yellow cake mixes, a can of dark chocolate frosting, and several tubes of black icing gel or black food coloring.

Prepare the cake mixes according to package directions and bake the four layers in round cake pans. Let the cakes cool. Open a can of chocolate frosting and tint it with black food coloring or black icing gel. (The object is to make the frosting look as black as you can.) Cover a sixteen-inch-diameter cardboard circle with black construction paper or black poster board for the brim of the hat. Place the first layer of the cake on the base. Apply a thin layer of icing on the top of this cake and add the next layer, until you have a stack of four layers. Now frost the entire cake with the black icing. Add a white six-by-eight inch rectangular sign and write on the sign "10/6".

Note: Participants will want to know what this sign means. You could tell them to look up the answer themselves or tell them that most authorities think it stands for the price of the hat, 10 shillings, 6 pence. (Is this a Victorian sign of bad taste reminiscent of Minnie Pearl wearing the price tags on her clothes?)

Chocolate Dormouse No-Bake Cookies

Form these cookies into the shape of a mouse or just in rounded tablespoons. You will need one stick of margarine, one cup of sugar, one-third of a cup of milk, two tablespoons of powdered baking cocoa, one cup of peanut butter, one teaspoon of vanilla, and a cup and a half of quick oats.

Melt the margarine in the microwave and stir in the next three ingredients. Microwave on high for two or three minutes, until the mixture boils. Be careful, this is hot! Remove the mixture from the microwave and stir in the peanut butter and vanilla. Then stir in the oats and drop the dough in tablespoons on waxed paper. Let them set until they are firm.

Note: Be sure to find out about peanut and any other allergies before serving these to children.

Tea Party Sandwiches

You will need about two slices of bread per party guest. Select thin sliced firm bread in white and whole wheat and trim off the crusts. Spread a slice of bread with one of the spreads suggested below and add a top slice of bread. Cut the full sandwich into four little squares or triangles.

Chicken Salad Spread

Purchase a roasted chicken from the deli and slice it thin or purchase one or two pounds of chicken from the deli department. Chop the chicken into small pieces and mix it with several tablespoons of mayonnaise and one teaspoon prepared mustard. Add a spoonful of chopped celery or pickle relish as you wish.

Cream Cheese with Additions

Purchase several eight-ounce tubs of whipped cream cheese and add these ingredients as you like several tablespoons of chopped fresh chives, several tablespoons of shredded cheddar cheese, or several tablespoons of chopped olives.

White Rabbit and March Hare Sandwiches

Add carrot curls or thin slices of carrot to cream cheese and spread on sandwich bread.

Cucumber Sandwiches

Spread bread with a thin layer of plain cream cheese or butter and add a slice of cucumber. Sprinkle a little chopped fresh parsley or mint on top if desired.

"Tea" Drinks for the Party

Prepare several choices of tea for party guests, such as mint, herbal, or lemon (using tea bags or loose tea), and a fruit punch. For the fruit punch, choose an herbal tea and add about one cup of fruit juice to each quart of tea. Serve from teapots or pitchers and use either paper cups or plastic teacups.

Party Games

Victorian children played with marbles, enjoyed hopscotch, and played hide and seek. Try one of these traditional games and a new one called "teacup relay." To play this game, divide kids into several teams and supply each team with a teacup filled with water placed on a saucer. The first member of each team is given a full teacup, and everyone waits until a bell is rung, indicating that teatime has begun. The child with the full teacup walks quickly to the opposite side of the room and back to the line, trying not to spill the "tea." Teacups are passed down the line, with each child repeating the action of the first. The team that finishes the race first and spills the least amount of "tea" is declared the winner.

Victorian Crafts

Jumping Jack Toy

Have kids cut out the jumping jack toy (see p. 99) and mount it on card stock to strengthen it. Assist them in punching out holes as indicated on the pattern. Show them how to assemble the figure and attach parts with brad fasteners and then attach separate strings to arms and upper legs as indicated. They may need extra help tying a third string vertically from these two strings. Instruct them to leave enough string to pull below so that the jumping jack will jump. Young people may color the toy.

Moving Picture Toys

Roget, the man who later wrote a famous thesaurus bearing his name, experimented with little inventions like this moving picture toy. It works on the principle of the persistence of vision, an idea that led to the development of motion pictures.

Instruct young people to cut out the circle pictures of the horse and rider (see p. 100) at the top of the photocopied pattern and glue the blank sides together so that they have one circle with two sides. Assist them in punching out the holes as indicated in the illustration. Have kids tie a string in each hole and pull strings so that the disk will spin. The images will look superimposed as if the rider is riding on the horse.

Victorian Collage

Victorians loved to cover boxes and plaques with fancy illustrations. Find fancy wrapping paper or photocopy the page (101) with the boy and girl on it. Have children decorate this page or several copies of the same page. Use the pages to glue on small boxes or on a shoebox for a collage decoration. You may wish to spray or paint the box with a special craft shellac for a final finish.

Victorian Lady Paper Doll with Two Outfits

Photocopy the paper doll and her clothes (pp. 102–4). Have kids cut out the doll and clothes and color them with pens, pencils, or watercolor paints. Instruct them to add little tabs to the outfits before they are cut out so that they can be folded back to hold the clothes on the paper doll. Tell young fashion designers they can create other outfits for the Victorian lady based on studying pictures in books about Victorian fashion.

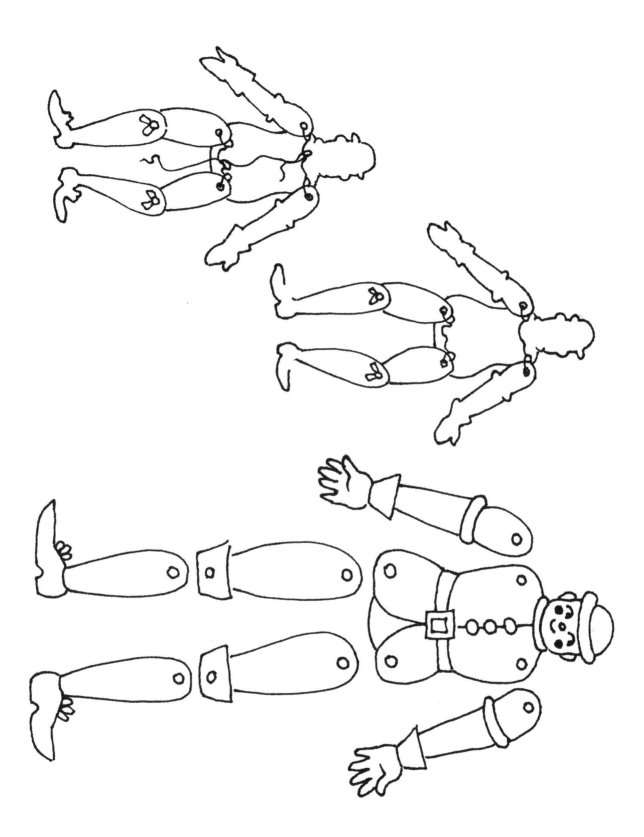

From *Story Celebrations: A Program Guide for Schools and Libraries* by Jan Irving.
Westport, CT: Libraries Unlimited. Copyright © 2008.

From *Story Celebrations: A Program Guide for Schools and Libraries* by Jan Irving.

6

Plagues That Changed History

When we think of the grand scope of history, we tend to think big events brought about change. We may recall the fall of the Roman Empire, the invention of the printing press, or the great age of explorations to the New World. But some things that are so small they are invisible to the human eye have had a far greater role in changing human history. These miniscule creatures are microbes, single cells of bacteria. Even smaller than bacteria is a virus, which consists of only a small amount of DNA, something found within a cell.

Bacteria and viruses live in dirt, in rivers, on rats, on mosquitoes, and even on you and me. They can make us sick, invade our bodies, and bring about death. In early times people were more nomadic, or lived isolated from one another, but over time they moved closer together, into towns and cities. This meant that a disease that may have previously affected only a small group of people could now sweep through entire cities and countries. These large diseases that spread through countries are known as pandemics. The Black Plague (the bubonic plague) is a prime example of a pandemic because it spread from China and India to Italy and throughout Europe.

Until fairly recently (within our grandmothers' memories), the causes of many deadly diseases were unknown. Sanitation is a modern practice. Medicine has only become well-grounded in science for about a century. However, even some diseases that had been previously controlled seem to be reappearing. Diseases can mutate and reenter the population in other forms.

Natural disasters such as floods and hurricanes may bring about contamination of water supplies. The filth that caused cholera to spread throughout the world ran rampant for hundreds of years. Water filtration and purification in the early twentieth century seemed to control the disease, but a new outbreak affected thousands of people in Central America as recently as the 1990s. Researchers found that when populations mushroom and economies cannot keep pace with necessary health practices, diseases like cholera come back, especially in tropical climates.

During war time, deadly diseases can kill as many people as war itself. In the Spanish–American War as many people died from the yellow fever as from war-related injuries. Another scary prospect often obscured from the public is the threat of biological or chemical warfare. This is not a new practice. During the Middle Ages, people living around the Black Sea believed they had been infected with the plague by Italian armies. In retaliation they catapulted infected dead bodies of their own soldiers over the Italians' fortress walls.

Most scientists today acknowledge that we will never eliminate all diseases. Mumps and polio epidemics, for example, have once again become public health hazards. The challenge will be for nations to remain vigilant, provide for the health care of all people, and continue to improve sanitation throughout the world. In his well-researched book *Outbreak,* Byrd Barnard reminds us: "We cannot ignore the elephant in our collective living room, unequal access to health care among the rich and poor . . . .The best medical care is lavished on the rich. Pharmaceutical companies cater to them. The poor get the crumbs." He concludes that "when health care is a public good, not a private perk, everyone is better off."

This chapter on plagues and pandemics combines the traditional disciplines of history and science, as well as addressing ethical issues associated with health. The focus here is on a few diseases that have become somewhat controlled. These diseases include bubonic plague, transmitted by insect bites; smallpox, an airborne disease; and cholera, carried by bacteria growing in unclean water. Since all disease is carried in one of these three ways, these examples serve as models for researching topics further. The bibliography will lead to books and Web sites about other diseases.

The school program "Plagues, the Story" involves science, history, and language arts teachers, as well as school media specialists, to lead students to an understanding of how disease has changed human history. Some activities lend themselves to role playing and writing in history and English classes. Science teachers could teach other facets of this project. Displays, oral presentations, and discussions happen in the library media center. For a brief program, the librarian may simply introduce this topic, read portions of appropriate books, and provide classroom teachers with related activities to pursue in their classrooms.

The public library program "You Were There" gives a lively view of history through interactive scripts, interviews, and conversations about the past. Engage young people in creating miniature museums with dioramas and objects related to plagues. Book discussion groups in public library programs can focus on some of the books in the bibliography for another extension of this topic.

A final note about this topic: Future bacteriologists and health care professionals will find the study of disease a fascinating subject to read about. This grim side of history also intrigues male reluctant readers. And there's plenty of excitement for those who like to unlock the mysteries of science and read about how doctors discovered causes and treatments for pandemics of the past. Along with the chapter on "grossology," this subject is bound to be a winner for kids who enjoy the quirky side of science.

Bibliography

Anderson, Laurie Halse. *Fever 1793.* Simon & Schuster, 2000.
(Reading Level: 4.4, Accelerated Reader)
Mattie Cook, a teenager in colonial Philadelphia, is forced to leave her widowed mother, who is sick because of the outbreak of yellow fever in the city. She and her grandfather must learn to cope with the ongoing threat of the disease.

Barnard, Bryn. *Outbreak: Plagues That Changed History.* Crown, 2005.
(Reading Level: Accelerated Reader, 8.9)
This fascinating book combines history and science through lively narratives, numerous maps, and meticulous dramatic paintings by the author. Among the diseases discussed are the Black Plague, smallpox, yellow fever, cholera, tuberculosis, and influenza. While details about the diseases are provided, this book's broad perspective about the effects of infectious diseases on history is its greatest strength.

Cooney, Caroline. *Code Orange.* Delacorte, 2005.
(Reading Level: Accelerated Reader, 6.2)
While Mitty is doing research on infectious diseases for a high school biology paper, he comes in contact with dried *variola major* scabs in an old book. As his continued research and fear escalate,

he contacts health and governmental agencies, in this suspenseful thriller ending with a terrorist encounter and a fight for Mitty's life.

Giblin, James Cross. *When Plague Strikes.* HarperCollins, 1995.
(Reading Level: Accelerated Reader, 9.8)
   Although the reading level of this text is slightly higher than other books in this bibliography, the narrative reads easily. Giblin, one of the most respected nonfiction writers today, provides the reader with gripping details of three epidemics—the Black Plague, smallpox, and AIDS. The book not only gives historical accounts of these diseases, it reveals insights about their effects on humanity.

Lynette, Rachel. *Bubonic Plague.* Kidhaven Press, Thomson Gale, 2005.
(Reading Level: Accelerated Reader, 6.9)
   The brief text (just under fifty pages) is set in large type and illustrated with numerous maps, paintings, and photographs. Students will find enough information for basic research and reports in this book, one in a series titled <u>Understanding Diseases and Disorders.</u>

Marrin, Albert. *Dr. Jenner and the Speckled Monster: The Search for the Smallpox Vaccine.* Dutton Children's Books, 2002.
(Reading Level: Accelerated Reader, 7.6)
   This detailed history of smallpox, with special attention given to Edward Jenner's research and treatment, includes a discussion of possible future outbreaks and their consequences.

Murphy, Jim. *An American Plague: The True and Terrifying Story of the Yellow Fever Epidemic of 1793.* Clarion, 2003.
(Reading Level: Accelerated Reader, 9.0)
   This carefully researched book describes the yellow fever epidemic that killed large numbers of people in Philadelphia. It further traces the horrifying events in other cities and throughout the eighteenth and nineteenth centuries. Pioneers who raised public awareness about the dangers of this disease include Dr. Benjamin Rush and President George Washington. Most laypeople as well as doctors could not accept early research that mosquitoes spread the disease, but finally in the twentieth century the causes were traced to both mosquitoes and infected monkeys in rainforests. Because different strains of this disease still exist in the world, we may never be truly safe from yellow fever.

Napoli, Donna Jo. *Breath.* Atheneum, 2003.
(Reading Level: Accelerated Reader, 4.2)
   This gripping novel set in medieval Hamlin, Germany, tells the chilling story of the town overrun by rats and the Black Plague from the perspective of a boy who has a mysterious cough, not related to the dread disease itself. Superstition and misery make Salz's life unbearable, even though he escapes death. This tale expands upon the legend of the Pied Piper.

Peters, Stephanie True. *Cholera: Curse of the Nineteenth Century.* Benchmark, Marshall Cavendish, 2004.
(Reading Level: Accelerated Reader, 8.8)
   One of five books in the <u>Epidemic</u> series, this informative text provides the history of cholera along with definitions and medical practices during the nineteenth century.

Ward, Brian. *Epidemic.* Dorling Kindersley, 2001.
(Reading Level: Accelerated Reader, 8.1)
   More than fifty topics, from the plague to germ warfare, are covered in the succinct text, with bright photographs and microphotographs of bacteria and viruses. Students reading below the eighth-grade level will find this book useful because of the prolific illustrations, typical of DK books.

Selected Web Sites

The Black Death: www.insecta-inspecta.com/fleas/bdeath/Black.html
  History of the disease and information on present-day incidences.

The Black Plague: A Hands-on Epidemic Simulation: www.mcn.org/ed/cur/cw/plague/plague_Sim.html
  Created for the Mendocino (California) United School District, this middle school curriculum contains many student activities and maps; inspired the game in this chapter.

Bubonic Plague Role Play: http://teacherlink.ed.usu.edu/tlresources/units/Byrnes-S2000/Symons/bubonic.htm
  Developed by students at Utah State University for students in grades 5–7. Objective: to help students form their own hypothesis for the cause of the Black Plague.

History of Medicine: www.annals.org/cgi/content/full/127/8_Part_1/635
  This link on smallpox was written by two doctors for the *Annals of Internal Medicine*. Extensive information about the history of the disease and present-day incidents is provided.

Kardinska Institutet: History of Epidemics: www.mic.ki.se/HistDis.html
  Swedish center for medical research provides histories of epidemics and plagues, with links to numerous other Web sites.

Plague: www.springfield.k12.il.us/scholls/springfield/eliz/plague.html
  Extensive discussion on Elizabethan England's plagues, by Liam Miller and Evan Orr of the Springfield, Illinois, schools includes historical data, drawings, and a lengthy annotated bibliography, with an additional article on the Black Plague.

Virtual Museum of Bacteria: www.bacteriamuseum.org
  Sponsored by The Foundation of Bacteriology and the Society for Applied Microbiology. Links to history of diseases, discussion of bacteria and the Black Plague, and student files.

Plagues, the Story: A School Program

This program is planned for five class meetings. The first three meetings are scheduled one week, with the final two sessions when students present their projects scheduled for a second week, but this can be shortened or lengthened as you wish. It is intended to introduce basic terminology in studying diseases, a history of selected diseases from the past, and an understanding of how science has sought remedies for these plagues and infections. The projects and suggested assignments that follow provide different learning methods, from writing and speaking to role playing and panel discussions on various topics. Map study, journal keeping, and interviewing are also suggested.

Materials Needed

Children will use their own materials with the exception of a few small items, which are optional:

- a black satchel or briefcase (something that slightly resembles a doctor's black bag)
- bulletin board or presentation boards (standard-sized triptych available in discount/craft stores, 36 inches high, center panel 22 inches long, two side panels, 13 inches each)
- dried beans (a small bag, about twenty each of the following kinds: Cuban black beans, black eyed beans or pinto beans, navy beans) and a pair of dice for game playing

Capes or large scarves (one for each student)

Copy of *Fever 1793,* by Laurie Halse Anderson, or *Code Orange,* by Caroline Cooney.

Index cards.

Procedure

Before You Begin

1. Write words or terms on index cards (at least one word percard per student)

2. Prepare handouts for the list of Web sites (p. 108) and guidelines for student projects (pp. 114–15).

3. Before the second session, you will prepare a bulletin board and set up a book display with maps and posters.

4. Arrange for guest speakers—e.g., the school nurse or cafeteria personnel—to give tours of the school and discuss sanitation and hygiene.

First Meeting

1. Introduce the topic of disease by reading the first two chapters of *Fever 1793,* by Laurie Halse Anderson, or a selection from *Code Orange,* by Caroline Cooney. You might read the first chapter or one of the chapters near the end of the book.

2. From a satchel or a black briefcase, select index cards that each contain a word or term that students need to define. Each student receives one card and looks up the term.

Second Meeting

1. Definitions are shared orally and then posted on a bulletin board or chart under the title: "Class Dictionary of Disease Terms" (p. 110).

2. If time permits, have students play the game "The Plague—A High Risk Adventure." The game will set the mood for this topic. Guidelines for this game appear on page 112.

3. Prepare a bulletin board with the "Little-Known Facts" (see p. 111) and set up a display of books, world maps, and posters.

4. Distribute lists of Web sites and guidelines for projects to students for small group research. .

Third Meeting

1. Guest speakers may present background to students. Allow time for students to research their topics in the media center and work with you for the remainder of the week. You may involve science, social science, and language arts teachers to assist in guiding kids through their research.

Fourth and Fifth Meetings

1. During the second week of this unit, students share the results of their projects with one another.

Little-Known Facts about Dread Diseases

Create interest in this topic by posting a sign with the title "Little Known Facts about Dread Diseases" and computer-generated information nuggets (see p. 111) printed on brightly colored copy paper. Students are encouraged to add to the pages as they do their research.

Class Dictionary of Disease Terms

Provide students with dictionaries, Web sites, and standard reference books, or simply challenge them to use the resources of the library to define the following terms:

1.	antibodies	16.	pandemic
2.	bacteria	17.	parasite
3.	bubo	18.	pathogen
4.	bubonic plague	19.	pustules
5.	chlorination	20.	quarantine
6.	cholera	21.	scapegoat
7.	endemic	22.	small pox
8.	epidemic	23.	typhoid
9.	filtration	24.	typhus
10.	immune system	25.	vaccination
11.	immunization	26.	vaccine
12.	inoculation	27.	variola virus
13.	lymphatic system	28.	virus
14.	miasma	29.	yellow fever
15.	microbe		

From *Story Celebrations: A Program Guide for Schools and Libraries* by Jan Irving.
Westport, CT: Libraries Unlimited. Copyright © 2008.

Little-Known Facts about Dread Diseases

Tropical Paradise?

Recent outbreaks of cholera in the 1990s caused Dr. Rita Colwell in the United States to study the disease. She discovered that this disease can reappear in tropical water that has the high sodium chloride content of ocean water.

Beautiful Bacteria?

Amazing photographs of bacteria show some that are shaped like little green gherkin pickles with white hair. But I wouldn't eat one, if I were you!

Curse of the Pharaoh

Some historians believe that Pharaoh Ramses V, who died in 1157 B.C., was the victim of smallpox.

Elizabeth I Was a Smallpox Victim

Historians tell us that Elizabeth I got smallpox when she was twenty-nine years old. Royal doctors put her in front of a hot fireplace to treat the disease. She survived, but she went bald and got ugly pockmarks. After that, she wore bright red wigs and wore heavy makeup, which made her look a little like a clown.

Fire Power

After the bubonic plague raged in England in 1665, another disaster actually helped eradicate the disease. The Great Fire of London in 1666 killed most of the rats that carried the disease, thus bringing the plague under control.

From *Story Celebrations: A Program Guide for Schools and Libraries* by Jan Irving.
Westport, CT: Libraries Unlimited. Copyright © 2008.

The Plague—A High Risk Adventure: A Game Simulation

This game, simplified from one created in the Mendocino Middle School in California, simulates pilgrimages during the Middle Ages, when people traveled to holy places. During the 1300s the Black Plague ravaged Europe, and people infected with the plague often passed it on to others as they traveled from one city to another.

In preparation for this simulation, place signs around the classroom or media center to designate inns in various villages where the pilgrims stop along the way. You could use names of actual towns that would have existed, such as "Chichester" and "Hastings," or you could use names of inns such as "St. George's Inn," "The Dragon," "The Flagon," "The White Horse," "Rose and Crown," and "The Red Lion." Collect twelve capes or large scarves to use as capes for the pilgrims. Collect dried beans of different colors and varieties (see supplies list) and a pair of dice.

Select a group of students from the class (perhaps ten or twelve) to begin play. They might wear capes to distinguish them from other students. Ask the "pilgrims" to stand by the classroom door and tell them they are going as a group from their home in Winchester to Canterbury and will make several stops along the way.

The teacher or librarian begins by describing the setting as students move from Winchester to the first stop. This explanation can be short or a longer mood piece, such as this one:

> Pilgrims, my name is Sir Gaunt, the leader of our pilgrimage.
> Please stay together as we travel this road ahead.
> The cobblestone path will end soon.
> Bow your heads for a moment of silence as we make our prayers
> for safety along the way.
>
> Now, we are entering a forest.
> Do not fear the falcons or the deer,
> but beware the wild boars and the wolves.
> Hover close as we walk.
>
> Ah! Sunlight will follow us. A good sign!
> Let us pause for a draught of ale from my flagon.
> [Pass a stein around the group.]
> We begin again.
> Press onward, watch your step as we are entering a rocky place.

When pilgrims arrive at their first inn, one pilgrim throws the dice to determine how many nights the group will stay at the inn. Each pilgrim then pulls a bean from the leader's pouch. The pilgrims who get a black bean have contracted the plague in this inn. They will die in this place and should indicate their fate by pulling their capes over their heads as if they are wearing death hoods. (If costumes are not used, you may give these students a black sign to wear around their necks.) Pilgrims who receive spotted beans have a milder form of the plague and may continue to the next stop. Pilgrims who receive white beans have escaped thus far.

The journey continues. Continue describing the journey as the remaining pilgrims travel to the next stop. Those who previously drew spotted beans will stop here. "Safe" pilgrims throw the dice to determine how many nights they will stay in this inn. At the end of the appointed time (allow one minute to represent a night), the pilgrims travel to the next stop, as play continues. At the third or fourth stop, the remaining pilgrims draw another bean from the pouch. Those drawing black or spotted beans must remain. Only those pilgrims drawing white beans may continue.

If any pilgrim continues to draw white beans, thus escaping the dreaded plague, by the end of the journey to Canterbury, this pilgrim is blessed by Sir Gaunt and receives a large key to the city of Canterbury.

Notes about This Simulation

This game may be expanded in various ways by having students discuss their concerns before they begin the journey. Ask what they know about the Middle Ages and the Black Plague. Chapter 1 in *Stories, Time and Again* (Libraries Unlimited, 2006) contains background information about this time period that you may wish to use with students as an introduction to playing this game.

Ask students to predict how long it would actually take for them to show symptoms of the Black Plague once they were exposed. How long would they live after the symptoms appear?

Another extension would be to have students write journals after they return from the pilgrimage, or the entire class could compose a class journal with ideas contributed by the pilgrims.

Other dramatic touches could underscore the intensity of the plague. Designate a class member as "scribe" who prepares a "Bill of Mortality" for each stop along the journey. Each bill lists the names of pilgrims who die in the inn on a particular date.

As various pilgrims are infected, Sir Gaunt, the leader, could conduct interviews. He could ask them how they think they contracted this disease and how they are feeling.

Student Projects about Disease

Most of these projects involve small group work. They can be conducted in the school media center or in classrooms, with research done in the library. Any posters, charts, maps, or visuals students create can be displayed in the media center for all students to learn more about this fascinating topic.

Although this chapter focuses on a select number of diseases, schools may choose to expand the scope by displaying books and pamphlets about other infectious diseases. An obvious focus might be on AIDS in communities and in the world today.

Sample Student Projects about Disease

- Work in a small group with other students to create a medieval newspaper titled *The Medieval Messenger*. Some articles will focus on diseases of the day; a lead article might announce the outbreak of the bubonic plague in a specific area in Europe. Include maps and interviews with citizens of affected cities. Some people on the committee might create advertisements for remedies of the day. Perhaps obituaries of deceased citizens could be included.

- Write articles for a science magazine for kids your age. A suggested topic is the effects of the Black Plague on Europe during the fourteenth century and during a later century. Prepare a graph or chart to show the percent of people who died over given time periods. Another topic might compare the number of deaths due to the plague in a specific city, such as Florence during the fourteenth century, to what that number might be on Florence today given the increase in population. You may want to check the stories written for the *Smithsonian* magazine for models. Check out www. smithsonianmag.com.

- Imagine you are a traveler in Italy during the Middle Ages who is sailing to France to escape the plague. Keep a journal and draw maps to describe your journey. Explain what you see and why you decide to go to another city or cities. Base your journal on research you do on the Internet and in books listed in the bibliography. This Web site may be helpful: www.mcn.org/ed/cur/cw/ plague/plague_sim.html.

- Do a "Science Investigators Report" for your principal. Working in small groups with science teachers, take the role of an investigator. Study symptoms of "mock" diseases—cramps, diarrhea, etc.—that have affected students in your school, then formulate possible causes, such as poor sanitation in restrooms, unsanitary kitchens, or infected classmates in the school. (This is a simulation only!) To learn more about school precautions, the school nurse and cafeteria personnel may take your class on tours of the school and describe what is being done to keep your school sanitary. The result of this project could be a report written to the principal about the status of health and safety at your school.

- Use a map of a country or a region within a country where a specific disease has been discovered. (An example might be a map of London in 1854, where 400 people died during a ten-day period of cholera.) In small groups, work with other students to decide how you would have organized the city to control the disease. Each group will make a separate report for the Lord Mayor. For example, some students, as news reporters, might explain how they gather information to inform the population of the dangers. Other students, as health professionals, can report how they would make hospitals ready to care for the sick. Check www.nationalgeographic.com/resources/ngo/education/ ideas912/912choleraho3.html for additional ideas.

- Disease detectives: Cases of the bubonic plague have occurred in the twenty-first century in the American Southwest. Find news articles about this subject and write articles for your school newspaper or the newspaper in your community.

- Disease mapping: Collect world maps and outline the path of the spread of a specific disease on each map. Accompany the maps with narrative explanations of the disease and its effects. Bar graphs may be used to show the number of deaths for five- and ten-year periods in specific countries.

Sample Student Projects about Disease
(*Continued*)

- Future careers in disease prevention and control: Organize student groups based on various careers, such as doctors specializing in tropical diseases, bacteriologists, and epidemiologists. Each person defines the specialty, lists the classes a student should take in high school and college to prepare for that career, and explains what happens during a typical day in the chosen career. If possible, interview people in the field, or a specialist might speak to the entire class.

- Disease preparedness: Dread diseases from the past have reappeared or mutated in our own times. Work in small groups to formulate questions to ask a student panel of experts. Before the panel assembles, give the "experts" the questions so they can prepare informed answers. A teacher or a student interviewer can ask the questions. Typical questions are:

  - What should I know about this disease?

  - Is it fatal?

  - What are the symptoms?

  - How is it spread?

  - How serious is the threat of catching this disease today?

  - Could I get treatment from my doctor if the disease were to break out this year?

  Note: This Web site of the Centers for Disease Control provides basic information: www.btcdc.gov/healthprofessionals/index.asp.

- When epidemics break out in various places in the world today, people are asked to contribute money to help. To learn what organizations are constantly working around the world to prevent and control disease, research world health organizations and what they are doing. Create posters, organize letter writing campaigns, or design activities you could do to assist in these efforts.

You Were There—Plagues in History: A Public Library Program

This program is planned for young people from ages eight to twelve. I advise advertising the program as one "for older students because of the mature nature of the subject." You may choose among the various program options depending on your skills, time limitations, and the participants' needs. Kids love to visualize history through artifacts!

Materials Needed

Objects for the history trunk described below, such as a chest, old bottles, a blanket, a rat puppet or stuffed toy, a red wig, etc.

Cloaks or capes, caps, hats, and shawls for the skit.

Black banner for the skit, with the words "The Black Plague" printed on it.

Procedure

Before You Begin

1. Prepare a history trunk of disease-related items to help participants visualize the subject. The trunk might contain some of the following items: a quarantine notice to place in the window of a home of an infected person; a disease mask worn by doctors during the Middle Ages; an old time cholera kit (small wooden chest filled with vials or bottles marked "opium," "laxative," "laudanum"—all dangerous drugs that were used to kill pain in the nineteenth century); a red wig, supposedly worn by Elizabeth I; old blankets; and a stuffed rat toy or puppet. (You will show this history trunk at the beginning of the program and talk to kids about the significance of each item.)

2. Invite a local history buff, science teacher, and a medical researcher to talk to kids about diseases in the past.

During the Program

1. Read portions of several novels about dread diseases. The first two chapters of *Fever 1793* are a good choice, or select a later chapter such as Chapter 11. Ask participants what they predict will happen in the following chapter and then read the next one. This novel works well for a program because the chapters are action packed and fairly short. Another novel, set in contemporary times, *Code Orange*, is also a good choice to read selections from.

2. Play the simulation game "The Plague—A High Risk Adventure," as described on page 112.

3. Have a guest speaker talk about diseases of the past.

4. Select kids to take parts in the history reenactment, "The Black Plague in History."

Note: If this program is part of a young adult program series, you may wish to have some teens plan their own script about the Great Fire of London, mentioned at the end of this program. They could create a skit of their own to present at a future date.

The Black Plague in History: A Readers Theatre Script

You may decide to invite some kids to practice this script (pp. 117–21) before the program, so it is presented as a more polished performance for others their age. Props and basic costumes can be added. (The costumes could be as simple as cloaks, shawls, aprons, capes, bonnets, berets, and tall hats.)

Black Plague Readers Theatre Script

Cast of Characters:

Narrator

Two peasants, who carry a sign

Marco, a merchant

Florence, a flower seller

Six children, who sing and dance

Farmer's wife, a plain-spoken woman

Dr. Galen, physician to the pope, a male

Dr. Arno, a second physician, male or female

Dr. Buono, a third physician, male or female

Dr. Siena, a fourth physician, male or female

Dr. Pisa, a fifth physician, male or female

Narrator: Good evening. This evening's special report will take you, our television audience, back to one of the most deadly times in human history: the days of the Black Death.

[Two peasants carry a black banner across the stage. The banner reads "The Black Plague."]

No one knows when this terrible disease began. Some say it may have started back in ancient Greece. Unfortunately, we have no reliable witnesses from that time. Let's begin our story then, in the year 1348 in the city of canals, the beautiful city of Venice, Italy.

Return with me to Venice. I believe we have a spice merchant who gives his name as simply Marco, who has agreed to talk with us. Marco, are you there?

Marco: Yes, I'm here, but please do not show a front view of my face. I'm afraid my family will be harmed if your viewers identify me. (He turns slightly to the side.)

Narrator: Yes, Marco, you have my word we will be discreet. Now, please tell us about this terrible disaster that has befallen your beautiful city.

Marco: Oh, woe, how can I tell you? It is too terrible. Terrible. People dying everywhere. First they get weak, then they get these lumps in their armpits. Big lumps! Big like hens' eggs! And the pain! They twitch and shake and the worst part is the skin. It turns BLACK. That's why it's called "The Black Death."

Narrator: How terrible indeed! Is there any explanation? How did it come to your fair city?

From *Story Celebrations: A Program Guide for Schools and Libraries* by Jan Irving. Westport, CT: Libraries Unlimited. Copyright © 2008.

Black Plague Readers Theatre Script (*Continued*)

Marco: You see those ships? They came from a city I will not mention. A city somewhere not far from here. I've never sailed there myself, but my uncle tells me it's a dirty place. No garbage collection! Trash everywhere! Piles of it in the streets! No clean water! Ach! And the smells! Uncle tells me even the rich men don't take baths! Can you imagine?

Narrator: And you're telling us that not taking baths in this unmentionable city is the reason for your problems in Venice?

Marco: No, no, I didn't say that! You see, no one knows, but I hear people talk about how those people live. They keep dogs in their houses, then they throw food to the dogs. When the dogs are full, what do you think eats the stinky food?

Narrator: Cats?

Marco: Yes, cats! And, worse than that! Rats! Big fat black rats!

Narrator: So, it's the rats' fault?

Marco: No, no, I didn't say that. No one knows, but I did see a sick rat or two running around the boats last year. At least, I think they were sick. No one paid any attention to me when I warned the city leaders about the rats. So, I say, what can you do?

Narrator: Marco, didn't the city leaders DO anything?

Marco: Ach! Politicians, you know about politicians! They tried to blame it on the weathermen.

Narrator: The weathermen? Why? Do your weathermen keep rats as pets?

Marco: No, no. I didn't say that! The politicians told the weathermen to blame it on the black clouds in the sky. Weathermen wouldn't do that. When the clouds went away, people still got sick.

Narrator: So then what happened?

Marco: The politicians came up with this dandy idea. They decided maybe the disease, they call the sickness "disease," did come from the ships. Whatever was on those ships was a DANGER. So, they said—Don't get off of the boat! Everybody on board, stay where you are for forty days and nights.

Narrator: And that helped?

Marco: No, no, I can't say that! People are still dying! Half of our people are dead in one year! I have to leave now. I've been here too long. Death is in the air, they say. I must go.

Narrator: Thank you Mr. Marco. And good luck!

[The people with the black banner parade across the stage again.]

From *Story Celebrations: A Program Guide for Schools and Libraries* by Jan Irving. Westport, CT: Libraries Unlimited. Copyright © 2008.

Black Plague Readers Theatre Script (*Continued*)

So, the plague marches on. We will now take you to Florence, Italy. City of flowers. We have a young woman named Florence to report on what's happening in her city.

Florence: Would you like to buy a few posies from my flower cart? They say that posies keep the plague away!

Narrator: Miss Florence, we're coming to you from far away. Keep your flowers for your own city. But tell us how flowers can help?

Florence: My mama (rest her soul) always said that roses keep away the evil spirits. It didn't help her, but listen to those children over there. They love to play the ring-a-rosy game!

[Children dance in a circle and sing:]

Ring-a-ring-a rosy

A pocket full of posies

A-tishoo!

A-tishoo!

We all fall down!

Florence: Isn't that just lovely? Children dancing and singing!

Narrator: But the children don't look very healthy to me. Do you think maybe they've got the disease?

Florence: Oh, dear. I didn't think of that.

Narrator: Thank you, Miss Florence. I think we'll talk with that farmer's wife standing behind you. Mrs. . . . ? What is your name?

Farmer's Wife: My husband told me not to talk with strangers! Be off with you!

Narrator: Please, Mrs. . . . . We don't have to know your name. Could you just tell me what happened at your farm yesterday? Someone at our television station heard that your pigs got into a terrible fight.

Farmer's Wife: Fight? It was a war! Never saw those pigs so mad! You see, we had this servant girl, lazy old Mary, I called her. She wouldn't get out of bed last week. Said she had a headache. Fancy that! She couldn't get out of bed because her head ached!

Narrator: Maybe she had the disease?

From *Story Celebrations: A Program Guide for Schools and Libraries* by Jan Irving.
Westport, CT: Libraries Unlimited. Copyright © 2008.

Black Plague Readers Theatre Script (*Continued*)

Farmer's Wife: Nah, she was fakin' it. Didn't look sick to me! I just told her to get up and feed the cows or else I'd tan her hide!

Narrator: So then what happened?

Farmer's Wife: Lazy old Mary. Clumsy old Mary. Didn't feed those cows. She were so clumsy she fell in the pig trough! Next thing you know the pigs were fightin' over her clothes. Mary ran off. Never saw her again. But those pigs. They fought and fought over her skirts and then—

Narrator: Then what?

Farmer's Wife: Yeah, those pigs snuffled her skirts. She fell on the pigs, pigs fell on the cows. Cows just plopped over and died.

Narrator: Then she did have the disease!

Farmer's Wife: Don't you go tellin' me! I know what brings about the plague!

Narrator: Then please tell our listeners!

Farmer's Wife: If you ask me, it's the stars. You watch 'em tonight! When seven of 'em line up in a row, means they're gonna rain down death.

Narrator: Sorry about your pigs, Mrs. . . . . I think we'll talk with someone else about this plague.

 We will now talk with a more distinguished guest, from Rome, Italy. Dr. Galen, are you there?

Dr. Galen: Yes, sir, I am here. What do you want to know?

Narrator: I understand you are a physician to the pope of the Church in Rome.

Dr. Galen: I am, but I tend to the people of this city, too. It's a hard job these days, with the plague killing off so many of our citizens.

Narrator: Yes, I'm sure that is true. As a man of science and healing, do you have any help? Any advice for your people? What can they do to avoid this dreadful disease?

Dr. Galen: Make a fire! Burn! Burn! Burn out the bad! Hot fires will burn out any bad fumes in the air, you know!

Narrator: Do your colleagues in the medical profession agree with you?

Dr. Galen: Why don't you ask them yourself? I'm much too busy to discuss this matter further!

Black Plague Readers Theatre Script (*Continued*)

Narrator: We turn now to the doctors outside of Rome. Dr. Arno, what is your advice to people to fight this plague?

Dr. Arno: Flee! Flee from the marshes. Take to the hills! Cool. Be cool and you will save yourselves!

Narrator: Dr. Buono! What is your advice?

Dr. Buono: Wash your hands. Always wash your hands!

Narrator: Dr. Siena! What do you recommend?

Dr. Siena: Do not bathe the body. Wash only the feet. Feet stink! Wash only the feet.

Narrator: I see. Only the feet. And, Dr. Pisa, what advice do you have for your city?

Dr. Pisa: Rest. Sleep. Do not exercise during the day. Stay cool, calm. And always carry flowers. They keep the nose free from bad air!

Narrator: Flowers? Bad Air? Stars? Bad Spirits? Keep cool? What do you think out there in our television audience? Stay tuned for our next series, "London, the Last Frontier." We will report from London in 1664, the year of the plague. The Great Plague. And our third series "Fire Conquers All," will end this dreadful disease. Thank you, and good night!

From *Story Celebrations: A Program Guide for Schools and Libraries* by Jan Irving. Westport, CT: Libraries Unlimited. Copyright © 2008.

Gross Science

This topic of gross science or "grossology" has taken United States by storm in the first decade of the twenty-first century. Kids bored by science in the past now can't seem to get enough of this offbeat way to study biology and its related fields. Upper elementary and middle school age boys become especially fascinated with the topic. Teachers and librarians eager to motivate this age group to read will find plenty of titles to appeal to kids in this chapter.

The word *gross* is not new to the English language. Even the use of the phrase "gross out" has been a favorite slang expression of young people for decades. The current term *grossology* was coined by scientist Sylvia Branzei. As a science teacher, Ms. Branzei sought a new approach to interest her students in science. She has written a series of books and performed workshops that grew into a wildly popular traveling exhibit all over the country. Thousands of children and their parents have visited museums and community centers to enjoy such interactive exhibits as a skin climbing wall, a huge stomach, and a larger than life nose they can walk through. While parents and teachers may wince at the grossology show, they need to understand that all exhibits are based on sound scientific information and teach kids about the human body and how it works.

Not all young people will be able to experience the exciting grossology show, but librarians and teachers can capitalize on the principles of gross science. Displays of books on the topic and lively booktalks by educators can lead young readers to books they might otherwise ignore. This chapter focuses on science projects and activities in the school setting, and it also encourages reading and writing appropriate to the theme.

As an educator and librarian, I suggest striking a balance between the kid friendly and obvious appeal of the topic and adult discomfort with the more gross areas involved. Older children love to push limits. The irreverent tone of poetry by Jack Prelutsky and outlandish consequences of eating worms or beetles in books by Thomas Rockwell and Phyllis Reynolds Naylor capture the kind of humor kids love.

Children have always enjoyed shocking their parents and teachers with behavior and language beyond what society deems appropriate. The limit of what is appropriate seems to stretch further with each new generation. How do we determine what will or will not be tolerated in schools, libraries, and society? It's not an easy question, and certainly not one that this book can answer definitively. Schools generally set stronger limits than public libraries because teachers and educators are in the business of setting boundaries. A teacher, for example, might caution kids to write stories with a "degree of gross" but keep in mind that such a story might be shown to the principal for approval. Public libraries are challenged to guide young people rather than let them take control of any program on this topic. Obscene language, graffiti, and acting out to embarrass and bully other kids and adults should not be tolerated.

I have focused on the spirit of gross science and gross activities in a lighthearted but controlled way. Some aspects of body functions are touched upon, but much of the slang is modified in this chapter. Recipes for gross food are mild compared to the majority of titles found in books listed in the bibliography.

Rather than design numerous activities about body fluids and wastes, I have created projects on insects and animals that some people find nasty or even vulgar. Each adult has a different tolerance for this topic, and you may choose to use whatever ideas you wish from books I have described.

In this chapter you will discover "The Yucky Center," a school program designed to prepare kids for doing science fair projects and research. This is not a science textbook approach, but it is an introduction to science through learning centers with books and materials. Poetry and art projects are included to teach this topic in other curricular areas.

"Gross Out," the public library program, combines stories, songs, and a play about bugs for kids to perform for their peers. Kids will also make gross food combinations in this program and be encouraged to try a taste of their own concoctions. If you want to pursue the cooking portion of this program, consult the cookbooks listed in the bibliography, or even create dishes of your own. Many of the recipes here are standard, like those found in any good children's cookbook, but simply have been given icky names. Youth librarians could plan cooking programs or contests for kids to submit their own food made at home, with groups of children voting on favorite names for the recipes.

Bibliography

Bulion, Leslie. *Hey There, Stink Bug!* Charlesbridge, 2006.
(Reading Level: Accelerated Reader, 5.5)
    This delightful collection of insect poems combines gross facts and literary fun for kids interested in science and poetry.

Dahl, Roald. *Roald Dahl's Revolting Recipes.* Viking, 1994.
(Reading Level: Dale-Chall, 6.72)
    With recipes compiled by Josie Fison and Felicity Dahl, Roald's widow, this delightfully revolting collection contains recipes for wormy spaghetti, hot frogs, and lickable wallpaper along with others inspired by the popular author's books. Quentin Blake's whimsical illustrations and clear instructions in the text add to the book's appeal.

Fontanel, Beatrice. *Monsters: The World's Most Incredible Animals.* Peter Bedrick, 2000.
(Reading Level: Accelerated Reader, 6.7)
    Appalling, grotesque-looking creatures are introduced in a lively text with stunning color photographs. Many creatures are among the world's most exotic species—a furry armadillo from Argentina, an armor-scaled Malayan pangolin from Africa and the Malay peninsula, and the dome-eyed tarsier (similar to a lemur) from several Indonesian islands.

Fredericks, Anthony. *Cannibal Animals: Animals That Eat Their Own Kind.* Franklin Watts, 1999.
(Reading Level: Accelerated Reader, 6.9)
    Fredericks describes animal cannibals, from the tiny to the very large. Tiny insects (the praying mantis and midges) lead to black widow spiders, guppies, horned frogs, and gerbils. The larger cannibals discussed include bears, chimpanzees, sharks, and even humans. The helpful bibliography contains books, media, and Web sites.

Gantos, Jack. *Jack on the Tracks: Four Seasons of Fifth Grade.* Farrar, Straus & Giroux, 1999.
(Reading Level: Accelerated Reader, 5.1)
    When fifth grader Jack moves to Miami with his family, he becomes embroiled in many gross adventures. He writes a story about a boy who eats a tapeworm, engages in such disgusting activities as picking his nose, and wears weird underwear. Elementary and middle school boys will love the yucky humor.

Haslam, Andrew. *Insects.* Two-Can Publishing, 1998.
(Reading Level: Dale-Chall, 6.5)

    Part of the <u>Make It Work</u> series that offers a hands-on science approach, this fascinating book is filled with craft and game projects useful for upper elementary and middle school students. Numerous color illustrations and instructions make the book easy to follow, but the difficulty of working with the variety of materials and tools calls for some sophisticated dexterity or adult guidance. Projects may be adapted for library programs with larger audiences.

Holt, David, and Bill Mooney, eds. *Spiders in the Hairdo, Modern Urban Legends.* August House, 1999.
(Reading Level: Accelerated Reader, 5.4)

    These legends that seem too outlandish to be true tell about such gross subjects as a cactus exploding with baby tarantulas and dead cats stuffed in sacks. Children and adults who enjoy the ghoulish will love reading and retelling these accounts, retold by two master storytellers.

Janulewicz, Mike. *Yikes! Your Body, Up Close!* Simon & Schuster, 1997.
(Reading Level: Accelerated Reader, 5.6)

    Short text, huge illustrations of microphotography, and the inviting format will coax reluctant readers to grab this book from the library shelf. The more detailed information is set in smaller typeface. The color photographs of body parts (follicles of hair, taste buds in the tongue, gastric glands) are so fascinating they might turn students into future microbiologists.

Kelley, True. *School Lunch.* Holiday House, 2005.
(Reading Level: Accelerated Reader, 3.3)

    In this picture book with wide reader appeal, the lunch lady Harriet goes on vacation. Instead of her nutritious and delicious meals, the students endure a dreadful number of gross or outrageous meals from substitute cooks.

Parker, Steve. *Shocking, Slimy, Stinky, Shiny Science Experiments.* Sterling Publishing, 1998.
(Reading Level: Dale-Chall, 6.86)

    Two of the four sections in this attractively formatted book apply to the gross theme: "Slimy Science" and "Stinky Science." Different kinds of slimes found in nature and ones that can be created are discussed along with easy to follow instructions. Several interesting experiments include making a slimometer to evaluate slime and testing smells by methods similar to the scratch 'n' sniff technology.

Porter, Cheryl. *Gross Grub: Wretched Recipes That Look Yucky But Taste Yummy.* Random House, 1995.
(Reading Level: Dale-Chall, 6.5)

    Delicious but gross-sounding recipes for brain cell salad, worm burgers, and toasted tongues are among the dozens of concoctions kids will want to make. Line drawings, cooking terms, and safety tips add to this book, useful for library programs.

Rhatigan, Joe, with Heather Smith. *Sure-to-Win Science Fair Projects.* Lark Books, Sterling Publishing, 2001.
(Reading Level: Spache, 4.43)

    From its lively introduction to more than fifty projects, this book sets out to tap kids' natural curiosity as they plan science fair projects. The projects are clearly laid out but "if you used one of them, you wouldn't be cheating, because it would still be up to you to do the work and figure out the results." Plans for implementation and presentation make this book invaluable.

Ross, Michael Elsohn. *Wormology.* Carolrhoda, 1996.
(Reading Level: Accelerated Reader, 5.5)
   This engaging text teaches kids to study worms and worm behavior with respect. Instructions for making a worm palace (a soil-filled jar with a sock cover) and a worm amusement park are given as well as suggestions for performing different worm experiments.

Scieszka, Jon, and Lane Smith. *Science Verse.* Viking, 2004.
(Reading Level: Dale-Chall, 4.2,)
   The zany verses, typical of this creative team's talents, cover many "gross" subjects—poems compared to spleens, gobblegooky, and mealworms. They will inspire kids to write their own gross poetry and make creative ugly art.

Scieszka, Jon, and Lane Smith. *Squids Will Be Squids: Fresh Morals, Beastly Fables.* Viking, 1998.
(Reading Level: Accelerated Reader, 3.8)
   Hilarious fables for the modern kid interested in grossology tell about a musk ox and cabbage who are appalled by a skunk's smell, an echidna who swallows her new friend ant, and lunch buddies no one wants to have around—shark, wasp, and bacteria. Upper elementary as well as middle school students will enjoy writing their own fables after reading these yucky examples.

Solheim, James. *It's Disgusting—and We Ate It!: True Food Facts from Around the World—and Throughout History!* Simon & Schuster, 1998.
(Reading Level: Accelerated Reader, 6.0)
   This positively "engrossing" text combines lively narratives, information, poems, sidebars, and cartoon art to inspire young scientists. Librarians and teachers can plan exciting programs using the numerous fun-filled ideas.

Vilicich-Solomon, Tina. *Gross Goodies.* Lowell House, 1996.
(Reading level: Dale-Chall, 6.2)
   These tasty treats are given detestable names (earwax on a swab, toe jam fondue, saliva slurp), and putrid presentation ideas are provided. Kids will love the gross humor and enjoy making these recipes at home or in the library.

Selected Web Sites

Carnegie Magazine: Grossology: www.carnegiemuseums.org/cmag/bk_issue/2002/novdec/feat5.htm
   Sponsored by Carnegie Museums of Pittsburgh. This issue of the magazine focuses on the "impolite science of the human body," with humorous details of the museum's exhibition on grossology. Ideas can be replicated by teachers and librarians.

Discovery School: http://school.discovery.com/sciencefaircentral/scifairstudio/handbook/scientificmethod.html
   Sponsored by the Discovery Channel, this site includes science fair rules, guidelines, tips from judges, and over 250 project ideas.

Grossology: www.grossology.org
   This Web site of educator Sylvia Branzei and illustrator Jack Keely has a virtual museum tour with fun facts, poems, quizzes, and links, along with kid-friendly illustrations.

Yucky Discovery: www.yucky.kids.discovery.com
   Sponsored by the Discovery Channel, games, facts, and activities will appeal to kids.

The Yucky Center: A School Program to Introduce Gross Science

This program can be set up in the school media center or in a science classroom to motivate students as they prepare for a science fair, but it also incorporates writing and art activities. Science students are required to write their reports clearly so that judges can follow the procedures they used. Language arts students will enjoy creative writing on the different yucky topics suggested here. Art students may create illustrations for the writing or they can make collages of strange insects, animals, and body parts.

The science projects presented here are sample experiments to peak student interest. Check science fair project resources in this chapter's bibliography for more complete procedures. This learning center will show students that science fair projects can explore offbeat topics and relate to everyday situations. Most suggestions will appeal to students in the upper elementary grades, but teachers of middle grade students can adapt the ideas for their students.

Not all students will want to choose a project of this kind, but the topic of gross science should interest everyone on some level. Reluctant students, especially boys, will be a target group to try these ideas. If some students are really squeamish about doing gross science projects, give them the alternative of another science project or doing a writing or art activity on this topic. Set ground rules, and be sure the projects are cleared with teachers and parents before you begin, since students in this age group often like to test limits.

This introductory program is different from those in other chapters in that the media specialist simply sets up learning centers for students to explore their favorite area: science, writing, or art. It may take just one class meeting in the media center, then science and language arts teachers use these ideas with students in the classroom. The media specialist will leave the displays in the school library for several days or a week so that students can explore the activities during the rest of the week.

Materials Needed

Display boards for ideas and pictures taken from the Internet or photos you have taken.

Art supplies (colored pencils, crayons, scissors, glue) and writing materials (paper, pencils or computers) for the yucky writing and arts centers.

Science project displays from previous years.

Ingredients and supplies for science projects:

- Food samples for Nosey Nosey Nosey! (p. 129): a small bag of spinach, two broccoli stalks, one green bell pepper, two cups each of cooked green beans and cabbage.
- Food samples for Color Makes All the Difference (p. 129): two cups of mashed potatoes; one dozen eggs, scrambled; one carton of whipped topping; one small carton of cottage cheese; one small package of food coloring.
- Nose clips (one for each student) and several blindfolds.
- Petri dishes (available from microtech labs on the Internet), mylar gloves, gelatin granules or milk for petri dishes, and three household cleansers for Bacteria Wars (p. 129)
- Used shoes, cotton swabs, and TSA (tryptic soy agar) for Stinky Feet (p. 130).
- Small tablets or spiral notebooks to use as journals and pencils to record in them for Color Makes All the Difference (p. 129).

Procedure

Before You Begin

1. Set up a display of science books, choosing many titles about science experiments (found under the Dewey classification number 507.8) and other books about the human body and insects. Consult the bibliography of this chapter for specific suggestions.

2. Set up display boards from past science fair projects as well as "idea boards" as described in this chapter.

3. Set up learning centers with materials, equipment, and a few partially completed projects to peak the interest of students. See suggestions in this chapter.

4. Choose books for read-aloud at the first meeting and review passages. The books by Jon Scieszka, especially the poems "Scientific Method at the Bat" and "Lovely" from *Science Verse*, will delight elementary students. Selections from *Hey There, Stink Bug!* are also good choices. Some of the urban folk tales from *Spiders in the Hairdo* work well with middle school students.

5. Arrange for a language arts teacher to assist with a creative writing project and for a science teacher to assist with the science projects.

First Meeting

1. Introduce students to the topic of gross science by reading from one of the books or reading the poems suggested in the materials list. Allow about fifteen to twenty minutes for the introduction.

2. Give students the opportunity to select a writing or art activity if they cannot "stomach" a science activity.

3. For the remainder of the class meeting, have science and language arts teachers use the activities suggested here with small groups in the learning centers.

Further Meetings (If Desired)

1. Work with classroom teachers on the projects introduced earlier or

2. Interact with students in the media center as they participate in the learning centers during the rest of the week.

Idea Boards

Display these questions and thoughts on signs or display boards around the room (or create some of your own):

Is science gross?

Bugs! Gross or Gorgeous?

I sing the body gross! (Sorry, Walt Whitman!)

Make signs with the following questions on them and place them on the learning center tables:

- Why does that bread stink?
- Look for yucky in your refrigerator!
- What is cleaner? Water from your toilet bowl or your drinking fountain?
- How slow is that worm in your backyard? Have a worm race!

Learning Centers

Set up learning centers with experimental projects such as those described below. The goal of these centers is to start kids thinking in questions. Next kids will begin research using library materials and Internet sources as well as interviewing experts in the field. You will help students frame the problem to be solved into an open-ended question to be solved experimentally. For example, the question "What is mold?" does not require an experiment to answer. The question "How does light affect the growth of mold on bread?" is a good one to answer experimentally. (See the worksheet on page 131.)

Next, the question should be stated as a hypothesis or a statement to be proved. Following the example above, a student might state this hypothesis: "I believe bread mold does not need light to grow." Experimentation follows, with students using a control factor and variables. In this case, the control factor would be bread (several pieces of the same kind) and the variables would be light, various gradations or periods of light, and dark.

For the learning centers, pose a question or title the experiment to be researched and include some of the equipment that will be used. *Note:* Have classroom teachers send home release forms for parents to sign if you are doing a food activity, since many children have food allergies.

1. Nosey Nosey Nosey!

Question: Does smell affect the taste of food?

Note: This experiment involves blindfolding participants and asking them to taste food as they use nose clips. Record responses as people taste food using only their tongues. Record responses again without the nose clips so that taste and smell reflexes can be used in the identifications.

Gross slant: Give kids food they originally said were "gross"—spinach, thin slices of broccoli stalk, raw green pepper, green beans, cabbage.

Sample equipment/materials: blindfold, nose clips, food samples

2. Color Makes All the Difference

Question: Does an unusual color affect food preference?

Note: Do this experiment with participants blindfolded first. Then have them remove the blindfolds and look at the food before they taste it. Record their responses at both times.

Gross slant: Add natural food coloring to food we eat everyday. Think of strange concoctions —blue mashed potatoes, green scrambled eggs, purple whipped cream, red cottage cheese.

Sample equipment/materials to display: blindfolds, journals with notes and pencils to show students the importance of recording results, blue mashed potatoes or cottage cheese.

3. Bacteria Wars

Question: Does Brand X cleanser fight bacteria better than Brands A, B, or C?

Note: This involves growing bacteria in petri dishes of gelatin and beef granules or milk or egg. Test different cleaners on the growth. Test bacterial growth after the petri dishes have been placed in dark places such as a closet for various periods of time—one day, two days, three days. The changes will be apparent to the naked eye. Caution: Be safe! Wear throwaway mylar gloves at every step in this experiment so as not to contaminate skin or the project itself.

Sample equipment/materials to display: petri dishes (available from microtech labs on the Internet), mylar gloves, three household cleansers.

4. Creepy Water

Question: Is the water in the school toilets dirtier (grosser) than the water in the sink?

Note: Test the water in both places—the toilet bowl and the sink—to answer this question. Put a small amount of water—such as a few teaspoons—from these sources into a petri dish filled with TSA sources. The answer might surprise you.

Sample equipment/materials to display: petri dishes, two jars of water labeled "water from the toilet bowl" and "water from the sink."

5. Stinky Feet!

Question: Whose feet are the worst sites of bacteria? At home children can test family members' shoes. At school, different teachers might allow students to test their shoes.

Note: This experiment involves swabbing shoes from different people with sterile applicators before shoes are worn and streaking the swabs across TSA petri dishes. (TSA stands for tryptic soy agar, a general growth medium for microbes.) Test shoes again after people have worn them 5-6 hours. Try this experiment with different kinds of shoes—canvas, leather, and plastic.

Sample equipment: petri dishes, at least three pair of shoes and intersoles

Other Tests with Bacteria:

Swab these places and place them in petri dishes.

1.   Check out bacteria on the surface of your desk.

2.   Swab the inside of your nose.

3.   Test the food in your lunch compared to food in the cafeteria

4.   Test the bacteria level inside your pockets compared to your backpack.

Yucky Writing and Art Corner

Provide students with several traditional poems that are now in the public domain, such as Joyce Kilmer's "Trees" or a Mother Goose rhyme such as "There Was an Old Woman Who Lived in a Shoe." Begin working in small groups or with the group as a whole to create yucky parodies of these poems. The following poem starters may need to be used to get elementary school students started, but middle school kids will be able to create their own with little prompting. The poems based on the "Trees" model need not be twelve lines long, but urge students to add at least two more couplets to complete the beginning idea and a final couplet to conclude their idea.

This exercise introduces the topic of grossology and also gives you an opportunity to discuss elements of quality in poetry. The original poem "Trees," first published in 1913 in the respected journal *Poetry,* has not stood the test of time as a good poem. The images are trite, the positions of the tree are awkward and inconsistent within the context of the poem itself, and the final couplet usually evokes a response from mature readers something like, "You bet you're a fool!" Despite modern criticism, this poem is fun to parody. Jon Scieszka's "Lovely" in *Science Verse* uses Kilmer's pattern. You may want to read this to students before or after this writing activity.

Note: The poem "Trees" by Joyce Kilmer may be found on the Internet at http://highsorcery. com/poems/trees.html. Mother Goose rhymes can be found at http://www-personal.umich.edu/ ~pfa/dreamhouse/nursery/rhymes.html.

Student Worksheet for Science Fair Projects

Use this worksheet as you plan your science fair report. It guides you through steps of the scientific method.

Step 1: What is the problem? Write this down as a question or state what you will be doing/what are you trying to solve. Think in terms of a control group and an experimental group.

Step 2: The Research. Look for background information in library books and on Internet sites sponsored by respected scientific organizations. Make notes and print pages from the Internet.

Step 3: The Hypothesis. State what you expect to find after you do your project. Be specific about this, giving numbers and using descriptive words.

Step 4: The Experiment. Record the daily (or more frequent) progress of your experiment, and do careful measurements.

Step 5: Compare the Hypothesis with the Experiment. Compare step 3 with step 4. (You may have to re-state your hypothesis.)

Step 6. Conclusion. Summarize what happened and what you learned.

Yucky Poem Starters for "Trees" Parodies

I think that I will never pick
A poem as yucky as a tick . . .

I know I will not delight
In poems as gross as a mite . . .

I hope I will never see
A poem as disgusting as a flea . . .

I know for sure that I will squirm
Reading poems that look like worms . . .

Yucky Poem Starters Inspired by Nursery Rhymes or Traditional Ballads

There was an Old Woman who lived in a Liver
When you knocked at the door, it gave a quiver . . .

Jack and Jill went up an intestine
To find a smelly lunch . . .

Hey diddle stomach ache
How many mealy worms does it take . . .

I know an old lady who swallowed a fly
I know why she swallowed a fly
And I'll tell you why . . .

I've been workin' in your stomach
All the live long day . . .

Here are some other kinds of silly yucky poems to share with your students.

- Shape poems, pattern poems, or concrete poems are visual display poems. They often are written in a shape or pattern appropriate to the subject of the poem itself. Give students an outline of a snake, a worm, or a tongue, and invite them to write their own poems about these subjects in free verse.

- Acrostic poems: The first letter of each line in an acrostic poem forms a word. Use this ancient form in new, gross ways for fun! For example:

  - Succulent tasting
  - Lovely smell
  - I love the touch of
  - Mucus-like snails
  - Every bite makes me drool

- Haiku is a Japanese form and traditionally captures a moment in nature. In order to write yucky haiku, students may not end up with the serene mood usually attributed to this form. The pattern of syllables in the three lines of a haiku is as follows: five in the first line, seven in the second line, and five in the third line. For example:

  Old maggot eating

  Rotten rotting sewer rats

  Not my kind of diet

Art Suggestions to Accompany Writing

Provide students with crayons, pastels, colored pencils, scissors, and glue to illustrate their poems. Collage art is a natural kind of illustration for these poems, as students can find photographs of body parts and gross-looking insects or animals on the Internet. Students may study Lane Smith's illustrations in *Science Verse* for inspiration.

Simple crayon drawings would also work well for this crude topic because crayon art is often associated with the naïve style of young children's artwork. Older students with more artistic ability may want to use pastels and colored pencils to draw more realistic intestines and stomachs for poems on these subjects.

You may want to suggest guidelines so that these projects do not spin out of control. A caution such as "create poems and illustrations that can be hung outside the principal's office" may be enough to guide imaginative kids.

Gross Out!: A Program for Public Libraries

This gross program combines a play for kids to perform for one another and cooking activities for the participants. You begin the program with songs and stories to set the mood. The program will last about an hour if you have children perform the play and make some of the yucky food.

Materials Needed

Basic costumes for the skit:

- brown T-shirt for Dung Beetle, three brown socks rolled into balls
- lime green T-shirt for Housefly, a flyswatter
- black T-shirt for Cockroach
- red T-shirt for Dust Mite
- camouflage shirt for Killer Mosquito
- striped shirt for Wasp
- bright colored cape for Madame Butterfly
- black cloak or cape or T-shirt for Old Man Fly
- crown and wings, purchased from discount store or costume shop
- scripts for ten children to perform the play "The Ugliest Bug in the World"
- a buzzer and mariachi music for cockroach's rumba dance
- kazoo
- pocket comb

Food as described in the recipes. *Note:* If you plan to do all the recipes, you will need these ingredients:

- hard boiled eggs, one per person
- green olives, one per person
- black olives, one per person
- flour, 1 cup
- 2 flour tortillas per person
- 1 can refried beans
- 1 8 oz carton of sour cream
- 1 jar salsa, poured into several small bowls
- 1 carton prepared guacamole
- 2 red peppers
- 2 cans tomato soup
- 1 can chopped tomatoes
- 44 oz. cooked spaghetti
- 1 small bag of gummy worms
- 1 package of chocolate wafers
- 1 can of chocolate pudding
- 1 Styrofoam™ cup per person
- 1 paper plate per person
- 1 paper bowl per person
- 1 paper napkin per person
- 1 plastic fork and 1 plastic spoon per person

Procedure

Before You Begin

1. Invite ten kids to come to the library a few days prior to the program (or an hour before the program begins) to try on costumes and practice the play.

2. Set up cooking stations with food and utensils as needed.

3. Make paste for icky eyeballs (Just mix a teaspoon of water with the flour and keep adding water until you achieve a good gooey consistency.)

4. Hard boiled eggs—one for each child attending.

On the Day of the Program

1. As children arrive at the library, lead the group in singing such songs as "The Ants Go Marching" and "Great Green Gobs of Greasy Grimy Gopher Guts."

2. Invite children to read selections from such books as *Squids Will Be Squids.* Or you might choose to tell a story from *Spiders in the Hairdo* and invite kids to read other urban tales from this collection. (See the bibliography for details and other books to use.)

3. Ten kids (who have been selected in advance and have practiced) perform "The Ugliest Bug in the World" (pp. 136–39).

4. Direct children to various cooking centers to make the food described in the gross grub recipe section of this chapter. Kids may eat the food at the program or take it home on the paper plates you provide.

5. To end the program, tell a gross story or read a chapter from one of the gross books in the bibliography of this chapter.

Play: The Ugliest Bug in the World Contest

Program note: Select ten children to perform this play and give them an opportunity to practice first. Colored T-shirts described below will make adequate costumes, but headbands with antennae could also be worn. You may wish to take the part of Queen Flea to keep the action going.

Cast of Characters with Costume and Talent Ideas

1. Dung Beetle wears a brown shirt. Talent: dung ball juggling.

2. Housefly wears a lime green shirt. Talent: performs gymnastics on a flyswatter.

3. Stink Beetle wears an old yellow shirt with holes. Talent: sings stinky songs.

4. Cockroach wears a black shirt. Talent: dances the roach rumba.

5. Dust Mite wears a red shirt. Talent: sings "I've Got You Under Your Skin."

6. Killer Mosquito wears a camouflage shirt. Talent: plays a kazoo.

7. Wasp wears a striped shirt. Talent: buzzes through a comb.

8. Madame Butterfly wears a brightly colored scarf or cape. Talent: dancing.

9. Old Man Fly wears a black cloak or T-shirt and hisses.

10. Queen Flea wears a crown and wings and flutters her wings.

The Ugliest Bug in the World Contest

Queen Flea: Welcome, viewers of the Vulgar Video Channel. This is me, Queen Flea, fearless and ferocious television star. I invite all you ugly bugs out there to come to my kingdom on the dog house for the time of your lives.

Bring your ugliest swimsuits! Practice your most disgusting talents! Join all your gross buddies in the First Annual Gross Bug Contest.

The winner who impresses me with the most unusual costume and original talent will take home a life supply of food from my very own garbage pile.

Come one, come all, but come as fast as your feet or wings can carry you.

[Actors buzz and flap as they march, run, and do cartwheels across the stage. They can make up different ways for these bugs to move.]

How beautifully yucky you all look. No biting, no fighting! There's plenty of room for all of you up here on the doghouse roof. My assistant will give each of you a number for our competition.

Old Man Fly: Ms. Dung Beetle, you are number one.

D.B.: I certainly am number one. I'm the best bug in the world!

Housefly: No way, beetle! I am twice as talented as you are.

Old Man Fly: Mr. Fly, didn't you hear the Queen? No fighting! You are number two in our competition. Unless you wish to fly away home right now.

Housefly: No way, old man. But I'm going to win.

Stink Beetle: Oh, no, you're just a common old housefly. I am far more talented. Just wait until you experience my special effects—stink-a-roo!

Old Man Fly: Stinky, you are number three, and behave yourself!

Cockroach: Did anyone see my swimsuit around here? I'm ready to make my appearance!

Old Man Fly: Is it this slinky little black number? (Holding up a black swimsuit.) I certainly hope it covers all of your big body. This is a decent video we're making, rated family friendly, you know! Oh yes, Cocky, you are number four in the competition.

Dust Mite: Here I am! Here I am! Your favorite bed bug! I'm one in a million you'll find in your bed tonight. What number am I in the competition?

Old Man Fly: Let's see, Dusty, you'll be number five.

DM: Perfect! I'll have time to practice my talent before we start.

The Ugliest Bug in the World Contest (*Continued*)

K. Mosquito: Oh, Mr. Mite, I wouldn't worry about practicing. My act is deadly. You won't come out of this competition alive.

Old Man Fly: Careful, Killer. There's not going to be any bloodshed on my watch. Just buzz off and take your number. It's six.

Wasp: Did anyone say deadly? Wait 'til you see my act. I'll knock you all dead!

Old Man Fly: Not you too, Wasp! No fighting, no biting! Just you buzz off too and take number seven. Your act is last in the show.

Queen Flea: Welcome bugs! As soon as Old Man Fly sounds the buzzer, we will begin. I will announce each beautiful bug as you come to the front of the stage. And may the best ugly bug win!

[O.M. Fly buzzes the buzzer.]

Queen Flea: Bugs of the world, may I introduce our first contestant, Ms. Dung Beetle. Ms. Beetle, show us your stuff! (Ms. Beetle struts across the stage with many twirls and curtseys to the audience.)

Ms. Dung Beetle, the youngest in an old line of famous beetles from ancient Egypt, is wearing her poopy brown bikini designed by Gross Designs. Notice the hip-hugging lines of her costume.

Ms. Beetle, would you now like to share your incredible juggling talents for our audience at home?

Ms. Beetle: Yes, I will now juggle three dung balls for your enjoyment. (Ms. Beetle juggles three balls of brown socks rolled into balls.)

Queen Flea: That was amazing, Ms. Beetle. Thank you.

Mr. Housefly, you are next. Come to the front of the stage and show your stuff! (Mr. Fly flutters across the stage with many flourishes.)

Mr. Housefly is wearing green swim trunks and a green tank top. He is not just your ordinary housefly. He is the fastest fly in the world.

Mr. Fly, would you share gymnastics with us?

Mr. Fly: SSSSS! I certainly will. I will now do cartwheels on the edge of a flyswatter.

[He does cartwheels across stage.]

Thank you, Mr. Fly. Why, I couldn't do that myself!

Mr. Stink Beetle, come to the front of the stage. (Mr. S. Beetle tiptoes across the stage.)

Mr. S. Beetle wears a yellow suit, the color of stinky cheese, and for his talent act he will sing a little song of stinky cheese.

From *Story Celebrations: A Program Guide for Schools and Libraries* by Jan Irving. Westport, CT: Libraries Unlimited. Copyright © 2008.

The Ugliest Bug in the World Contest *(Continued)*

S. Cheese: [singing to the tune of "This Old Man"]

Hold your nose

If you're smart

I'm a stink bug

With smelly farts.

With a stinky

Stinky smell

Like rotten cheese

I'm a stink bug, if you please! [Bows and makes a bad sound as if farting.]

Queen Flea: Oh, my gracious! That was a real-l-l-l-l-y gross act! How exciting!

OK, Mr. Cockroach, you're next. [Cockroach crawls across the stage.]

Mr. Cockroach is wearing a slinky black set of swim trunks and he will dance the roach rumba. [Music begins as Cockroach makes grand steps around the stage and does a dance.]

Thank you, Mr. Roach. Folks, time is running out. Miss Dust Mite, run up here to the front of the stage and strut your stuff. [Miss Mite takes little steps to the front of the stage.]

Miss Mite wears a skintight swimsuit made of dead skin. For her talent she will sing "I've Got You Under Your Skin."

Miss Mite: [singing out of tune to the song "I've Got You Under My Skin"]

I've got you under your skin.

I'll make you itch

From your toes to your chin—

Queen Flea: That's enough, Miss Mite, you're driving me crazy. Now, our time is really short. Killer Mosquito and Wasp, will you come to the front of our stage and strut your stuff together?

[Mosquito and Wasp flap their wings and make buzzing sounds really LOUD until Queen Flea claps her hands.]

Stop! This is too much. I'll have to ask you bugs to bow and buzz off.

M. and W.: No fair! We didn't get to play our songs.

Queen Flea: Very well, can you make this a duet?

[Mosquito and Wasp make loud buzzing songs as they play the kazoo and the comb.]

The Ugliest Bug in the World Contest (*Continued*)

Queen Flea: Thank you killer bugs. And now, it's time for my decision. Wait! Who is flying in from the stage wings?

M. Butterfly: Oh, Queen Flea, it is I, Madame Butterfly. I know I'm not really a bug, but I have a ballet dance created just for your show. Please, will you let me perform?

Queen Flea: You are not very welcome here, Madame, but because I am Queen I shall make an exception. But make it a very fast dance.

M. Butterfly: Oh, thank you, Queen Flea. I shall do my very own Butterfly Ballet.

[She twirls on her toes. She pretends to suck juices out of the bugs. She sticks out her tongue. And she throws kisses to Queen Flea.]

Queen Flea: Oh, my Madame Butterfly. That was truly unusual. Beautiful. Slightly gross. But oh so fetching. Bugs of the world, I have made my decision. Madame Butterfly has stolen my heart and wins the show. To her I give the grand prize of my entire garbage pile.

Butterfly: No! No! No! I only dine on flower juice! Give that garbage to your bugs!

Queen Flea: How generous of you, Madame Butterfly! Bugs, be my guest.

[The bugs mime eating large handfuls of the garbage pile.]

Home viewers, this concludes our show tonight. Thank you, bugs. And now, buzz off!

[All bugs including Queen Flea and Old Man Fly bow and buzz as they exit the stage.]

From *Story Celebrations: A Program Guide for Schools and Libraries* by Jan Irving. Westport, CT: Libraries Unlimited. Copyright © 2008.

Gross Grub Recipes

Note: When you advertise this program, ask parents to notify the library if their children have food allergies.

Icky Eye Balls

Ingredients

hard-boiled eggs (one per kid)

green olives stuffed with pimento

black olives (without pits)

flour and water paste (to hold the "iris" of the eye in place)

Note: Make little bowls of this ahead of time. This is edible, but you may want to caution kids to use just a little since it tastes sort of icky by itself.

Directions

1. Hard boil several dozen eggs, enough so that each participant will have an egg.

2. Give kids the opportunity to peel eggs carefully so the peeled egg will remain intact.

3. Cut eggs in half vertically (cut through the egg, including the yolk, in the same way you cut eggs for deviled egg halves) and very carefully remove the yolk without tearing the white. (If this happens, the eyeball will look even more gross.)

4. Tilt the yolk back in the center of the egg so that the "eye" will look slightly bulgy.

5. Slice the green olives horizontally and add them to the center of the yolk to resemble an iris. Hold the iris in place with a little flour and water paste.

6. Slice black olives in strips and place them vertically on the yolk. This resembles a reptilian eye.

Note: Suggest to kids that they may wish to make one green iris eyeball and one black eye slit as a reptilian eye rather than combining the olives on one eyeball.

Gooey Nose (or Snotty Nose)

Ingredients

>   flour tortillas
>   refried beans
>   sour cream
>   salsa
>   guacamole.

Directions

1. Spread a tortilla with beans, sour cream, guacamole, and a little salsa. (Caution kids to not use too much.)

2. Roll up the tortilla lengthwise.

3. Bend the tortilla in half to resemble a snout or ugly nose.

4. Put the snout on a plate and carefully poke two holes in them to resemble nostrils.

5. Squeeze the snout a bit so the goo comes out of the nostrils. Yuck!

Bloody Fingers

Ingredients

>   flour tortillas
>   canned refried beans
>   sour cream
>   salsa
>   guacamole
>   pieces of red bell pepper for fingernails

Directions

1. Spread tortillas with beans, sour cream, and guacamole as in the gooey nose recipe.

2. Roll tortillas lengthwise to make fingers. Tuck in one end of the tortilla for the smooth end of each finger.

3. Add red pepper fingernails to end of each finger (hold this in place with a little salsa).

4. Add a little more salsa to the fingers to suggest blood.

5. Serve fingers on paper plates.

Blood Soup with Worms

Ingredients

    canned tomato soup

    chopped canned tomatoes

    cooked spaghetti (fat round noodles, not flat)

    green food coloring

Directions

1. Prepare tomato soup according to directions (adding a little water to the condensed soup). Heat, but not to boiling. (In a library setting, you may want to use slow cookers and Dutch ovens with separate electric units. If this is not convenient, cover large pots of warm soup and place on serving tables.)

2. Add small chunks of chopped tomato to soup to resemble blood clots.

3. Give kids bowls of already cooked fat spaghetti (not flat pasta since the spaghetti should look like worms). Place a small amount of spaghetti in the bowl so there will be room for plenty of the blood soup.

4. Add a few drops of green food coloring to the spaghetti and stir so that the worms will become a nasty green color.

5. Ladle blood soup on top of the spaghetti.

6. Enjoy!

Worms in Dirt

Ingredients

    gummy worms (purchased)

    chocolate wafers

    chocolate pudding (prepared ahead)

    white Styrofoam cups

    waxed paper

    several rolling pins for the group

Directions

1. Crush chocolate wafers on sheets of waxed paper with rolling pin.

2. Put several spoonfuls of pudding in bottom of Styrofoam cups.

3. Add chocolate wafer dirt to top of pudding. Be sure to cover the pudding with plenty of the crumbs.

4. Stick a gummy worm or two into the dirt so part of the worm will be sticking out.

5. Enjoy!

From *Story Celebrations: A Program Guide for Schools and Libraries* by Jan Irving.
Westport, CT: Libraries Unlimited. Copyright © 2008.

8

In the Spotlight: Public Speaking for Kids

What is most people's greatest fear? It's not the fear of heights, the fear of facing wild animals, or the fear of going to the dentist. It causes your throat to become dry, your palms to get sweaty, and your stomach to jump with butterflies. You guessed it! Most of us say that our greatest fear is getting up to speak in public.

While even professional speakers experience some degree of nervousness, speech coaches assure us that developing good skills and getting experience in the field lessens this common fear. A favorite saying to share with beginning speakers is that the only difference between novices and pros is that professional speakers train their butterflies to fly in formation. Training can make the difference. This chapter introduces skills necessary for successful speaking activities with young people.

Why is public speaking such an important skill to develop at a young age? With so many vital curricular topics and skills to crowd into the curriculum, shouldn't units on public speaking be put off until high school or college? Or why not let students wait to learn public speaking until they enter their chosen careers? Introducing public speaking at a young age gives kids skills and helps them gain self-confidence. Learning good oral skills helps kids in high school and college, not just in their careers. Teaching public speaking is not just important, but today it may be even more vital than in times past.

But wait—isn't this the most connected generation? Because of cell telephones, text messaging, and blogging, aren't kids already pretty savvy about communication? Don't students write better today because they use e-mail frequently? These questions assume that frequency of using electronic media equates with better, more skilled communication. Research tells us that using e-mail, for example, does not advance student vocabularies or grammatical skills. The growth of many communication companies in the twenty-first century highlights the fact that many corporations feel new employees lack the ability to express themselves in public speaking situations.

Yes, communication styles are changing, but clear speech is always in fashion. Learning how to evaluate one's audience is basic. Learning to speak with as little jargon as possible is not only courteous to an audience, but it helps the speaker develop a more expansive vocabulary useful in communicating with broader groups of people. We live in a society with many new language learners, a diversity of ethnic groups and social classes. The need to be able to interact in this tapestry of complex cultures requires us to learn more about effective speaking and social interaction.

This chapter focuses on the basics of public speaking—and specifically on speeches. It provides warm-up exercises and oral exercises to ease students into the actual experience of getting up in front of the audience to give prepared remarks. It focuses on introductory speeches, informative speeches, demonstration speeches, and simple persuasive speeches. Because the emphasis is on overcoming anxiety, organizing the speech, and learning basic delivery, using props and PowerPoint™ presentations are not included here. Once students are confident with the basics, they can more easily master the "extras." As a former high school speech teacher and frequent public speaker myself, I have found this approach works best.

The bibliography is shorter in this chapter, for obvious reasons. This is a less "content rich" subject in which skills practice takes center stage. Selected texts listed here provide enough material to help teachers and librarians set up their own programs on the topic. Included are exercises and numerous tip sheets that can be reproduced for student use. A brainstorming sheet, an evaluation page, and an outline for organizing topics are added to the chapter.

Here's a special note for teachers in helping students become good audience members for speakers. Storytelling experts like to remind audiences that they are as much a part of the storytelling process as the storyteller. Author Norma Livo describes this interaction as "story negotiation," a kind of informal contract between the storyteller and the audience, which agrees to listen actively to the story being told. This "agreement" needs to take place in the public speaking world as well. Remind kids that they will appreciate having an attentive audience when they speak in front of a group; therefore, they need to be alert and courteous and give such positive feedback as nodding in agreement when appropriate. Good audiences contribute to good speeches!

Bibliography

Dietz, Joan. *It's Not What You Say, It's How You Say It.* St. Martin's Griffen, 2000.
(Reading Level: Flesch-Kincaid, 9.4)
    Although this book is not specifically written for young people, much of the information will be helpful to middle school and high school students. It will also help the teacher or librarian who is teaching speech making. Speech-writing skills, delivery techniques, using storytelling, and doing research are all covered.

Juskow, Barbara. *Speakers' Club: Public Speaking for Young People.* Dandy Lion Publications, 1991
(Reading Level: Flesch-Kincaid, 8.0)
    This practical guide consists of all the instructions and evaluation forms necessary to teach a unit on public speaking to kids in grades 4 through 8. They can use the book on their own to plan speeches. The pages are scored so that they can be easily reproduced for classroom use.

Podhaizer, Mary Elizabeth. *Painless Speaking.* Barron's Educational Series, 2003.
(Reading Level: Flesch-Kincaid, 12.0)
    This guide intended for adults will be a welcome resource for teachers and librarians. It is filled with information about all aspects of speaking, contains brain teaser exercises, discusses the art of conversation, and explains how speech happens.

Ryan, Margaret. *Extraordinary Oral Presentations.* Franklin Watts, 2005.
(Reading Level: Flesch-Kincaid, 10.1)
    Designed as a student guide to teach creative speaking, this book provides clear instructions for developing drafts, doing research, writing effective introductions, and organizing speeches. Helpful tips, quotes, and guides to presenting hot topics and making note cards make this an invaluable resource for teachers and librarians to use with middle school students.

Ryan, Margaret. *How to Give a Speech.* rev ed. Franklin Watts, 1994.
(Reading Level: Flesch-Kincaid, 6.8)
    Written by a professional speech writer, this book guides kids through an easy course in learning how to write and deliver the speech and how to conquer stage fright, and includes ways to use humor, props, and visual aids.

Ryan, Margaret. *You Mean I Have to Stand Up and Say Something?* Atheneum, 1986.
(Reading Level: 8.5)

Ryan sets forth seven excuses for not speaking, then refutes each one with humorous answers. In this simple, straightforward guide she discusses audience analysis, gives helpful hints for preparing and delivering the speech, and encourages kids.

Selected Web Sites

Lesson Plans Page: www.lessonplanspage.com/LAPublicSpeakingTongueTwistersIdea67.htm

Among the various units available on this Web site is a unit on public speaking designed for grades 6 to 7. Suggestions include using tongue twisters and self-evaluation with students.

Lesson Tutor: www.lessontutor.com/dppersuasive.html

This Web site link is based on a public speaking unit planned for grades 7 to 12 by Douglas A. Parker. It covers procedures, presentation techniques, and strategies for giving persuasive speeches.

Public Speaking Resources: Syndicated Content Powered by FeedBurner: http://feeds.feedburner.
   com/PublicSpeakingResources

Free information provided by Ray DuGray and Maria Ngo, "The Entrepreneur Doctors," is designed for professional development with plenty of ideas on speech delivery and using tongue twisters. Useful for librarians in program planning.

Toastmasters International: www.toastmasters.org/tips.asp

The well-known international organization provides ten helpful tips for successful public speaking at this Web site.

Speak Up: A School Program

This program unit builds on a series of warm-up exercises and discussions so that students will be able to give several short speeches in front of their peers. The idea of working with a "speech buddy" encourages kids to provide useful feedback to one another and teaches supportive listening. Watching videos and listening to audio recordings also provides models for good speaking, but nothing replaces the practice students get by giving formal presentations. The activities are planned for class periods of approximately fifty to fifty-five minutes. Educators may adjust these to their own schedules.

Note: Fourth- and fifth-grade teachers may wish to substitute several days of reading aloud, improvisational activities, or perhaps another informational speech instead of the persuasive speeches described in this plan.

Materials Needed

Duplicate handouts for students.

Camcorders, if desired. (One camcorder for each speech buddy team is best. *Note:* If camcorders are used, they will be used for six of the class sessions. The plan given here suggests using them for meetings 3, 6, 7, 9, 11, and 12.

Procedure

Before You Begin

1. Duplicate the handouts and evaluation forms in this chapter (pp. 149–57) for students.

2. Duplicate short stories and poems for reading aloud (see first meeting).

3. Gather newspaper clippings, magazine articles, and books on controversial topics for displays that generate interest in subjects for student speeches.

4. Purchase or borrow videos of famous speakers for classroom study. If your school has camcorders and tapes of student speakers, plan to borrow these for this unit.

First Meeting

1. Pass out short stories and poems for students to read through then read aloud to fellow classmates. See list of suggestions on page 147.

2. Ask students to stand in front of the room to read so they experience performing in front of an audience.

3. Give students the television reporter's assignment described on page 149, with handouts.

Second Meeting

1. Discuss student responses to the television news and weather reporting.

2. Listen to one or more videos of good speeches. *The Speeches Collection,* available on DVD, contains several volumes. Volume 1 includes speeches by Jacqueline Kennedy, and *The Greatest Speeches of All Time* has speeches by Martin Luther King Jr. and John Kennedy as well as other famous people. Public libraries often collect these for patron checkout.

3. Assign speech one, the short introductory speech (see "My First Speech," pp. 150–51), giving students the handouts, and assign "speech buddies," pairing children in groups of two.

4. If time permits, let speech buddies exchange their ideas for the introductory speech.

Third Meeting

1. Have students give their first speech and have them evaluate each other.

2. Videotape students if desired.

3. After students do their evaluations, give comments of your own as a model for the evaluation process. Show the videos as time permits.

4. Give assignment two, the informative speech, and distribute handouts (pp. 153–55). The "Information Isn't Boring" sheet (p. 151) gives ideas for topics.

5. After showing students the brainstorming web on mummies, ask them to brainstorm one or more topics as time permits.

Fourth Meeting

1. Present information and distribute the handout on organizing the speech (p. 155).

2. Allow students time to research their topics in the library and complete the "speech plan" to be turned in during the next class period.

Fifth Meeting

1. Have students present one-minute summaries of the informative speech they will give.

2. Discuss simple delivery techniques with students. Consult the books by Margaret Ryan in this chapter's bibliography. Main points to emphasize in delivery include establishing good eye contact with the audience, speaking slowly and clearly, and using expression in one's voice.

3. Have speech buddies practice the speech with each other.

Sixth and Seventh Meetings

1. Have students present their speeches.

Eighth Meeting

1. Set up the display on persuasive speeches

2. Have students select one of the topics listed on page 151 for research.

3. Ask students to research their topics and write a summary statement to turn in for teacher comments.

Ninth Meeting

1. Have students present the first two minutes of their speeches and evaluate each other.

Tenth Meeting

1. Have students practice speeches with speech buddies.

2. Show another speech video in the <u>Speeches Collections</u> series or check with high school speech teachers, since many teachers keep a library of student speeches. For variety, you might invite an outside speaker such as a member of the local Toastmasters group to talk to the class. (You may also choose to invite the outside speaker to the last day of this program/unit. See information about Toastmasters later in this chapter.)

Eleventh and Twelfth Meetings

1. Have students present their persuasive speeches.

Selections to Read Aloud

1. Poems from Liz Rosenberg's collection *Roots and Flowers* (described in chapter 3).

2. Almost any book by Dr. Seuss with lots of verbal play. These will limber up the tongue and give students practice in reading clearly.

3. Stories from Rudyard Kipling's *Just So Stories* (described in chapter 5), since they are short and also involve verbal play.

4. Puns, games, and wordplay from books described in chapter 2, such as Richard Lederer's *Pun and Games* (see p. 21).

5. Stories, chants, and riddles found in Virginia Tashjian's *Juba This and Juba That* (Little Brown, 1995).

6. Tongue twisters found in books or at www.geocities.com/Athens/8136/tonguetwisters.html.

7. Improvisational activities from Paul Rooyackers *101 More Drama Games for Children* (Hunter House Publishers, 2002).

Organizing Your Speech

The form on page 155 will help you organize your speech. If you write out your speech and type it up on the computer, use a larger typeface such as 14 or 16 point so you can easily read it without losing your place. Use wide margins and end your typing several inches from the bottom of the page, so your eyes will not need to look down as you speak.

Consider writing out only the introduction and any direct quotes, along with the main points of the speech, and practice saying your speech several times so you can speak from notes only. Experienced speakers recommend this approach and use a few note cards (four by six inches is ideal). If you do this, write on one side of the card only, and number your cards so you won't get the sequence mixed up.

Use the outline on page 155 as a guide.

Watch the Weather Woman/See the TV Newsmen

As you watch a television reporter and weather person for this assignment, listen and look for the following:

1. Eye Contact:
   - How effectively did the person look into the camera and seem to be speaking to the audience?
   - Were there any distractions or ineffective practices?

2. Vocal Qualities
   - Was the speaker's voice expressive or monotonous?
   - Was the voice clear and precise in pronunciations?
   - Did the speaker use effective pauses?
   - Was the rate of speech slow enough for you to follow what was being said?

3. Gestures and Other Matters
   - Did the speaker use gestures, and if so, how were they effective?
   - If the speaker was standing, was the posture good?
   - Did the speaker use facial expressions appropriate to the situation (or was the person "deadpan"?)

Write down your comments to share in class.

From *Story Celebrations: A Program Guide for Schools and Libraries* by Jan Irving. Westport, CT: Libraries Unlimited. Copyright © 2008.

My First Speech

Before you give your first speech, remember three things:

• First, you know more about this subject than other students. This is a speech about yourself!

• Second, stand tall with both feet on the floor so you'll look confident.

• And, third, speak slowly and clearly so that everyone in the room can hear you.

Your speech will be very short, only one minute, so you don't have to say very much. Remember how much fun you had in "show and tell" when you were in first grade? Show your audience through example how fun you still are!

Parts of the Introductory Speech about You

1. Your name and something about that name. (Were you named for someone? Do you have a nickname? Are there other famous people who share your first name?)

2. What I like to do when I'm not in school. (This may be your hobby, such as "collecting stamps" or practicing the guitar. Maybe you volunteer at your church or read to your younger brother. What can you say in a few short sentences about this interest?)

3. A skill you have that you can show. (You may have a unique skill, such as being able to memorize numbers easily. This could be demonstrated by having your teacher give a series of numbers you can repeat. Maybe your skill is one that other people have too, but demonstrate your special skill briefly. You could demonstrate some tennis strokes or how to tie a bow.)

Note: Other parts of an introductory speech might include telling about your family or describing an interesting place where you've visited. These topics have not been included in this assignment because the focus is on the speaker—you!

Information Isn't Boring . . . It's Finding Out About Things You Want to Know

This kind of speech invites you to think about topics you'd like to know more about. Use the following brainstorm list to get started. Other topics will probably pop into your head as you read the list. Just add them and explore a few ideas before you decide.

Airplanes	Frogs	Politics
Art	Hawaii	Pollution
Astronauts	Inventions	Reptiles
Astronomy	Jokes	Robots
Ballet	Juggling	Sea, the
Baseball	Kites	Soccer
Basketball	Libraries	Stars
Birds	Magic	Swimming
Bugs	Mice	Technology
Castles	Mountains	Tennis
Cats	Movies	Toys
Cooking	Mummies	Trains
Crafts	Music or musicals	Veggie diets
Crocodiles	Pets	Violins
Dragons	Photography	Yoga
Egypt	Pigs	Zoos
Fishing	Plays	

Student Evaluation Form

Name of Speaker _____

Title or Type of Speech _____

Please rate the following on a scale of 1 to 5, with 5 being the highest score:

I. Voice

Clear and distinct	1	2	3	4	5
Not too fast or slow	1	2	3	4	5
Good expression	1	2	3	4	5
Good volume	1	2	3	4	5

II. Eye contact

Appropriate	1	2	3	4	5

III. Content

Well organized	1	2	3	4	5
Held my interest	1	2	3	4	5

What I liked about this speech:

One suggestion for improvement:

Sample Brainstorming Sheet for Informative Speech on Egyptian Mummies

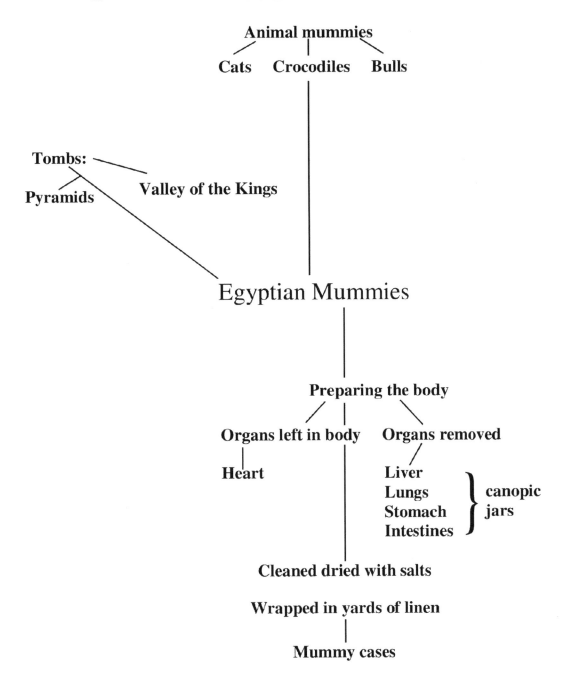

Funeral/Burial Ceremonies

Note: The speaker selected a topic he knew something about. This brainstorm sheet shows basic details that the student can use in completing research and organizing the speech.

Let's Get Started: Introductions

1. State purpose of speech, or

2. Begin with a story linked to the topic, or

3. Tell why you chose this topic, or

4. State a startling fact or statistic, or

5. Ask the audience a question (a rhetorical one to which you don't expect an answer), or

6. Find a good quotation on the topic (even better if the quote is from a well-known person), or

7. Refer to information the audience may already know ("Some of you remember our class trip to the natural history museum last year when we saw a mummy . . ."), or

8. Tell your audience why this is a crucial or important topic for them to know about.

Speech Title

Introduction: (Use a startling fact, quote, or other technique mentioned above previous page.)

Main Point of Speech: (Tell them what you are going to say.)

Middle of Speech: (Tell them or just give them the facts.)

Fact One:

Fact Two:

Fact Three:

End of Speech: (Remind them what you have told them.)

The Persuasive Speech

Build on your experience of giving an informational speech with this assignment. You will still give information, but you will try to persuade your audience to do something—adopt your viewpoint on a subject or move them to act on a belief. Letters to the editor in newspapers, political speeches, and editorials in school newspapers do this. Advertisements also persuade us either directly or subtly to buy products and services.

Study the display your librarian has set up with sample topics and clippings for ideas. Write down some of your own ideas on these subjects and talk through them with your speech buddy. This kind of exchange will help you clarify your position. Then use research materials in the library and Internet sites to support your argument.

Write down the main point of your speech as an argument or a position, such as, "I believe cell phones should not be used when driving automobiles." An excellent Web site to research this topic is www.theautochannel.com/news/2005/07/12/137294.html.

Another way to phrase the point of a persuasive speech is to put it in the form of an action statement, such as, "Become a vegetarian. It's fun!" Two good resources to use are Judy Krizmanic's *The Teen's Vegetarian Cookbook* (Viking, 1999) and Stephanie Pierson's *Vegetables Rock! A Complete Guide for Teenage Vegetarians* (Bantam, 1999.)

Maybe you'll want to take an active political stand on a subject of national or international scope. If you're interested in saving endangered species, you may want to do a speech on global warming or on a specific animal that is becoming endangered, like the polar bear. Check out the resources in the last chapter of this book. Two good resources on endangered animals are Richard Mackay's *The Penguin Atlas of Endangered Species* and Steve Pollock's *The Atlas of Endangered Animals.* You will need to narrow your topic a bit so you can make a short, focused speech. Another interesting topic is saving the rainforests of the world. An effective persuasive speech might be, "Kids like us can do a lot to save rainforests of the world." An especially good Web site on this topic is http://ran.org.

In addition to stating your position at the beginning of your speech, you will probably make several subpoints—that is, statements that support your argument. For each of these points, you will need "supporting evidence" such as quotations, facts, statistics, or well thought out solutions. Your outline will look something like the one on page 157.

Persuasive Speech Outline

Speech Title

Brief Introduction:

Main Argument:

Point (reason or position) One:

    Supporting evidence for this point (statistic, expert opinion, research study, testimony, or a powerful press release):

Point Two:

    Supporting evidence

Point Three:

    Supporting evidence

Conclusion (call to action or restatement of main arguments or a dynamite quote at the end):

The Yaks: A Speech Club for Public Libraries

This section outlines a complete speech program in the form of a series called "The Yaks: A Speech Club." The plan outlines six weekly programs. You may choose to schedule the six meetings two weeks apart or one meeting a month. Each program might last between 1 and 1½ hours.

Older kids in this age group are beginning to narrow their interests in areas of expertise. Some kids join tennis teams and chess clubs. Others take guitar lessons or art classes. Others genuinely like to be "on stage" performing drama or giving speeches. Plan the club for either kids in grades 4 through 6 or grades 6 through 8. Your decision may be based on your community's school structure. For example, if middle schools in your town include grades 6 through 8, this might be a logical group for your speech program focus.

The program can also be structured as a one-time speech contest in which kids give prepared speeches to an audience of their peers. However, it would be helpful for you to do a workshop for kids based on some of the ideas in the school portion of this chapter before announcing a speech contest, in which case it would run to two or three sessions.

Adapt the following general ideas and suggestions to your needs and library. For example, you might choose to combine the program with creative dramatics. If so, check out the chapters "Child's Play: Creative Dramatics and Story Theatre" in *Stories, Time and Again* (Libraries Unlimited, 2006). The chapter "Storytelling Sampler" in *Stories NeverEnding* (Libraries Unlimited, 2004) could also be consulted.

Materials Needed

A meeting room with chairs.

A performance space is not really needed, as chairs can be arranged to create a comfortable space.

You may wish to use a speaker's podium or a music stand so students can use notes.

Procedure

Before You Begin

1. A couple of weeks before your first meeting, start inviting kids to come to the library's "Speech Club," which will be having regular meetings with fun activities that kids help plan. Hand out flyers and post a notice in your library newsletter or on the Web site. Encourage children to become active club members. Some children may decide after a few meetings that this is not something they want to do. Be flexible. Remember, this isn't a school requirement.

2. Plan a few warm-up exercises such as reading aloud or playing charades. Refer to suggestions under the school program (pp. 145–47).

First Meeting

1. Do warm-up exercises that you have planned, allowing children to offer ideas as well.

2. Ask kids to find poems or short stories to read aloud for the next meeting Or you may provide the readings using those listed under the school program on pages 145–47.

Second Meeting

1. Invite club members to read aloud the poems or short stories.

Third Meeting

1. Ask kids to divide into pairs to interview one another.

2. You might have several suggestions for these introductions, such as What is your partner's favorite activity? His favorite song? Her earliest memory? A scary experience she or he had in kindergarten?

3. Then ask for volunteers to stand up to introduce their partners, using the information they gleaned from their interviews.

Fourth Meeting

1. Use the Speech Grab Bag with club members during this meeting.

Fifth Meeting

1. Invite an outside speaker to talk with kids. Someone from a local Toastmasters club or a high school speech student or drama coach would be pleased to encourage young speakers.

Sixth Meeting: Party and Entertainment

1. Plan a pizza party for the final meeting and pass out certificates to all club members. Then play the following game with a "Whatsit Bag" for giving impromptu speeches.

2. Your bag can be filled with unusual kitchen gadgets such as egg separators, cake testers, and vegetable peelers. Include an odd tool from the garage. Add anything that may be obscure. The first person in the circle of speakers takes an object from the Bag, stands up, and does an "instant ad" selling the audience on the importance of the "Whatsit" and why they need to buy one.

Note: You may want to schedule another event in the evening or on a weekend so that parents and adults in the community can see kids perform. Club members could choose their favorite activity from the series to share at this public event.

Speech Grab Bag

Grab bags challenge kids to take a risk. You might even introduce this activity by telling kids they will become successful in life if they learn to make good choices and then take calculated risks. Set up conditions for safe risk taking by using the "Rules of the Game" (p. 160).

Copy the quick pick speech topics (p. 161) on a piece of paper and cut it into strips. Or write them in bold marker on large index cards. Place paper strips or cards in a bright-colored laundry bag or a decorated grocery bag for students to begin play.

The Rules of the Game for Speech Clubs

1. Discuss how audience attention is important to public speakers. Have an outgoing kid (maybe someone who tends to be a "showoff") demonstrate the following rude behaviors, which are turn-offs to the speaker.

   Sit up. Cross your legs. Swing one foot wildly. Shake that leg to show irritation.

   Look at your feet.

   Roll your eyes.

   Look out the window.

   Look at your cell phone. Pretend to text message.

   Put your head down on the table or close your eyes.

   Look at your watch.

   Sigh deeply.

   Look around the room.

2. After these rude behaviors have been demonstrated, ask students to list points for good listeners.

3. With the children, set limits for a positive experience in Speech Club, such as no profanity, no vulgarity, and no gross gestures or words that could make people feel uncomfortable.

4. Talk about not "upstaging" others in giving speeches or being in the audience. This is not an arena for drama kings and queens. Everyone participates, shares, and is cooperative.

5. Explain the idea of coaching. In sports, the leaders "coach" players to do their best, to practice skills with side assistance. In speech club, the librarian and club members "coach" or guide each other in helpful ways.

6. Talk about the merits of positive evaluation, not negative criticism. Ask students to write out at least one positive comment for speakers when formal speeches are given.

7. Set an atmosphere for a fun experience, but let kids know this is not a place for wild horsing around or rowdy behavior.

8. Give students opportunities to help you plan the club, but tell them that you as adult in charge may need to make adjustments to plans at times.

Quick Pick Speech Topics

- Everyone has a wacky relative. Tell us about one of yours.

- If you could join a circus, what entertainment would you choose to do?

- What appliance in your kitchen do you feel describes you the best?

- What was the best gift you ever gave to someone?

- If you could turn into an animal, what would it be?

- You have been given a magic fortune cookie. What fortune do you wish you would find inside?

- You are going on a trip around the world, but you can only take your backpack. What would you put inside, and why?

- On your birthday you can choose your favorite dinner in a restaurant in town. Where would you go, and what would you order?

- You want to start your own business next summer. What will the business do, and how will you start it?

- An airline ticket arrives in the mail addressed to you. When you open the envelope, you discover that it's a ticket to anywhere you want to go over summer vacation. Where will you go and why?

- Heroes aren't always celebrities. Tell us about a hero of yours who is not well known.

- Tell us why phone books are fun to read.

- You have just been given an Academy Award as Best Actor or Actress in a film. Give us your acceptance speech.

From *Story Celebrations: A Program Guide for Schools and Libraries* by Jan Irving.
Westport, CT: Libraries Unlimited. Copyright © 2008.

9

Chew on This: Healthy Eating Kids Like

While eating a carrot will not literally turn a person into a carrot, there is truth in saying "you are what you eat." Humorous consequences of eating too much spaghetti or making a pizza the size of the sun, as described by talented poets Shel Silverstein and Jack Prelutsky, cause kids to laugh. But eating a diet of too much junk food is no laughing matter. Overweight children in the United States now number 20 percent. Could this grow to 25 percent by 2010?

What contributes to this scary phenomenon? How many ads can you name that make burgers and fries sound tempting? What expressions encourage listeners to eat even more of these foods? How many commercials extol the virtues of carrots and yogurt? Answering these questions gives young people much to think about.

It's a fact that sugar and fat sell. Sugared cereals will probably not go away—not in the near future, anyway. More chips loaded with fat fill grocery shelves every year. Check out grocery store shelf space devoted to sugared cereals. Write down all the different kinds on one aisle. How many varieties of chips can you list? Make a grocery list of every variety you can find. Ask kids to tell you what they learn from this basic research. Unless parents and educators help children make better food choices, consuming junk food is hard to resist.

Nutrition is a hot topic today. In the past, nutrition education simply promoted eating from the four food groups of meat and fish, milk products, fruits and vegetables, and grains and bread. Today, since the introduction of the new food pyramid in 1994, the focus is more defined and more complex. An illustration of the pyramid, with helpful suggestions, appears at http://kidshealth.org/kid/stay_healthy/food/pyramid.html. Some experts (including the Kids Health Web site) suggest even finer distinctions—what "a serving" of food means, healthy fats versus trans fats, the difference between recommended servings for men and for women.

Practices and policies in American schools are moving to address the most current findings. Progress varies from state to state. Nutritional education programs vary widely, from the comprehensive California guidelines to sketchy standards in most other states. A typical standard prior to 2006 might state that schools encourage healthy eating in the cafeteria or provide for free breakfast. By contrast, California's guidelines enumerate nutrition competences and describe specific learning activities by grade level.

Generally, attitudes about food and nutrition improvement lag behind the availability of current information in books and Internet sources. At the beginning of the twenty-first century, school cafeterias represented a wide range of practices. In some districts, vending machines with carbonated soft drinks were taken out of elementary schools, but allowed in high schools. Schools not selling junk food might allow local PTA groups to sell it as a fundraiser. Other districts set up salad bars, offered "light plates" of fruit and cottage cheese, and promoted "cool food" programs. A milestone act brought about real change.

One section of the Child Nutrition and WIC Reauthorization Act of 2004 required that all school districts participating in the National School Lunch Program have local wellness policies by July 2006. These policies include goals for nutrition education, physical activity, and nutrition guidelines, with a plan for implementation. While the new law does not specify details, it required that policies be in place by the beginning of the 2006 school year.

This chapter provides information and fun activities in a lighthearted style so that students will be energized rather than bored or turned off by the topic. In this chapter you'll find a bibliography of print sources on the topic of nutrition for children from upper elementary grades through middle school. More nonfiction titles are listed than fiction, and a few picture books of interest to this age group have been included. Several titles specifically address a young adult audience, because upper elementary kids today consider themselves in this age group. The bibliography is selective, and the sources listed are some of the best books on the topic. Take note of the book *Chew on This* as you prepare activities on this theme. It is a unique title that directly addresses the topic of the dangers of eating a diet filled with fast food. Related areas such as food disorders are not covered, although you may wish to address these topics in health classes. Pertinent Web sites are also included.

The school program "Food for Thought," planned for a school media center, describes learning center activities to engage kids in lively interactive approaches. Writing, speaking, cooking, and doing art address some of the different learning styles of children. The inspiration for these activities is grounded in California's nutrition guidelines, but the actual descriptions are original.

The public library program "Cool Kids Cooking" capitalizes on kids' fascination with food preparation and eating. Four cooking stations are set up in the library, with suggestions to modify the program according to local resources.

Although this topic has a serious side, both programs avoid a didactic approach, so that young people will be motivated to learn through enjoyable activities and perhaps change their attitudes about food as they grow.

Bibliography

Barrett, Judi. *Cloudy with a Chance of Meatballs.* Atheneum, 1978.
(Reading Level: Accelerated Learner, 4.3)
    This modern classic picture book imagines that food comes to the citizens of Chewandswallow through strange weather patterns. The exaggerated text, accompanied by hilarious illustrations, can best be appreciated by older children.

Barron, Rex. *Showdown at the Food Pyramid.* G. P. Putnam's Sons, 2004.
(Reading Level: Accelerated Reader, 4.3)
    In this lively picture book for younger and older kids, junk foods take over the food pyramid. As Candy Bar and Donut knock healthy foods off the top of the pyramid, fruits, veggies, grains, and meat cooperate to rebuild the pyramid, which has collapsed under the weight of the junk food.

Bass, Jules. *Cooking with Herb, the Vegetarian Dragon: A Cookbook for Kids.* Barefoot Books, 1999.
(Reading Level: N.A.)
    Twenty-two delicious recipes with amusing titles appear, with tips and brief narratives appropriate to each recipe. The whimsical illustrations add to the fun. Recipes are created for vegetarians who eat eggs and dairy products. The clever acronym the author coins is LOVE—Lacto-Ova-Veggie-Eaters.

Faiella, Graham. *The Food Pyramid and Basic Nutrition: Assembling the Building Blocks of a Healthy Diet.* Rosen Publishing, 2005.
(Reading Level: Accelerated Reader, 8.8)
    Brief chapters describe the elements of nutrition, digestion, metabolism, and the food guide pyramid. This source will be useful in science reports as well as in nutrition education. The formula for calculating a person's body mass index is included.

Gregson, Susan R. *Healthy Eating.* Capstone, 2000.
(Reading Level: Accelerated Reader, 6.0)
    Appealing photos and format complement the text, which discusses how foods are used in our bodies and how to make healthy eating part of a kid's lifestyle. Illuminating scenarios, such as a boy losing his temper because he missed lunch, will show young people real-life situations to influence their choices.

Haduch, Bill. *Food Rules: The Stuff You Munch, Its Crunch, Its Punch, and Why You Sometimes Lose Your Lunch.* Dutton, 2001.
(Reading Level: Accelerated Reader, 6.1)
    This informative text approaches the topic with zany humor and sprightly writing. Sidebars, numerous cartoon illustrations, and wordplay will appeal to kids in super ways. Parts of the book, such as the "Using Chyme" section, can be used with activities in chapter 7, "Gross Science."

Jukes, Mavis, and Lilian Cheung. *Be Healthy! It's a Girl Thing; Food Fitness and Feeling Great.* Crown, 2003.
(Reading Level: Accelerated Reader, 7.4)
    Sidebars, format, and appealing covers combine with a chatty, informative text to guide young teens in eating healthy food. The authors' "Cactus Plan" illustrates specific suggestions for forming healthy habits.

Kelley, True. *School Lunch.* Holiday House, 2005.
(Reading Level: Accelerated Reader, 3.3)
    In this picture book with wide reader appeal, the lunch lady Harriet goes on vacation. Instead of her nutritious and delicious meals, the students endure a dreadful number of gross or outrageous meals from substitute cooks.

Krizmanic, Judy. *The Teen's Vegetarian Cookbook.* Viking, 1999.
(Reading Level: Fleisch-Kincaid, 8.7)
    Loaded with recipes and suggestions for breakfast, lunch, dinner, and snacks, this cookbook also provides a useful substitution chart for young vegetarians who don't like milk, tofu, grains, or leafy green vegetables.

Landau, Elaine. *A Healthy Diet.* Franklin Watts, 2003.
(Reading Level: N.A.)
    This easy-to-read text will be helpful in doing basic research on nutrients, the food pyramid, and the importance of exercise. A glossary and bibliography are included as well as several Web sites.

Pierson, Stephanie. *Vegetables Rock! A Complete Guide for Teenage Vegetarians.* Bantam, 1999.
(Reading Level: Fleisch-Kincaid, 9.3)
    Solid information, tips, and dozens of recipes help teens who make this nutrition choice for their lives. This kid-friendly guide encourages those interested in becoming vegetarian and addresses the topic humorously.

Prelutsky, Jack. *A Pizza the Size of the Sun.* Greenwillow, 1996.
(Reading Level: Fleisch-Kincaid, 7.5)
    Humorous poems on all topics include several about food that upper elementary and middle school students will enjoy.

Rosen, Michael J., ed. *Food Fight: Poets Join the Fight Against Hunger with Poems to Favorite Foods.* Harcourt Brace, 1996.
(Reading Level: N.A.)
Forty-five poems from American's best-loved poets celebrate food for young people. This project is sponsored by Share Our Strength, an antihunger organization.

Salter, Charles A. *The Nutrition-Fitness Link.* Milbrook Press, 1993
(Reading Level: N.A.)
This book for teens active in sports focuses on nutrition and dietary guidelines from a more specific perspective than most books. Traditional myths such as eating large amounts of meat prior to sports participation are exploded. Pros and cons of some foods are presented so that kids can make their own decisions.

Schlosser, Eric, and Charles Wilson. *Chew on This: Everything You Don't Want to Know about Fast Food.* Houghton Mifflin, 2006.
(Reading Level: Accelerated Reader, 8.1)
Here, in the teen version of the popular adult book *Fast Food Nation,* young people can read the horrifying facts and stories behind the fast food they devour and how teen obesity can shorten their lives. The eye-opening facts about advertising gimmicks and how people spend their money on burgers and fries give students plenty of information for discussions, public speaking, and changing their lives.

Scott, Emily, and Catherine Duffy. *Dinner from Dirt: Ten Meals Kids Can Grow and Cook.* Gibbs, Smith, 1998.
(Reading Level: N.A.)
This unique approach to healthy eating combines gardening and meal preparation. The illustrations and attractive page layouts add to the appeal of such meals as a "Sandwich Garden," "Salad Garden," "Pizza Garden," "Stir Fry Garden," and "Soup Garden."

Swinden, Liz. *Look Great, Feel Good.* Franklin Watts, 1997.
(Reading Level: N.A.)
This book on health and hygiene covers more than healthy eating. Food and behavior are linked. Sidebars and personal stories will attract young people.

Ward, Brenda C., and Jane Cabaniss Jarrell. *Good 'n' Healthy.* Word Publishing, 1995.
(Reading Level: Fleisch-Kincaid, 3.3)
Part of the Teachable Moments Cookbooks for Kids series, this spiral-bound cookbook targets teaching values along with preparing healthy food in a family setting. It reinforces math and language skills and encourages sequential thinking. It also incorporates religious thinking, such as the importance of praying with children. While particularly useful for religious schools and parents who homeschool, the general principles and recipes have wider appeal.

Westcott, Patsy. *Diet and Nutrition.* Raintree Steck-Vaughn, 2000.
(Reading Level: N.A.)
This clearly written introductory book about food groups and the importance of vitamins and minerals uses color photographs and numerous charts. Upper elementary students will be attracted to the photos of kids their own age as they participate in sports and enjoy good food.

World Book's Managing Your Teenage Life: Eating for Health. Word Book, 2003.
(Reading Level: N.A.)
This informative text briefly covers over two dozen topics on food and related issues such as weight, eating disorders, and vegetarianism. Numerous pictures, sidebars, and an attractive layout contribute to the book's appeal.

Selected Web Sites

Annie Appleseed Project: www.annieappleseedproject.org
   Nonprofit organization for people who have cancer or are interested in alternative medicine. Many links to food and nutrition, including an excellent listing of vitamin sources in different foods.

Center for Nutrition Policy and Promotion: www.usda.gov/cnpp
   Sponsored by the U.S. Department of Agriculture, this site has spotlights on the food pyramid for kids, with interactive tools

Center for Young Women's Health: www.youngwomenshealth.org
   Sponsored by Children's Hospital Boston. Includes health guides, quizzes, and information on food and fitness.

Keep Kids Healthy: www.keepkidshealthy.com
   A pediatrician's guide for parents (and teachers), with guidelines and numerous links about nutrition.

Food for Thought: A School Program

This program is planned for a school media center as an adjunct to the school nutrition curriculum, where the librarian and teachers work together. Classroom teachers in grades 4 through 8 can use the activities, making adaptations for their specific grade level. The school media specialist sets up learning centers, adding others as needed. Over several sessions, students work to complete the activities, then present their projects with the other groups. Ideas for the following centers were inspired by nutrition competencies and learning activities developed by the California Department of Education.

The program is planned for three class sessions, with the librarian introducing the topic during the first meeting. Students are given a second class period to research and plan their projects based on the different learning centers set up in the media center. During the third meeting, students present their projects. An additional meeting might be needed if the class is large.

Materials Needed

Students provide their own materials for projects as suggested:

Food Skit Center I: Access to computers and space to practice skits.

Food Skit Center II: A copy of the book *Cloudy with a Chance of Meatballs,* access to computers, and space to practice the skit.

Cookbook Center: Display of cookbooks in the library. Students purchase food and partly assemble it at home. For the fruit tart recipe on page 171, you need a purchased baked pie shell with fruit (one pint of strawberries, one-half pint of blueberries, one can of mandarin oranges, one can of pineapple slices, one kiwi, sliced, and one-quarter cup of apricot or peach preserves, melted).

Food Journal Center: A loose-leaf notebook for students to add their journal pages to. The completed notebook is kept in the media center.

Ad Writing/Art Project Center: Copies of old magazines such as *Family Circle, Woman's Day,* or *Good Housekeeping*; local newspapers; and poster board for each student to make a poster.

Ethnic Cookbook Center: A basket filled with slips of paper with different cultures/geographical places written on them (Caribbean Islands, Central America, Mexico, Spain, Brazil, East Africa,

North Africa, South Africa, West Africa, China, Japan, Thailand, Korea, Israel, Lebanon). Collection of ethnic cookbooks from the media center. *Note:* Lerner Publications' Easy Menu Ethnic Cookbooks are excellent. A loose-leaf notebook to compile each students' recipes and interviews. If students prepare food to bring to class, they will compile their own ingredient list and cook at home.

Copies of the following books: *Cloudy with a Chance of Meatballs, Showdown at the Food Pyramid,* and one of Norah Dooley's books (*Everybody Serves Soup* or *Everybody Brings Noodles*).

Procedure

Before You Begin

1. Set up learning centers as follows:

    • Food Skit Centers: access to computers and a copy of the book *Cloudy with a Chance of Meatballs.*

    • Cookbook Center: Display of cookbooks.

    • Food Journal Center: Loose-leaf notebook.

    • Ad Writing/Art Project Center: copies of old magazines, posterboard

    • Ethnic Cookbook Center: A breadbasket with names of cultures written on index cards or slips of paper for students to choose their projects and a substantial collection of cookbooks such as the Lerner series Easy Menu Ethnic Cookbooks (second editions).

2. Prepare a display of informational food books and cookbooks (see bibliography on pages 164–66 for some ideas and select books from your library's collection).

3. Gather books needed for read-aloud (e.g., *Cloudy with a Chance of Meatballs*)

First Meeting

1. Briefly introduce some of the titles on your display to students.

2. Read a short humorous book such as *Showdown at the Food Pyramid,* by Rex Barron (Putnam, 2004), about the food pyramid, or a book about ethnic food. Norah Dooley's books are good choices. Her most recent titles are *Everybody Serves Soup* (Carolrhoda, 2004) and *Everybody Brings Noodles* (Carolrhoda, 2005).

3. A food game may be played. (See Food Games section on page 170 for specific ideas.)

4. Have students choose a project from one of the food learning centers (pp. 169–70).

5. As a group, students begin working on the projects in class.

Second Meeting

1. Students work on their projects.

Third (and Possibly Fourth) Meeting(s)

1. Students present their projects.

Food Learning Centers

Food Skit Center I—The Food Pyramid

Write a script or create a skit based on the book *Showdown at the Food Pyramid*. This can be written as a play or as a readers' theatre script, with narrators reading the background or telling the story. Add nasty dialogue for the different junk food characters—donuts, candy bars, cookies. Make up songs or chants for the fatty foods—hot dogs, French fries, and chips. Add conversations between the vegetables and fruits about how they might overturn the unhealthy food. Make up dialogue for the meats and grains as they take on leadership roles in rearranging the whole pyramid back in its proper place.

Practice reenacting the story from your script and plan simple costumes if you wish.

Food Skit Center II—Cloudy with a Chance of Food Storms

Using the book *Cloudy with a Chance of Meatballs* as inspiration, write a weather report for a rain shower of lunch ingredients. Add segments to the basic weather report, with several "on-site" reporters interviewing local residents about what they plan to do with the ingredients raining in their yards.

Write the weather report and added news segments and practice aloud in preparation for a class performance.

Cookbook Writing and Cooking Center

Study healthy food cookbooks (choose from the display in the media center) and plan three dinner menus. Each menu should incorporate all the food groups described in the food pyramid. Prepare at least one recipe for each menu and distribute samples to the entire class. Compile the menus and recipes into a class cookbook to keep in the school library.

Food Journal Writing Center

Keep a food journal of everything you eat for one day. Write an evaluation of your eating habits compared to the guidelines in the food pyramid. Select several representatives to make a joint presentation to the class about your group's findings.

Ad Writing and Art Project Center

Make several poster collages of food ads found in magazines and newspapers. One collage could contain unhealthy foods and another could focus on healthy food ads. Then make individual posters on fruits, vegetables, grains, and fish or meat with slogans and ad copy. Choose one or more members of your group to explain the posters to your entire class, and display the posters in the library.

Ethnic Cookbook Writing and Cooking Center

Draw a slip of paper with the name of a culture that has been placed in the class "bread basket of the world." Research the culture for a class report and describe its food and some typical recipes for a class report in three or four pages. If you have family members or neighbors from this culture, interview them about their favorite foods for extra credit. Gather the recipes from each member of your group for a class cookbook. If possible, prepare two or three foods from the cookbooks to bring for each class member to enjoy a taste.

Food Learning Centers (*Continued*)

Food Games

"Name That Food Group": The librarian will call out the name of a food such as "noodles," and you must respond with the name of the food group in the food pyramid that applies. Noodles, for example, are in the grains group. Here are some foods and their food groups to include: zucchini (vegetable group), watermelon (fruit group), tomatoes (vegetable group), shrimp (meat group), and bagels (grains group).

"On the Ball": This is the reverse of the previous game, with the addition of a ball. The librarian tosses a medium-sized ball (not as small as a tennis ball or as large as a basketball) to students seated in a circle. As the ball is tossed, the leader calls out a food group such as "grains," and the student catching the ball names a food within that group.

"Vitamin Trivia": The librarian as cheerleader calls out a vitamin by its letter in this manner, "Give me a (C) (A) (K) . . . " then points to a student, who names a food source of that vitamin."

From *Story Celebrations: A Program Guide for Schools and Libraries* by Jan Irving. Westport, CT: Libraries Unlimited. Copyright © 2008.

Suggested Recipes for Kids to Make for Class Cooking Centers

Healthy Fruit Tart

Ingredients

2 prepared pie shells

fruit assortment:

> 1 can mandarin oranges
>
> ½ pint of fresh strawberries
>
> ½ pint fresh blueberries
>
> 1 kiwi, sliced
>
> 1 can pineapple slices
>
> ¼ cup apricot or peach preserves

Directions

1. Bake pie shell and bring to school.

2. Cut up fruit in bite-sized portions (slices of strawberries, half slices of pineapple rings, leave blueberries and mandarin orange pieces whole)

3. Arrange fruit attractively in a circular fashion in the pie shell just before you serve.

4. Heat the preserves in a microwave oven (usually available in a teacher's lounge) and pour over the arranged fruit.

Healthy Vegetable Stir Fry

Ingredients

    1 tbsp cooking oil

    1 green bell pepper, chopped

    1 carrot, sliced thinly

    ½ cup fresh broccoli, chopped

    ½ cup red cabbage or Chinese cabbage, sliced thinly

    1 celery stalk, sliced

    1 cup miniature corn (canned Chinese variety)

    1 red bell pepper, chopped

    ½ cup fresh bean sprouts (optional)

    1 slice fresh ginger, grated or ½ tsp. ground ginger

    1 cup canned chicken broth

    ½ tbsp cornstarch

    1 tbsp soy sauce

    ½ tsp sesame oil (optional)

Directions

1. Heat oil in electric skillet or wok.

2. Carefully add vegetables and cook quickly in oil. (*Note:* Add the bean sprouts and corn at the end since they don't take as much time to cook.) The vegetables should be crisp-tender, so total cooking time will be about 5 minutes.

3. Stir in the broth, cornstarch, and soy sauce. Sir until the sauce thickens.

4. Add the splash of sesame oil just before you serve the vegetables.

This recipe is healthy, vegetarian, and adapted from Chinese cookbooks.

Cool Kids Cooking: A Public Library Program

This public library program encourages healthy eating through cooking and tasting food from the different food groups. Involve participants in planning this program by having a few kids shop for food ahead of time, and ask for their ideas in setting up the food stations. Introduce the program by reading some of the picture books that treat the topic of nutrition in a lighthearted manner. Kids never appreciate a didactic approach to learning , and they expect a public library program to be fun. You can introduce this age group to cookbooks and books on healthy eating as it applies to feeling great and looking good. Because many preteen kids become interested in vegetarian eating, you can also use this opportunity to set up a display of books on this topic.

Materials Needed

Food for the veggie sandwich food stations and salad bar

- **Veggie Sandwich Station**

  - ½ bagel per person
  - ½ tortilla per person
  - 1 pita bread half per person
  - 1 jar peanut butter
  - 4 apples
  - 1 green bell pepper and 1 red bell pepper
  - 1 eight-ounce carton of cream cheese
  - 1 sliced cucumber
  - 1 bunch of fresh parsley
  - 1 can of garbanzo beans
  - 2 cups of shredded lettuce
  - 2 chopped tomatoes
  - 1 bottle of low fat ranch dressing and 1 bottle of low fat Italian dressing

- **Salad Bar Station**

  - 3 bags of torn lettuce
  - 1 bag of spinach leaves
  - 2 cups of shredded red cabbage
  - 1 each, green, yellow, and red bell peppers
  - 3 chopped tomatoes
  - 1 chopped cucumber
  - 1 bunch of green onions
  - 1 1-pound package of carrots, peeled and shredded
  - ¼ cup of sesame oil
  - ¼ cup of vegetable oil
  - 2 to 3 tablespoons of soy sauce
  - ¼ cup of rice vinegar (or apple cider vinegar)
  - 4 to 6 cups of cooked pasta (curly, shells, or corkscrew shapes)

Small paper plates, napkins, and plastic forks.

Health-oriented cookbooks and recipes for soups, salads, and sandwiches, to give you inspiration.

Chopping boards and knives if kids will do this part of the preparation. Or you can do this before the program for less mess.

Copies of the three Veggie Bingo Boards (pp. 177–79) and note cards with the titles B-Broccoli and all the other game spaces shown on the sample bingo games. A small bag of pinto or navy beans for game tokens.

Procedure

Before You Begin

1. You may wish to have children preregister for this program to ensure you have enough food on hand.

2. Choose recipes for food stations and make a list of ingredients you'll need.

3. Shop for food for the food stations as well as paper plates and cups.

4. Assemble any cooking utensils if program participants will be preparing the food.

5. Photocopy bingo boards, make index cards as described above, and purchase a small bag of dried beans (pinto, navy, for example) for game tokens.

The Day of the Program

1. Set up the food stations on long tables with ingredients and utensils (Many libraries have kitchens or sinks in their program rooms. If these facilities are not available, you may simplify the program with some food demonstrations by volunteers and set up ingredients for kids to make simple recipes.)

2. Read one of the suggested picture books or booktalk several books about healthy diets found in the bibliography of this chapter.

3. Play a game of Veggie Bingo. See the Bingo Boards on pages 177–79.

4. Divide participants into two groups so that each food station is fairly equal in size. Six to eight per group is ideal. If more than sixteen kids attend the program, you may need to set up an additional salad bar station.

5. Instruct groups to prepare foods as they consult the recipes and instructions on the table. They may sample the food, but should prepare extra servings so that everyone will be able to have a taste.

6. At the end of food preparation time (about twenty minutes), have each group "advertise" its concoction and pass out small tastes to the rest of the kids at the program. Share some of the sample slogans on pages 175–76, and encourage children to create their own slogans, jingles, and songs.

7. Allow twenty minutes for this tasting and sharing. Kids will enjoy reading the food puns and jokes and making up their own during the program.

8. Allow five to ten minutes for participants to help clean up. This is an excellent opportunity for young people to learn that library programs may involve messy activities, but clean up is part of the program, too!

Literary Food

Because many tantalizing books about food are published every year, you may already have favorites. Two picture books about food that older children will enjoy are *Showdown at the Food Pyramid,* by Rex Barron (Putnam, 2004) and *School Lunch*, by True Kelley (Holiday House, 2005). These books are specifically about healthy eating. Numerous books about food (not necessarily on nutrition) may be found in this chapter's bibliography.

Food Stations

The Veggie Sandwich Kids

At this food station kids will prepare sandwiches using ingredients with no meat. Since some vegetarians eat eggs and milk, some recipes include these ingredients. Other vegetarians refrain from eating all dairy products and eggs, choosing only vegetables; fruits; and meat substitutes made from grains, legumes, and vegetables (such vegetarians are called vegans). Provide a variety of foods so kids can concoct their favorite combinations.

Make-It-Yourself Sandwich Creation Suggestions

1. Half a bagel (or a mini-bagel) spread with hummus or peanut butter, topped with apple slices or green and red pepper slices.

2. Tortillas spread with low fat cream cheese, chopped cucumbers, tomato chunks, and fresh herbs. Roll up tortillas and slice into one-inch pieces so everyone can have a bite.

3. Pita bread halves filled with garbanzo beans, lettuce, tomato, low fat ranch dressing, or an oil and vinegar dressing. Add shredded cheese if desired.

Kids can make their own hummus from a simple recipe or a mix and chop the vegetables to make this an active food preparation workshop.

Advertising the Veggie Sandwich Kids

Encourage kids to make up their own chants, cheers, jingles, or songs. Here are some ideas to inspire kids:

"Peas try our pea pods. Peas? Peas?"

"Barney's Green Beans, buy some today. You've been away from our market too long!"

"Rosie's Roasting Ears for Sale. So sweet you'll think they grew in heaven. And that's no corn!"

Salad Bar Slims

Participants at this food station concoct their own salad combinations. The make-it-yourself ideas below serve as guidelines, but young people will probably want to create their own sensations.

Make-It-Yourself Salad Creation Suggestions

1. Salad Garden Salads: lettuce, fresh spinach, shredded red cabbage, yellow and red peppers, tomato chunks, carrot coins, and fresh herbs with oil and vinegar or low fat ranch dressing.

2. Pasta-bility Salads: cooked shell or curly pasta; chopped green onion; chopped cucumber; chopped green or red pepper; shredded carrots; and a dressing of cider vinegar, sugar, salt, pepper, garlic salt, and mustard.

3. Oriental Salads: cooked fine noodles such as vermicelli or softened cellophane noodles, green onions, strips of peppers, shredded carrots, and fresh spinach with a dressing of sesame oil and teriyaki sauce.

For a more active workshop experience, ask children to chop the ingredients, and provide salad dressing ingredients with small jars for mixing. A cautionary note: You may want to chop ingredients before the program or have older students do this for you.

Advertising Salad Slims

Encourage participants to make up their own chants, cheers, jingles, or songs. Here are a few slogans to inspire kids:

"Lettuce serve you at our Salad Bar!"

"Olive the kids you know will love our salad fixings!"

"What is a rich woman's favorite salad? Answer: 24 carrots (carats)."

"What kind of cabbage should be eaten raw? Cole slaw. Try ours today!"

"Lettuce dress your salad! Sally's Designer Salad Bar!"

Bingo

Note: The leader should distribute game boards and handfuls of dried beans to each participant. Then the leader draws cards, one at a time, from a box or bag, reading the cards aloud, such as "B—Broccoli * Vitamins A & C," "I—Cantaloupe* Vitamins A & C." Students place dried beans on their game boards when the name read matches the square on their board. Play continues until someone has a vertical, horizontal, or lateral line of five tokens on the board, making a "B-I-N-G-O." Note that an asterisk denotes food containing more than one vitamin.

Vitamin Bingo Card 1

B	I	N	G	O
Broccoli* Vitamins A & C	Cantaloupe* Vitamins A & C	Strawberries Vitamin C	Tomato* Vitamins C and A	Oranges* Vitamins C & K
Milk Vitamin D	Yogurt Vitamin D	Asparagus Vitamin A	Green pepper Vitamin A	Peaches Vitamin A
Potatoes Vitamin C	Brown Rice* Vitamins B & D	Eggs* Vitamins A, B & D	Beef Liver* Vitamins A & B & E	Grapes Vitamin K
Corn Vitamin E	Tuna Vitamin D	Peanuts* Vitamin B & E	Carrots Vitamin A	Whole Grain Cereal Vitamin B
Peas Vitamin B	Yogurt Vitamin K	Oatmeal Vitamin E	Grapefruit* Vitamins C & K	Kiwi Vitamin C

Vitamin Bingo Card 2

B	I	N	G	O
Kiwi Vitamin C	Cantaloupe* Vitamins A & C	Oranges* Vitamin C & K	Tomato* Vitamins C and A	Strawberries Vitamin C
Milk Vitamin D	Yogurt Vitamin D	Asparagus Vitamin A	Green pepper Vitamin A	Peaches Vitamin A
Potatoes Vitamin C	Brown Rice* Vitamins B & D	Eggs* Vitamins A, B & D	Beef Liver* Vitamins A & B & E	Grapes Vitamin K
Corn Vitamin E	Tuna Vitamin D	Peanuts* Vitamin B & E	Peas Vitamin B	Whole Grain Cereal Vitamin B
Carrots Vitamin A	Yogurt Vitamin K	Oatmeal Vitamin E	Grapefruit* Vitamins C & K	Broccoli* Vitamins A & C

From *Story Celebrations: A Program Guide for Schools and Libraries* by Jan Irving.
Westport, CT: Libraries Unlimited. Copyright © 2008.

Vitamin Bingo Card 3

B	I	N	G	O
Broccoli * Vitamins A & C	Tomato* Vitamin C & A	Strawberries Vitamin C	Cantaloupe* Vitamins A & C	Oranges* Vitamin C & K
Asparagus Vitamin A	Yogurt Vitamin D	Milk Vitamin D	Green pepper Vitamin A	Potatoes Vitamin C
Peaches Vitamin A	Brown Rice* Vitamins B & D	Eggs* Vitamins A, B & D	Beef Liver* Vitamins A & B & E	Grapes Vitamin K
Corn Vitamin E	Whole Grain Cereal Vitamin B	Peanuts* Vitamin B & E	Carrots Vitamin A	Tuna Vitamin D
Peas Vitamin B	Yogurt Vitamin K	Oatmeal Vitamin E	Grapefruit* Vitamins C & K	Kiwi Vitamin C

10

Is This Goodbye?: Studying Endangered Animals

Children are wild about animals. They often want pets, from typical ones like dogs and cats to more exotic species like lizards and birds from the rainforest. They flock to zoos to see animals from far reaches of the world, often because they may never travel to an African savannah or to Australia. They read stories about endangered animals from wolves to condors, and they become concerned. This topic does not need to be "sold" to students. Because young people already care about endangered animals, they will be automatically interested in finding out more and in participating in activities suggested in this chapter.

Some of the areas students will encounter in their research involve controversial matters. Environmentalists provide impressive studies regarding the dangers of global warming for animal species in arctic areas of the world. Many people choose to ignore those warnings, argue about the scientific basis of the premise, and may even become hostile about such scientific findings. Drilling for oil in Alaska concerns naturalists who care about animals living there. Oil companies generally discount these arguments because they say "people need oil" and also because they stand to profit from the drilling. Some nations and religious groups become edgy about talk of overpopulation in the world, whereas naturalists like Jeff Corwin warns, "If the global population of human beings continues to grow at such an astronomical rate, it will only be a matter of a few more decades before our planet is no longer adequately fortified with the natural resources to sustain us." Corwin insists it's not too late for wildlife in places like Africa because nongovernmental (and governmental) organizations are working hard on conservation efforts.

As an educator, you have a special part to play as students pursue research on this subject. You can guide children to well-written articles, books, and Internet sites. You can search for answers to troublesome questions, and you can help kids sort through research that is too biased or opinionated to be of value. You can also teach by example that finding easy answers is never a wise approach. And you can warn against such negative thinking that young people begin to despair that it's too late for change to be made. Even the most concerned scientists and environmental advocates, such as former Vice President Al Gore, point to hopeful trends in our complex, challenging world. Level-headed thinking and genuine concern are admirable. Panic doesn't solve problems.

Some areas that you will want to explore with students include these factors contributing to animals becoming endangered: pollution, nonbiodegradable waste, global warming, over-hunting, poaching, overpopulation, and introducing non-native animals to other areas of the world. Kids need to know some history of conservation in the United States and in the world. They should research private conservation groups such as the World Wildlife Federation and government agencies like the U.S. Fish and Wildlife Service in the Department of the Interior; encourage them to check the Web sites of these organizations for up-to-date information.

This subject is a lively one in which information becomes quickly outdated. Many books found in reputable libraries were published about fifteen years ago, but they have not been revised as of the publication of this book. Fortunately you can find more current information through Internet sources and magazine indexes, such as the SIRS *Discoverer* subscription database. A few of these articles are listed along with books in this chapter's bibliography. I have not included many books on specific endangered animals; rather, I have cited atlases of animal groups or books that describe many animals.

The two programs created for this chapter capitalize on older kids' interest in "cool" lingo to talk about the topic. "E.S. World Link," the school program, describes a student newspaper titled *The W.W. Report,* because young people use acronyms constantly in their fascination with text messaging and in their daily conversations. The suggested television talk show *Animals in Jeopardy* builds on the popularity of a television game show and various nature programs. Having students interview one another and videotape the results of this presentation gives them practice in oral literacy. There are other academic benefits to doing research for the school program. This topic, in particular, requires that students use higher order thinking skills, sort out facts from opinions, and recognize propaganda techniques.

Note that there are two different levels for schools. Younger students in grades 4 and 5 will do mapping projects and simple reports. The newspaper and talk show programs are designed for older students in grades 6 through 8.

"The E. S. Kids Club," the public library program, will appeal to young people particularly interested in wildlife and the natural world. It is set up as a program series in which young people plan their own meetings under the guidance of a librarian. Different nature games and creative dramatics are offered along with general suggestions for program planning according to the interests and budgets of individual libraries and communities.

Bibliography

Anderson, Bob. *Endangered Species: Understanding Words in Context.* Greenhaven Press, 1991. (Reading Level: Flesch-Kincaid, 7.8)

    Part of the Opposing Viewpoints Juniors series, this brief text discusses four questions about endangered species, including "Should endangered species be saved?" and "Are humans responsible?" For each question, two viewpoints are given.

Corwin, Jeff. *Living on the Edge: Amazing Relationships in the Natural World.* Rodale, 2003. (Reading Level: Flesch-Kincaid, 12.0)

    Although the text is intended for adult readers, this fascinating account of a television naturalist's journeys to Africa, Arizona, and Central and South America is such a lively read that teachers and librarians will want to read portions aloud to students interested in saving parts of the natural world that have many endangered species living in them.

Dobson, David. *Can We Save Them?: Endangered Species of North America.* Charlesbridge, 1997. (Reading Level: Accelerated Reader, 6.2)

    This brief discussion of twelve endangered species poses questions about animals such as peregrine falcons and gray bats and includes several plant species as well. It also describes the various environments in North America.

Jenkins, Steve. *Almost Gone: The World's Rarest Animals.* HarperCollins, 2006.
(Reading Level: Accelerated Reader, 5.7)
      Jenkins, a Caldecott Honor illustrator, briefly describes twenty-eight animals that are either endangered or extinct. For each animal, he has created a stunning collage illustration. A world map locating the homes of all these animals appears at the end of the book.

Mackay, Richard. *The Penguin Atlas of Endangered Species.* Penguin Books, 2002.
(Reading Level: Flesch-Kincaid, 12.0)
      Although this text is advanced, teachers will find the discussion of animals and their habitats invaluable, along with the numerous color maps and lists of threatened species arranged by country.

Maynard, Thane. *Saving Endangered Mammals.* Watts, 1992.
(Reading Level: Flesch-Kincaid, 8.8)
      Arranged alphabetically by the names of endangered mammals of the world, this concise text describes the characteristics of each animal, its habitat, its size, its diet, and the threats to its existence. A general discussion of overall threats and efforts to conserve species will guide students researching this topic.

Pollock, Steve. *The Atlas of Endangered Animals.* Facts on File. 1993.
(Reading Level: Flesch-Kincaid, 9.7)
      Arranged by areas of the world, this concise atlas briefly discusses endangered animals and provides brief histories of each. The author includes the particular symbol set by the International Union for the Conservation of Nature (IUCN) for each animal, such as E = endangered, V = vulnerable, and T = threatened.

Swinburne, Stephen. *Once a Wolf: How Wildlife Biologists Fought to Bring Back the Gray Wolf.* Houghton Mifflin, 1999
(Reading Level: Accelerated Reader, 7.5)
      This gripping story of the gray wolf traces the history of wolves and their controversial relationship with people in the natural world. It relates the ways in which scientists have helped to preserve this once plentiful species that has recently been removed from the endangered species list.

Thacker, Paul D. "Come and Get It! It's Feeding Time at the San Diego Zoo." *The Christian Science Monitor* (January 7, 2003).
(Reading Level: Flesch-Kincaid, 6.7)
      Typical and unusual efforts to feed and grow food for endangered species at the zoo include feeding wax worms to birds, growing bamboo for pandas, and growing eucalyptus for koalas.

Vergoth, Harin, and Christopher Lampton. *Endangered Species.* rev. ed. Watts, 1999.
(Reading Level: Accelerated Reader, 9.1)
      This detailed account explains how and why species become endangered and extinct and ways in which people can help threatened species. Full-color photographs and a glossary add to the useful text.

Weir, Kirsten. "Quiet Forests." *Current Science* (December 6, 2002).
(Reading Level: Flesch-Kincaid, 5.5)
      Informative article about how illegal hunting in the African bush is endangering such species as forest antelope and leopards. Without these animals the entire ecosystem is threatened.

Yeh, Jennifer. *Endangered Species: Must They Disappear?* Thomson Gale, 2003.
(Reading Level: Flesch-Kincaid, 12.0)
      This advanced text is used by high school students, but it is an invaluable reference source for teachers and librarians working with this topic. It discusses endangered species and environments—all issues involved in an understanding of this area—as well as providing charts, maps, and a wealth of animal lists.

Selected Web Sites

Endangered Animals for Kids: www.fws.gov/endangered/kids/index.html
   Sponsored by the U.S. Fish and Wildlife Service, this site features links for teachers and kids about the Endangered Species Act and threatened species.

International Fund for Animals Welfare: www.ifaw.org
   Locate news stories about endangered animals by clicking on countries or regions on a map of the world.

Kids Planet: www.kidsplanet.org
   Web site of the Defenders of Wildlife has facts, games, and teacher ideas.

Kids Saving the Rainforest: www.kidssavingtherainforest.org
   A nonprofit organization founded by children in Costa Rica. Appealing pictures and information about animals in the rainforest include efforts to save the rainforests.

National Wildlife Federation: www.nwf.org/wildalive/index.html
   Resources of this well-respected group include information about specific animals, nature's web, and activities sponsored by this group.

Oracle Think Quest: http://library.thinkquest.org
   Innovative Web site with 6,500 sites for students. Several hundred links to endangered animals.

ES World Link: A School Program

ES World Link is the short name for "Endangered Species World Link," a multifaceted program that involves students from different grade levels in learning about specific endangered or threatened animals and where they live in the world. Younger children identify animals, learn basic terminology, and research those animals to write short reports for a library or classroom display. They make maps of the world for a large wall mural showing where endangered animals live. Older students turn their research into news reports and do an interactive talk show that can be presented to other classes or be videotaped for the school library

Three meetings are planned for younger students and three meetings are planned for older students. Each class session will last between forty-five and fifty minutes. Adjust this according to your school's schedule.

Materials Needed

Large wall maps of the world or an atlas and seven six-foot-long sheets of brown paper for making maps.

Colored markers for map making.

Computers and printers for writing reports and printing colored photographs of endangered animals.

Video equipment to tape the interactive television talk show (optional).

Procedure

Before You Begin

1. Find maps or purchase map-making supplies for the map exercise. Gather books for read-aloud (see first meeting notes for suggestions).

2. Photocopy handouts (pp. 187–93) for students.

3. Find a science teacher who can give a short talk on endangered animals for younger students during the first meeting.

First Meeting for Younger Students (Grades 4 and 5)

1. Read from one or more of the following books to introduce this topic: *The Great Kapok Tree,* by Lynne Cherry (Harcourt Brace Jovanovich, 1990), *Songs for Survival,* compiled by Nikki Siegen-Smith (Dutton Children's Books, 1996), or *Keepers of the Earth*, by Michael Caduto and Joseph Bruchac (stories such as "Awi Usdi, the Little Deer").

2. Have a science teacher talk to fourth and fifth graders about endangered animals.

3. Have younger students select animals (from the list on page 187) to research for the mapping project and begin research.

Second Meeting for Younger Students

1. Younger students work on their maps and reports.

Third Meeting for Younger Students

1. Younger students present their reports to the class, then display their maps on the wall murals.

First Meeting for Older Students (Grades 6–8)

1. Have a science teacher discuss endangered animals and environmental studies with older students.

2. Distribute the handout "Terms Students Need to Know" (p. 186) for background homework.

3. Give students assignments to participate in the "Animals in Jeopardy" project (pp. 191–93).

4. Students research their topics and write remarks for a preliminary taping the following day.

Second Meeting for Older Students

1. "Animals in Jeopardy" is given as an oral presentation in class. This can be taped, if desired.

2. Students sign up for assignments in compiling *The W.W. Report,* a class newspaper. They begin research.

Third Meeting for Older Students

1. Students finish research, write articles, and "publish" the paper.

Mapping the World of Endangered Animals

Divide your class into groups by areas of the world suggested below. Give each group a large map or a six-foot length of brown paper to create a map of the specific land mass it is assigned. Have each group research basic geography and climate of this area. Individuals within the group should find color photographs of the endangered (vulnerable, threatened, or rare) animals living in this area and display pictures of these animals on the map with the animal's name and its status on the endangered list. Display the maps around the room and place a composite map of the entire world on a table in the middle of the room.

Have students type class reports neatly on a single sheet of computer paper and place them in a notebook for library use. You can also have students give oral reports about the animals or have students keep animal journals for their reports.

Terms Students Need to Know

Give students the list of terms on page 188 to define for class discussion as you begin this program/unit. Add other terms as desired.

The W.W. Report: A Class Newspaper

Create sections for a class newspaper titled *The W.W. Report* (*World Wildlife Report*) and ask students to sign up for different assignments suggested on page 190. This newspaper could appear in an electronic or a printed version for other students to read.

Animals in Jeopardy: A Simulated Television Talk Show

Use this outline of a talk show with your students. The media specialist and a teacher or two students may serve as co-anchors. Students should be the panel of experts. (Names of the experts should be fictional.) Have other students prepare questions as audience members. All students must prepare for this exercise. Even the audience needs to be well informed, so they should research their questions before you tape or present this television talk show. Comments by the panel are not provided, as they need to be researched and written by your students. This format lends itself to videotaping.

Suggested Areas and Selected Animals

I. The United States and Canada
- Red wolf
- California condor
- Black-footed ferret
- Whooping crane

II. Central and South America
- Golden lion tamarin
- Giant anteater
- Manatee
- Jaguar
- St. Lucia Amazon parrot
- Spix's macaw
- Leatherback turtle

III. Europe
- Gray wolf
- Loggerhead turtle
- Dalmatian pelican

IV. Africa
- African elephant
- Nile crocodile
- Black rhinoceros
- Okapi
- Mountain gorilla
- Cheetah

V. Asia
- Cheetah (also in Africa)
- Bactrian camel
- Tiger (Siberian, Sumatran, and Chinese)
- Arabian oryx
- Snow leopard
- Asiatic lion
- Giant panda
- Orangutan
- Komodo dragon

VI. Australia
- Numbat
- Northern hairy-nosed wombat
- Kakapo

VIII. The Arctic and Antarctic
- Blue whale
- Polar bear

Terms Students Need to Know

1. biodiversity

2. captivity

3. biome

4. endangered

5. evolution

6. extinct

7. game reserve

8. habitat

9. habitat destruction

10. threatened

Symbols Set by the International Union for the Conservation of Nature (IUCN)

Ex = Extinct: Species has not been sighted in fifty years. Occasionally used for recently extinct species.

E = Endangered: Species is so low in numbers (or its habitat is so badly destroyed) that it will become extinct if nothing is done.

V = Vulnerable: Numbers are still numerous but species is under threat.

R = Rare: Animal found in only one or two places in the world.

I = Indeterminate: Animal known to be endangered, vulnerable, or rare but not enough information is known to place in a definite category.

K = Insufficiently Known: Animal may belong to one of the other categories but little information exists about the species.

CT = Commercially Threatened: Animal is numerous but is being hunted.

The World Alert

- Write a headline story about a weather condition or immediate threat to wildlife in a country or area of the world. Research a situation that has actually occurred during the past decade.

- Write a sidebar column about a weather condition or threat to wildlife fifty years ago for a historical perspective in understanding the lead story.

Help Column

- List and briefly discuss the major governmental and private environmental organizations around the world. Organizations you might include are: The U.S. National Park System, IUCN, World Wildlife Federation, U.S. Fish and Wildlife Service, The Wilderness Society, Center for Reproduction of Endangered Wildlife, Conservation International, Cousteau Society, National Audubon Society, The Nature Conservancy, Rain Forest Action Network, The Sierra Club

- List names and contact information for your state's organizations, governmental agencies and groups concerned with wildlife.

Most Wanted List

- Identify and describe the ten most endangered animals around the world or in one area of the world. Find photographs of these animals to display along with your listing. Tell where the animal can be found and why it is threatened or endangered.

Letters to the Editor

- As a concerned citizen, write one or more letters to the editor of *W.W. Report* about an animal you are concerned about. Briefly tell why you are concerned and suggest action to improve the situation, if you can.

- Response from the editor: After you have read the above letters, respond briefly to each one.

Animals in Jeopardy

Television Anchor: Hello, this is _____, your television co-host for Animals in Jeopardy. May I introduce my co-host, _____.

Co-Anchor: Thank you, _____. We are excited to have you with us this evening. Our topic is "Endangered Animals:

Will We Say Good-bye?" This series is brought to you by your local TV station and concerned citizens around the world.

Anchor: Before we introduce our panel of experts, I would like to give some background information to our audience here in the studio and to our audience all over the globe.

Hello Friends of Animals in Jeopardy! As you know, we all share this earth, a biosphere of living species, richly supplied with a diversity of life.

Co-Anchor: You mean, we are an enormous stew of stuff—thousands and thousands of plants and animals, different kinds of animals, that have to share this one planet.

Anchor: That's right. It's not simple. But we all depend on each other for food, shelter, and a way to survive.

Co-Anchor: Right! But it's not easy, is it?

Anchor: Right! Removal of even one species can set off a huge chain of events.

Co-Anchor: Could you give us an example?

Anchor: Yes, I can. Let's say we get rid of the leatherback turtle in oceans from the Caribbean to Australia. What happens?

Co-Anchor: OK, what happens?

Anchor: Big things! Did you know that the leatherback turtle is very important to the balance of nature? If this creature did not prey on jellyfish in the ocean, it would be a catastrophe.

Co-Anchor: Why?

Anchor: Because jellyfish would overpopulate the ocean, eat too much fish, and then there would not be enough fish for the rest of the world.

Co-Anchor: Wow! I see what you mean.

Anchor: The point is, we need a huge diversity of life on our Earth. We are all connected to one another in this fragile world of ours.

Co-Anchor: What can we do?

From *Story Celebrations: A Program Guide for Schools and Libraries* by Jan Irving. Westport, CT: Libraries Unlimited. Copyright © 2008.

191

Animals in Jeopardy (*Continued*)

Anchor: Let's ask our panel of experts, who have done extensive research on this topic!

Co-Anchor: May I introduce the following people to our audience: first, John Snow, professor of zoology at one of our leading universities; next, Anne Spring, Ph.D. research scientist for the Department of the Interior; next, Grace Brown, director of an independent think tank on environmental science; and finally, Dr. William Winterhouse, scientist, author, and speaker on endangered species of the world. Who would like to introduce our topic?

Professor Snow: I will. Let me tell our audience about the web of life, and how all life is interrelated. Then I'll say a few words about the problem of endangered animals.

[Students have researched this topic and now present Professor Snow's remarks.]

Dr. Winterhouse: Professor Snow, may I comment next? I'd like to talk about the major threats to endangered species a little more specifically.

[Students have researched this topic and now present Dr. Winterhouse's comments and cover the areas of loss of habitat, global warming, and over-hunting.]

Anchor: Thank you Professor and Doctor. But isn't anything being done at all to help?

Grace Brown: Let me talk next about what government and private agencies exist and what legislation is in place. That may answer your question.

[Students have researched this topic and now present Grace Brown's comments.]

Anne Spring: Could I speak next? I'd like to tell you about what research labs and zoos are doing to help endangered species so that they won't become extinct.

[Students have researched this topic now present Anne Spring's remarks.]

Co-Anchor: Thank all of our experts, audience, with your applause. Now, what questions do you have for our panel?

[Students in the audience have researched these topics and formed their own questions. The following examples may guide them. After each question, one or more of the experts answer.]

Question 1: Isn't death just a part of the life cycle? Maybe it's not possible to save all endangered species, is it?

Question 2: I'm a logger. I could lose my job if any more forest area is put into a preserve. What about that?

Animals in Jeopardy (*Continued*)

Question 3: I'm a wilderness lover and I fish. I pay lots of money in fees to be able to enjoy my hobby. Isn't this money going to the government so they can re-stock rivers and lakes with enough fish?

Question 4: People will always break the law! Have laws outlawing poaching really done any good?

Question 5: I like my fur coat! Are you people trying to infringe upon my rights?

Question 6: Isn't all this talk about global warming exaggerated?

Question 7: I'm worried that the United States depends too much on foreign oil. Isn't it justified to drill for oil in Alaska?

Question 8: I've heard that some of these laws like the Endangered Species Act don't really work because animals become extinct anyway. What do you experts think?

Question 9: So what is the biggest threat to endangered species, anyway?

Question 10: What can we, as individual citizens, do to help?

Anchor: Thank you all for an exciting program. Next week we'll bring you another episode of Animals in Jeopardy. Join us!

The ES Kids Club:
A Program Series for Public Libraries

Older kids will enjoy using an acronym for this special club for kids interested in animals and wildlife. The ideas and procedures suggested here are not intended to be followed slavishly, but they serve as suggestions for typical activities young people enjoy doing. After a first meeting, guide students in planning subsequent events and programs. Some librarians may choose to preregister participants as a method of planning for enough supplies or snacks, if these will be provided. Other libraries think registration of any kind discourages walk-in participation. Consult your library's policies for parental permission forms if you plan to take kids on a trip to a local zoo or animal preserve. In many cases, it may be easier to bring the expert to your library.

Materials Needed

Depending upon what activities are selected:

Basic art supplies and poster board will be needed for the Poster Parade.

Computers and printers will be needed for printing color photographs of endangered animals from the Internet.

Snack food such as Rainforest Crunch and tropical juices or plain popcorn and apple slices, if desired.

Procedure

Before You Begin

1. Gather materials and prepare a display of books and various media for an initial meeting of The ES Kids Club (see pages 182–83 for books and other media).

2. Make copies of "Fifteen Nifty Things ES Kids Club Can Do" (p. 195) and have kids discuss their preferences.

On the Day

1. Hand out "Fifteen Nifty Things ES Kids Club Can Do" and have children select activities they wish to do. Tell them this series will be a three- (or four-) month series, so they will need to choose one to three activities from the list.

2. Decide with participants the length and frequency of meetings: once a month for three or four months, for example. Allow one hour per session.

3. Meetings are held according to the group's plan, but the librarian may need to change the plan as this program series progresses.

4. Plan a special event such as a storytelling performance for the public, a party, a library sleepover, or an awards evening with every member of the club receiving a certificate and small incentive for participating. Incentives might include a free book from a book exchange of club members, zoo passes, or discount coupons to visit a local museum of natural history or science.

Fifteen Nifty Things ES Kids Club Can Do

1. Write a tip sheet for ways to save energy and print copies to have available for library patrons.

2. Write an *ES Kids Newsletter* featuring different endangered species in every issue.

3. "Adopt" an acre of land in the rainforest or a tree in the rainforest. Check out this Web site about donations and adoptions: www.kidsavingtherainforest.org.

4. Earn money to help endangered animals or help rainforest concerns. Earn money by holding a bake sale, raking yards around town, pulling dandelions this summer, and so forth.

5. Do nature projects: Make bird feeders in winter. Start a butterfly garden on the library's lawn or somewhere in town in the summer.

6. Play nature games. (See pages 196–98 for ideas.)

7. Start wildlife or nature journals

8. Invite guest speakers (environmentalists, scientists, local wildlife experts).

9. Read books about different endangered animals to discuss with the group.

10. Decorate the library with pictures of endangered animals in our own country.

11. Write a play or a skit about endangered animals and perform it for the public.

12. Have a crafts day. Make posters for a poster parade. Each club member should choose an endangered animal to feature with a catchy phrase. Display the posters around town on Earth Day. Paint T-shirts. Make masks of endangered animals.

13. Visit a local animal preserve.

14. Read Native American tales about caring for the earth and its animals.

15. Start a rainforest or nature store to distribute books and information about endangered animals. Sell the young people's art and local artists' work featuring wildlife. Read about the Kids Saving the Rainforest organization at www.kidssavingtherainforest.org.

From *Story Celebrations: A Program Guide for Schools and Libraries* by Jan Irving.
Westport, CT: Libraries Unlimited. Copyright © 2008.

Nature Games

Rainforest Story

Read Lynne Cherry's *The Great Kapok Tree* to students. Seat kids in a storytelling circle and ask one to begin retelling the story from the beginning. After about one minute, say gently, "Thank you. Will the next person in our circle continue the story from this point?" Continue telling the story until it has been retold. Ask kids if they would like to change or add to the story. Retell the story again, giving children the opportunity to add dialogue. You may want to use a "storytelling stick" (a bamboo stick with seeds inside or an ordinary stick you have found) to pass from one child to the next as each child is encouraged to speak.

Arctic Story

After children have retold the rainforest story, begin another story set in the arctic. Describe the setting and explain that the polar ice caps are melting because of global warming. With participants seated in a story circle, ask one to take the part of an animal living in this biome. This child might say: "I'm penguin. I depend upon this cold world to live, to lay my eggs and protect them so the world will have penguins for not just my lifetime, but for years to come. Is any other animal out there concerned?" Some other animals are polar bears, Artic foxes, and caribou.

Have students continue in this manner until many animals have spoken about the threats to their environment. (You may want to have students browse books about arctic animals before you play this game. You could also give them fact sheets about animals from this part of the world.)

Web of Life Game

The purpose of this game is to increase participants' awareness of interdependence in an ecosystem. Write the names of different animals and plants on separate index cards. One child receives a card that says "tree." Give that child a ball of twine and instruct "the tree" to read the card then toss the ball of twine to another kid, who reads his or her card and tells how that species relates to "tree." Another card might read "squirrel," another might read "owl," and another might read "chipmunk." If the tree is in a tropical rainforest area the cards would read differently (e.g., "kapok tree," "anteater," "tree porcupine," and "sloth") . The first student should continue to play until everyone has had a turn at catching the twine. By this time the twine will be tangled and complex, graphic illustration of how interrelated all the species in the ecosystem are. You may also want to have a science teacher or a nature specialist from a park or an environmentalist talk to kids about the interdependence of species.

Ocean Action

Select a group of five or six kids to do a mini-drama for the rest of the group. Take them aside and explain that they will be silently acting out a "living ocean" environment. Some may want to mime ocean waves. Other may decide to build sand sculptures on the "beach" in front of the ocean. Others may mime creatures living in the water. After several minutes of play, the audience should ask questions that can only be answered by "yes" and "no" by the actors. How long will it take for the audience to guess what environment is being portrayed?

Endangered Animal Trivia Quiz

Prepare endangered animal question cards such as those on pages 197–98. Copy the question on one side of the card and the answer on the other. Award individual points or divide your group into teams. Or just play for the fun of it!

Sample Cards

1. When was the last California condor seen in the wild?
   a. 1900   b. 1955   c. 1987

2. Where have white rhinoceroses been bred most successfully?
   a. The U.S.   b. Africa   c. Asia

3. Leopards can climb trees, but they can't swim.
   True or False?

4. Giant pandas live on eucalyptus and bamboo.
   True or False?

5. What is the largest living lizard on earth?

6. What U.S. bird has been taken off the endangered species list recently because DDT has been banned for so long?

7. What Australian animal has become endangered because its food source is limited?

8. Name two birds that have become endangered because their plumes are sought for ornamental purposes.

9. What kind of U.S. wolf has become critically endangered?

10. What shy bird has recently been taught how to do a courtship dance by people dressed in bird costumes?

11. What turtle has existed for over a hundred million years but is now facing extinction?

12. What kind of camel found in the Gobi Desert is endangered?

13. About how many giant pandas live in the wild?
    a. 100   b. 500   c. 1,000

14. Pandas usually give birth to many pandas, but they are weak and die young.
    True or False?

15. The passenger pigeon was once endangered, but it has been successfully bred so that it is no longer on the endangered species list.   True or False?

16. The quagga, a kind of zebra, is now extinct.
    True or False?

17. The golden lion tamarin, a little Brazilian monkey, is endangered because rainforests are threatened.
    True or False?

18. Name an American crustacean that is endangered because many people like to eat it.

Number 1
Answer: c

Number 2
Answer: a.

Number 3
Answer: False

Number 4
Answer: False (They do not eat eucalyptus.)

Number 5
Answer: The komodo dragon

Number 6
Answer: The bald eagle

Number 7
Answer: Koalas, because they only eat eucalyptus

Number 8
Answer: Scarlet macaws and birds of paradise (other answers are possible)

Number 9
Answer: The red wolf

Number 10
Answer: The whooping crane

Number 11
Answer: The leatherback turtle

Number 12
Answer: The bactrian camel (the one with two humps)

Number 13
Answer: c

Number 14
Answer: False. Pandas do not have many offspring.

Number 15
Answer: False. It is extinct.

Number 16
Answer: True

Number 17
Answer: True

Number 18
Answer: The American lobster

Index

About the Author

JAN IRVING is a writer and consultant in the field of children's literature and library services. She was formerly a children's librarian and library supervisor in Iowa, Kansas, and Colorado. For more than twenty years she has been active in ALA, and has presented workshops and trainings nationwide. Among her previous Libraries Unlimited publications are *Mudluscious* (1986), *Stories NeverEnding* (2004), and *Stories, Time and Again* (2005).